STANISŁAW WYSPIAŃSKI

ACROPOLIS
THE WAWEL PLAYS

GLAGOSLAV PUBLICATIONS

ACROPOLIS
THE WAWEL PLAYS

by Stanisław Wyspiański

Translated from the Polish and introduced by Charles S. Kraszewski

This book has been published with the support
of the ©POLAND Translation Program

Book cover and interior design by Max Mendor

Publishers
Maxim Hodak & Max Mendor

© 2017, Charles S. Kraszewski

© 2017, Glagoslav Publications

www.glagoslav.com

ISBN: 978-1-911414-54-4

A catalogue record for this book is available from the British Library.

This book is in copyright. No part of this publication may be reproduced, stored in a retrieval system or transmitted in any form or by any means without the prior permission in writing of the publisher, nor be otherwise circulated in any form of binding or cover other than that in which it is published without a similar condition, including this condition, being imposed on the subsequent purchaser.

Contents

INTRODUCTION 5

ACKNOWLEDGEMENTS 71

WANDA 72

BISHOP, KING. BISHOP 169

ACROPOLIS. 318

ACROPOLIS – A PROPOSAL FOR THE RENOVATION
AND EXPANSION OF WAWEL. 464

APPENDICES 478

GLOSSARY 486

BIBLIOGRAPHY. 494

ABOUT THE AUTHOR. 496

ABOUT THE TRANSLATOR 497

ILLUSTRATIONS 499

STANISŁAW WYSPIAŃSKI

1869 – 1907

INTRODUCTION

Two lyric poems by the multi-talented artist and poet Stanisław Wyspiański (1869—1907) will serve to place the works included in this book in their proper historical context. The first is a reminiscence of his childhood and of his father Franciszek, a well-known sculptor:

> U stóp Wawelu miał ojciec pracownię,
> wielką izbę białą wysklepioną,
> żyjącą figur zmarłych wielkich tłumem;
> tam chłopiec mały chodziłem, co czułem,
> to później w kształty mej sztuki zakułem.
> Uczuciem wtedy tylko, nie rozumem,
> obejmowałem zarys gliną ulepioną
> wyrastający przede mną w olbrzymy:
> w drzewie lipowym rzezane posągi.

> [At the foot of Wawel my father's atelier was placed. / A great white vaulted chamber, / Animated by a crowd of images of the dead; / There, as a little boy I wandered, and what I felt, / Later I forged in the shapes of my art. / At that time, by emotion only, and not rational understanding, / I grasped the outlines, moulded in clay, / which grew before my eyes into giants: / statues, carved in lime wood].

Franciszek Wyspiański's art can still be seen in Kraków: for example, in the church of St. Anne, on St. Anne's street, stands his sculpture of St. Jan of Kęt, very much in its appropriate place, for the church of St. Anne is associated with the Jagiellonian University, and St. Jan is one of its most worthy alumni. The influence of the sculptor-father on the young Stanisław Wyspiański cannot be overstated, of course. Although he did not follow in his father's footsteps per se, as a sculptor, he superseded him as an artist, becoming not only one of the most important dramatic poets of the Polish nation, but also the most important painter of the fauve-like, Art Nouveau period, which took on the name of Młoda Polska, Young Poland, in that portion of the Austro-Hungarian Empire.

Yet in consideration of the development of this most Cracovian of artists, it must not go unmentioned that the house too, in which the young Wyspiański wandered about those developing sculptures, must have made its own deep impressions on the boy. It still stands today, on the corner of Kanonicza Street and Podzamcze, literally at the foot of Wawel Hill, that centre of princely and royal power that predates the Polish nation itself. Originally built in the fourteenth century, it is known as the House of Długosz, named after one of its most well-known inhabitants: Canon Jan Długosz (1415—1480), who both served at the cathedral on Wawel Hill, and composed one of the most important chronicles of the Polish nation. That chronicle, which commences with the legendary times of the Cracovian region, and strives to reconstruct a memory of the ancient pagan traditions of the Polish nation, is one of the precursors of the dramatic fantasies that Wyspiański went on to compose. When one reads the introductory didascalia to Wyspiański's play on King Bolesław the Bold, it is as if that little boy comes alive before us:

> *I had a dream, and in my dream I saw*
> *Such things to which my heart leapt yearning:*
> *There ghostly figures trod, all bearing swords,*
> *Shields of leather, and some heavy items*
> *Of leathern armour. Dressed in glowing robes,*
> *The train, wrapped in the colours of the moon,*
> *Stood before Wawel castle, and my eyes.*

That little boy never stopped gazing up at the imposing castle on the hill across the street from his father's atelier. It was always to enjoy an almost obsessive place in his consciousness. As a young artist, he won a competition to create stained glass windows for the Wawel Cathedral; as a recruit of the Austro-Hungarian Army, the hill was the location of the main garrison in the city; images of the castle constitute an important element in his oeuvre as a painter, and, of course, it is there that he set the action of the four plays included in this translation. In 1904, when Emperor Franz Josef agreed to withdraw the troops from the hill and return it to the Polish people, Wyspiański, along with his friend Władysław Ekielski, set about reimagining the Castle and the adjacent buildings as a centre of Polish nationhood, which was to contain both cultural and religious structures, as well as a seat of government for the Polish lands — the autonomy of which was one of Wyspiański's great desires (although he was to die more than ten years before that goal was finally achieved).

The mediaeval centre of Wyspiański's hometown of Kraków remains today much as it appeared during the poet's lifetime. Wyspiański was exceptionally sensitive to the history and the ancient monuments of his city. As a student of the great historical painter Jan Matejko, he participated in the conservation of many of the mediaeval structures in and around Kraków, including the polychrome walls and vault of the Basilica of St. Mary on the Main Market Square. One of the newer buildings which was to play an important role in Wyspiański's life was the Municipal Theatre, whose imposing bulk still stands at the end of Szpitalna Street. That street itself takes its name from the Hospital of the Holy Ghost, a mediaeval structure that was razed in the 1890s to make room for the new theatre. Wyspiański's master, Matejko, who was no less sensitive to the sacredness of the remnants of his city's past, protested vigorously against this move. One of Wyspiański's younger contemporaries, Tadeusz Boy-Żeleński, recorded the following exchange between Matejko and the municipal authorities during his unsuccessful campaign to halt the destruction: *Panie artysto, rzekł jeden z dygnitarzy miejskich urażony, przecież i my każdy kamień w Krakowie znamy i kochamy. — Tak, każdy kamień, który prowadzi od Hawełki do Wentla* ["My dear sir," replied one of the exasperated municipal dignitaries, "we know and love every single stone here in Kraków!" — "Sure you do," rejoined Matejko, "Every paving stone between Hawełka and Wentzel's!"] — two popular cafés on the Main Market Square.

Which returns us to that second poem of Wyspiański's, composed in accord with Matejko's sentiments (who returned his honorary citizenship in protest of the destruction of the ancient building, and swore never to exhibit his paintings in the city more):

> O, kocham Kraków — bo nie od kamieni
> przykrości-m doznał — lecz od żywych ludzi,
> nie zachwieje się we mnie duch ani zmieni,
> ani się zapał we mnie nie ostudzi,
> to bowiem z Wiary jest, co mi rumieni
> różanym świtem myśl i co mnie budzi.

Im częściej we mnie kamieniem rzucicie,
sami złożycie stos — stanę na szczycie.

[O, I love Kraków — for never by stones / have I been offended — only by living people. / But the spirit in me will never waver or change, / Nor will the enthusiasm in me ever cool, / for these are from that Faith, which nourishes / my thought with its rose-coloured dawn, and which invigorates me… / The more stones that you throw at me / the higher grows the stake — at the summit of which pedestal I shall stand.]

Today, the poet does indeed stand on a pedestal, surrounded by figures from his dramas, in the form of a 1982 statue by Marian Konieczny erected outside the main building of the National Museum in Kraków. The central figure of Wyspiański seems to be musing, summoning to life the sculpted characters at his feet. Both this dream-like quality captured by Konieczny, and the poet's own professed preference for stone people over those of flesh and blood, characterise his approach to drama. After all, no human figure makes its appearance in the play *Acropolis* at all. Rather, the stage of this unusual, magical-realistic play is entirely populated by the statues and embroidered figures of Wawel Cathedral, who come alive during the night stretching from Holy Saturday into Easter Sunday.

WYSPIAŃSKI AND POLISH MONUMENTAL DRAMA

Such fantastical characters — be they the magically awakened silver angels, who patiently bear the weight of St. Stanisław's reliquary tomb during the daylight hours in *Acropolis,* or the Werewolves and other "Water Folk" that appear in *Wanda* — set Wyspiański's plays firmly in the tradition of Polish Monumental Drama, which was initiated by Adam Mickiewicz during the Romantic era.

To define it simply, Polish Monumental Drama is a theatrical tradition that widens the stageable area of the theatre to include the world of the dead, of eternity. It is more than just a morality play, although that mediaeval dramatic tradition is quite near to Monumental Drama in its philosophical underpinnings. Both the morality play and Polish Monumental Drama start from the position that man is more than an animal moving through this earthly life, from birth until extinction. They put forth the teachings of the Christian tradition, which form the basis of European culture, asserting that man is a composite being of body and soul. Death does not bring existence to an end; it is merely a transition into a different state of being, in which man will interact directly with the beings that belong to the spiritual realm — God, angels and saints, the departed — who are hidden from his earthly eyes. This is not to say that these inhabitants of eternity do not, at times, manifest themselves among the living here and now. From the perspective of Polish Monumental Drama, we inhabit the shaded area of a Venn diagram: that area in which the worlds of the living and the dead, of time and eternity, intersect.

As we note above, Polish Monumental Drama provides us with a wide "stageable area;" in fact, one that is almost limitless. Werewolves and Witches appear in *Wanda; Acropolis* comes to an apocalyptic end with the glorious irruption of Christ/Apollo onto the scene. As a theatrical tradition that urges us to willingly suspend our disbelief in favour of the spiritual and extraordinary, Polish Monumental Drama draws on a wide range of supernaturally-focussed writing, from the Lenore-like folk ballads of the dead hero returning to reclaim his lover, to the sophisticated cosmology of Dante's *Divine Comedy*.

Polish Monumental Drama is an exceptionally vibrant current in Polish theatre. Coming into existence in the 1830s, examples of it can be noted throughout the twentieth century. It spans literary and cultural periods, but it is not monolithic, in that it is not immune from the surrounding ideological atmosphere; it is constantly in flux, as the decades come and go. During the Romantic age, which in many respects was an age of faith, the Dantean character predominates. Both Adam Mickiewicz's *Dziady* [Forefathers' Eve] and Zygmunt Krasiński's provocatively entitled *Nie-boska komedia* [Undivine Comedy] are morality plays in that they accept the Christian cosmology enunciated by Dante, and the message they deliver to the reader is an affirmation of the eternal hierarchy of right and wrong, reward and punishment, proffered by the Christian *Weltanschauung*.

Skipping some hundred and fifty years, the most recent practitioner of Polish Monumental Drama is Tadeusz Kantor. Like Wyspiański, almost exclusively associated with Kraków, the painter-dramatist Kantor is best known for a trilogy of "theatrical spectacula" staged to great acclaim in the late 1970s and early 1980s. *Umarła klasa* [The Dead Class], *Wielopole, Wielopole* and *Niech sczezną artyści!* [Let the Artists Croak!] introduce to the stage an odd mélange of characters both living and dead. But while it would be wrong to suggest that Kantor was *not* affected by religious speculations in his work,[1] the contemporary, sceptical approach to the supernatural that characterises the twentieth-century mind reduces the reality of the otherworldly characters to an exploration of memory. As he refers to it in the theoretical writings that accompany *Let the Artists Croak!*, our memory does not proceed in a chronological fashion. When we come across the dead sharing the stage with the living in one of Kantor's spectacula, or various versions of one character — child, man, aged man — on stage at the same time, we are to understand the stage as a kind of box of negative photographic plates, tossed on top of one another without rhyme or reason, with the disparate images superimposed on the screen of our imagination.

With Wyspiański, who appears at nearly the midway point between the Romantics and the twentieth century avant-garde, the Monumental approach is different as well. Wyspiański introduces his "eternal" characters neither from the pages of Christian hagiography, nor from the theories of psychoanalysis, but rather from the traditions of Polish/Cracovian legend, as a way of understanding what it means to be "Polish" in a Europe where the country that bears that name no longer exists. Influenced by Nietzsche in the realm of philosophy, and by Wagner in the fields of synaesthetic art,[2] Wyspiański is most interested in exploring the mythical essence of his nation. It is legend and ethnic lore which most fully make up the eternal, and fantastic, portions of his Monumental stage.

---

[1] After his mother was abandoned by her Jewish father, Kantor was raised in the rectory of his uncle, a Catholic priest, in the small town of Wielopole. His youth was permeated by the religious observances of both the Catholic and the Jewish inhabitants of the town, and — as I assert in the article "Kantor's Crucifixions: the Use of the 'Village Lexicon of Suffering' in the Theatrical Works of Tadeusz Kantor," *The Polish Review* XLIV (1999) 2:151-182, Kantor makes use of familiar Jewish and Christian motifs in order to give voice to the sufferings and aspirations of the simple people who populate his intimate dramas. It gives his characters a way to understand their world and express their role in it.

[2] See Czesław Miłosz, *The History of Polish Literature* (Berkeley: University of California Press, 1983), p. 353.

THE PLAYS

Before we move on to a discussion of the individual plays included in this translation, a quick orientational note may be necessary. Our book presents four of Wyspiański's most important dramatic works dealing with Wawel. In Polish, they are *Legenda II* (1904), *Bolesław Śmiały* (1903), *Skałka* (1907) and *Akropolis* (1904). The dates given here relate to the publication of the plays in book form. Some of them premiered on stage only after they had been long available to the reading public. In the case of *Akropolis*, for example, its theatrical debut did not come about until 1926 — long after the poet's untimely death in 1907.

As the title of the play dealing with Cracovian prehistory suggests, *Legenda II*, the story of Wanda, was preceded by *Legenda (I)*, an early unfinished play from 1897, which Wyspiański completely overhauled two decades later. We have retitled our English version *Wanda*, in order to avoid unnecessary confusion arising from the ordinal number.

No doubt the reader will have noticed that, although we list four Polish titles in the paragraph above, our translation seems to contain only three plays. This is because of our conflation of the two works dealing with the bloody struggle between the crown and the altar, *Bolesław the Bold* and *Skałka*, into the composite drama entitled *Bishop, King. Bishop*. This is not a whim of our own. *Bolesław the Bold* was written first; later, Wyspiański returned to the topic in *Skałka*. Although both plays are integral dramatic works in their own right, we have it on good testimony — from the poet Leopold Staff, among others — that Wyspiański intended to combine both plays into one, as we do here, and was only prevented from doing so by his death. Our rearrangement of the two plays into one follows Wyspiański's instructions to the letter. It opens, as he wished, with Act I of *Skałka*, which is followed by Act I of *Bolesław*, then Act II of *Skałka* ensues, with the two plays alternating until all six acts have run their course.

In reading these plays in this interlocking fashion, the reader is struck by Wyspiański's deft pen. Although *Skałka* is a dramatic whole of its own, the poet must have had this composite plan in mind while writing the new play. Act by act, the action of the later drama flows seamlessly into the action of the earlier, and vice versa, like snug-fitting pieces of one puzzle. At no point do the interlaced plays jar; there is no need for explanatory notes or fudging so as to smooth the flow from one play into the other, and back again. We have not tinkered with the action or the words of either play one iota. The only exception to this rule deals with didascalia.

As Wyspiański was writing his works to be read as well as seen on stage, he developed the curious habit of composing stage directions in verse. *Bolesław the Bold* is fronted by a long verse introduction in which the poet describes, in somewhat mystical fashion, the "dream" he had one night concerning the ancient kingly seat on Wawel, and how he was entrusted with the theme by some none-too-defined spirit of the nation. Because Act I of *Bolesław* begins after we have already submerged ourselves in the action of *Skałka*, the sudden, extended appearance of the narrator's voice would interrupt the dramatic flow of the composite play. For that reason, I have excised those three pages of descriptive verse, which add nothing of value to the drama itself. The reader who wishes to consult them may do so in the Appendices, where I have moved them. The only other minor adjustment I have made to the text is in Act II of *Skałka*. Towards the middle of that act, Wyspiański describes the collapse of the pagan temple into the waters of the pond, and the resurfacing of two of the pagan idols, who circle the pond to meet in the centre of the stage and embrace. Wyspiański's description of this event veers into the overly-mechanical, as if he were sketching out how the complicated scene might be staged, for the benefit of those carpenters and mechanics who would be building the apparatus. It seems to me that this too disrupts the flow of the play, and for that reason I have simplified the description.

As I note above, the conflation of the two plays into one is no mere caprice of my own. It was Wyspiański's idea. I do not know if this is the first book to present the plays in this fashion, but I have not come across any earlier such arrangements. If the reader approaches *Bishop, King. Bishop* as we offer it, he or she will be reading the plays as Wyspiański wished them to be read. However, our arrangement does not overly impede the progress of such readers who wish to read the plays as separate dramatic works. It will be noted that each of the divisions into acts is followed by a subtitle indicative of the original placement of the act, i.e. "Act II (Act I of *Bolesław the Bold*)." All one needs to do, in order to separate out the plays into their original order, is to follow the directions of the subtitles. Again, no planing was necessary to get the individual acts of both plays to fit together into the composite form: both *Bolesław the Bold* and *Skałka* are presented here in their entirety. So, however the reader chooses to read them, the integrity of the poet's words has been preserved.

Both of the plays are three acts long. It should be noted, however, that although the acts of *Bolesław the Bold* are further divided into individual scenes, those of *Skałka* are not.

Nothing needs to be said here, in general, about the *Acropolis* texts, save that Wyspiański did consider Wawel, both castle and cathedral, as a potential focal-point for Poland and Poles, no matter where they lived. It should be remembered that Wyspiański lived and died a citizen of the Austro-Hungarian Empire, at a time when the historical lands of the once large Polish Kingdom had been subsumed into Austrian, Prussian, and Russian partitions. Looking forward to that day when these three Polish sectors would be reunited, in independence or some sort of autonomous whole, Wyspiański offers Wawel (with its grand necropolis beneath the cathedral, containing the tombs of nearly all Polish kings, as well as that of the national bard Adam Mickiewicz),[3] as a special place of pageantry and reverence, analogous to the Acropolis of Athens. It is for this reason that we append *Acropolis. A Proposal for the Renovation and Expansion of Wawel* to this collection of dramatic works. The grand ideas for the rebuilding of Wawel Hill as a de facto centre of Polish nationhood and government, drawn up by Władysław Ekielski according to the discussions he had with the poet, provide thrilling evidence of the central place of Wawel in the work, and thought, of Stanisław Wyspiański, as well as a fitting context for the cycle of dramas we present to the reader.[4]

---

[3] Mickiewicz's remains were transferred from Paris to Wawel in 1890. Wyspiański did not live to see the re-interment of the second great Romantic, Juliusz Słowacki, which took place in 1927. While we are on the subject of entombments, Wyspiański himself was interred in the crypts of the church on Skałka, a pantheon of Polish artists, which also includes the final resting places of Jacek Malczewski, J.I. Kraszewski, Czesław Miłosz and Jan Długosz, among others.

[4] Speaking of cycles, Wyspiański saw *Acropolis* as the third and concluding portion of a cycle of dramatic works beginning with *Wesele* [The Wedding Feast] and stretching through *Wyzwolenie* [Liberation]. Although *Liberation* is tangentially connected with Wawel, its real focus is not on Wawel per se, as a historical locus and focal point of Polish legend. Rather, it is a continuation of the poet's polemics with the Polish poetic tradition, and for that reason we do not include it here. It has more in common with *Legion*, Wyspiański's play dealing with Mickiewicz's political aims. Perhaps, in the future, I will turn my hand to another anthology of the poet's works in English, which will be grouped around his interest in Mickiewicz: *Legion, Liberation,* and his notes on his groundbreaking production of *Forefathers' Eve*.

Wanda

The play that we entitle *Wanda* is called *Legenda II* in the original Polish. It is our English translation of the second version of Wyspiański's treatment of a familiar Cracovian legend, which he had first attempted in 1897, only to abandon it as unsatisfactory. In a letter to the Cracovian historian Adam Chmiel, dated 19 August 1901, Wyspiański writes: "You ask what's new. Well then, in my opinion, *Legenda* is wretched. It is my intention to destroy the entire thing, save for maybe three ballads and the character types. In general, my point of view has sharpened."[5]

The myth of Wanda, one of the very earliest folkloric accounts in the Cracovian tradition, is one of the foundational myths of both Kraków and Wawel Hill, which towers over the city and its rich historical past. It is not surprising at all that Wyspiański should be haunted by the story of the self-sacrificial warrior princess Wanda. Although he released the play in print in 1898, his dissatisfaction with his poetic expression haunted him for six full years. He returned to it in 1904, and, as a letter to Chmiel from that year points out, he was enthusiastic about the new version: "I am rewriting *Legenda*, and am having such a pleasant time doing it, that I will be sorry to finish it... It's too bad that I publish things like this. I know that I do it only for my own satisfaction — it's the only way to read, in thought, what was, and what is to be."[6] Rather enigmatic, that coda referring to the past and the future; are we to understand from it that the poet never really finished the play to his satisfaction? Is he suggesting that even publication in book form was, for him, a way of ordering his thoughts, developing them, until they should bear fruit in a work that would finally find approval in his eyes? We might be excused for thinking so. As late as 1905, when the actor Ludwik Solski, who had recently been appointed Artistic Director of the Municipal Theatre in Kraków, was determined to stage the play as his inaugural offering, Wyspiański was still unsure of the play's quality, and hoping to come to a better understanding of what he'd written himself from the theatrical production. As he wrote to Solski:

---

5   Quoted in Stanisław Wyspiański, *Dzieła zebrane* [Collected Works] ed. Leon Płoszewski, et al (Kraków: Wydawnictwo Literackie, 1962-1982), Vol. 6: *Bolesław Śmiały, Legenda II, Skałka*, p. 359.

6   Wyspiański, Vol. 6, p. 360.

> The act that takes place on the banks of the Vistula, or more precisely, everything that takes place on the banks of the Vistula, is so weak, so limitlessly wretched [*bezgranicznie liche*], that one simply despairs. Fortunately, I do not have a copy of the book to hand, otherwise I might take out my frustrations on it. And yet I think that the Kraków production will to a great extent help me, finally, to puzzle out the play [*posłuży mi w znacznej części do ostatecznego odgadnienia tego dramatu* — (the italics are the poet's own)].[7]

One might be tempted to see the poet as an over-finicky perfectionist. Yet the general consensus is that, as works to be staged, Wyspiański's retellings of the Wanda myth are rather wanting. In 1926, the Cracovian bibliographer and historian Stanisław Estreicher wrote that the unstaged *Legenda I* "made no impression on anyone."[8] No less an experienced man of the theatre than Józef Kotarbiński, writing in 1909 of a production of *Wanda* (that is, *Legenda II*) staged in Lwów by popular demand, wrote of it as a failure:

> As a work for the stage, the second version of *Legenda* did not possess a living vitality. Produced in Lwów in 1905, it failed, despite the beautiful stage decorations and a cast made up of artists of the highest quality [...]. As an experienced director, Tadeusz Pawlikowski, who was at that time the artistic director of the theatre, certainly knew that neither the talented interpretations of the actors, nor the decorative effects, had any hope of redeeming a theatrical work outfitted with so little action, and no theatrical nerves at all.[9]

Solski himself, one of the most popular and accomplished Polish actors of his generation, seems to agree with the opinion voiced by his immediate

---

7   Wyspiański, Vol. 6, p. 428.
8   Stanisław Estreicher, "Narodziny *Wesela*" (1926) quoted in Leon Płoszewski, *Wyspiański w oczach współczesnych* [Wyspiański in the Eyes of his Contemporaries] (Kraków: Wydawnictwo Literackie, 1971), Vol II, p 19.
9   Józef Kotarbiński, "Rzecz o Stanisławie Wyspiańskim" (1909) quoted in Płoszewski, II, 276.

predecessor in the Municipal Theatre. Given that during the Lwów production, he had directly experienced the problems involved in staging what is preeminently a closet drama, it is surprising that he would still pursue the project again, once he took control of his own theatre. As he later recalled: "I was cast in the role of Krak, who for the entirety of Act I is to sit motionless on a platform representing the bier. This tired me out to such an extent that I fainted, and awoke only at the very end of the act, when the time came for Krak to speak."[10] Yet pursue it he did. *Legenda II*, our *Wanda*, was to be his first play to be staged in Kraków, to be followed shortly thereafter by the more successful, and dramatic *Wesele* [The Wedding Feast]. But then, the poet himself pulled the plug. Convinced, perhaps, that even though seeing it on stage would help him to understand what he was trying to say, the play would still be incomprehensible to the public, Wyspiański halted the progress before the production was even underway. His sentiments are conveyed in the following communiqué:

> The author of *Legend* has arrived at the conviction, that, as of now, the play cannot be given on the stage of the theatre in Kraków. The author confesses that to a great degree the play is weak and poorly structured. For this reason, he wishes to reserve more time to himself for its further, advantageous development and organisation. By this note, he wishes to apologise to both the public, and the administration of the theatre, for any disappointment this may cause. However, his own mind is set at ease by the knowledge that the theatre administration shares in his opinion of the play.[11]

And so, the play was never performed in the poet's native city during his lifetime.

This does not mean that *Wanda* is a failure. Rather, it a closet drama; a poetic consideration, in dramatic form, of the foundational myth of Wawel. Wyspiański's mistake was not in his poetic expression of the myth, but rather in his determination to set it on any stage other than that of the reader's mind.

---

10   Ludwik Solski, "Wspomnienia o Wyspiańskim" (1932) quoted in Płoszewski, II, 372-373.

11   Antoni Chołoniewski, "Wspomnienia o St. Wyspiańskim," (1907) quoted in Płoszewski, II, 95.

THE LEGEND OF WANDA, AND WYSPIAŃSKI'S ELABORATION

In the window of the Goethe Institute on the Main Market Square in Kraków hangs a poster designed by the satirical cartoonist Andrzej Mleczko. It depicts Wanda hurling herself to her death from the walls of Wawel Castle, while the German knight Rytygier rushes up, too late, arms outstretched, (with the incongruous, yet touching addition of Cracovian peacock feathers waving from his helmet), crying out: *Ich liebe dich!* Two people in the foreground look on, and the elder man says to the younger, *Gdyby Wanda uczyła się niemieckiego, nie byłoby problemu* ["If only Wanda had learned German, all of this could have been avoided."] A humorous and good-natured advert for the Institute's German language courses, the immediacy of the succinct joke testifies to the permanence of the ancient myth of Wanda in the consciousness of Poles — especially Cracovians. As we have noted earlier, if there is a spiritual aspect to the Wawel plays of Stanisław Wyspiański, as there must be to any expression of Polish Monumental Drama, the Catholic, Christian characteristics, which so define Polish culture, take a back seat to the stressing of Polish legend.

Although the Austro-Hungarian partition was much more open — and opening ever wider — to the expressions of the national characters of its varied ethnic regions, Wyspiański continues to think according to the tropes of nineteenth century Poles: the Polish nation has been subjugated; Polish language and culture are under attack from Russifiers and Germanisers; both Polish language and Polish cultural traditions must be incubated, nourished, fostered so that they do not disappear, so that the Polish nation will arise integral and take up where it left off, once the partitions disappear and the country is re-united. And thus, Wyspiański packs his prehistoric drama chock-full of legend; legends both appropriate, and somewhat anachronistic. Wanda, who over the ages developed into a symbol of Polish racial purity (there's no other way to put it) and resistance to German pressure from the West by hurling herself to her death in the Vistula, rather than marrying the German Prince Rytygier (and thus binding her nation to the Germans in a personal and political union) takes pride of place in the play that bears her name. And while the original title of the play in Polish suggests that this story is a "legend," Wyspiański still effects two purposes: first, he underscores the antiquity of Polish culture (in the face of those scholars, particularly Germans, who would deny Poland any sort of meaningful history before German civilisational influence in the area), and second, Wanda's determination to "beat back the raiders" at all costs sends a similar message, in no uncertain terms, to the poet's contemporaries: "Resist the Germans, come they as conquerors, or suitors." The ambivalent figure of Krak, the legendary first king of the area, who supposedly gave the city its name, is one of the more intriguing aspects of *Wanda*. True, Wyspiański gives the legendary king his due: he is described as a doughty warrior, loved by his people, who weep in despair at his approaching death, which occurs at precisely the worst moment: when his town and his castle are being besieged by the German "raiders." And yet, after the old king's death, as Wyspiański moves on to the fantastic scenes, with werewolves, witches, and water-folk, the praise of Krak melts away into farce. As Leon Płoszewski puts it: "Whereas the character of Krak, who, in *Legenda I* was a great warrior-leader, and after his death became the genius loci of Wawel, in the second version, he was developed toward the grotesque."[12] He becomes something of a simple-minded fool: doddering, nervy in the scene with the three Fates; and he is positively degraded by the water-folk who steal his corpse from his bier, to sink him in the river after dressing him up like a scarecrow. Despite all the grotesque, there is a chilling threat that one senses in following the water-folk's treatment of the dead king. So much so, that it is tempting to see these scenes as a "passion of Krak" based on the familiar tropes of the Holy Week story: as Jesus was jeered at and degraded by the soldiers of Pilate, and then nailed to the Cross to suffer for our sins, so is Krak mocked and denuded of his implements of power by the fantastic creatures of the Vistula, after which Act II begins with the long soliloquy of his abandoned Corpse among the reeds: suffering, aching for death — a death that finally seems to come when the Werewolf submerges him in the river.

And yet although Wyspiański seems to return to Krak the glory he had been stripped of — the final scenes of *Wanda* include the Princess' vision of the majestic "azure and gold" realm ruled by her father beneath the waves of the Polish river — the scene is equivocal in and of itself. As Wanda prepares to follow the encouragement of the Rusalkas and disappear beneath the waves, the people looking on from the bank debate whether or not she is mad. Is she a visionary? Or is she hallucinating? It is impossible to know, from the text as it is written. What is certain is that she has achieved the liberation of her people, and her end is tragic, heroic.

---

12   Wyspiański, Vol. 6, p. 363.

If the play does have a compositional flaw, it is that we do not witness Wanda's heroism. The play is basically an elaboration of ideas. While the didascalia ask us to imagine the fierce battle raging around the castle on Wawel Hill while Krak lies dying, very little of this is presented on stage — and stage action is the very heart of dramatic composition. Rather than placing us in the exhilarating mix of hordes warring about the portcullis, Wyspiański sets us safely behind it. We are in the inner chamber with the frightened princess, and, almost as in the case of a Greek tragedy, all the fun bits we'd like to see with our own eyes are related to us at second hand. The most dramatic thing that occurs is the symbolic, vicious sacrifice of the tame deer by Wanda, as part of her vow of self-immolation to the goddess Żywia. After this she is transformed. She calls down the power of the lightning and chases the stunned invaders from the walls. This too is mainly transmitted to us through didascalia, which again underscores the fact that the proper stage for *Wanda* is the reader's imagination, rather than the proscenium arch of the Municipal Theatre on Szpitalna St.

It might be argued that there is very little of the heroic in the character of Wanda anyway, even at this point. We like our heroes to be human beings: faulty, nervous, imperfect: men and women who overcome some inner conflict at the do-or-die moment of crisis. Wanda, here, is like some sort of comic-book super hero, who touches the right sort of mystical stone, ingests the proper amount of some magical liquor, and, literally, becomes someone else. In such a case, where is the heroism? Stanisław Brzozowski would convince us that "The superhuman world of *Legenda II* is, for that battling community, a source of energy [...] and the community knows how to engage the power necessary for their battle — one must only *dare*."[13] Yet although we would not wish to deny Wanda bravery, given her drastic decision, this is still setting the heroic bar far too low. For the power, here, is located not in the heroine's breast, but remains outside her: it is the goddess's power, it is the power of the lightning bolt, and is no more hers, than the lightning can be said to belong to the lightning rod it strikes.

And yet, that is exactly the point at which the poet is aiming. Wanda is not a heroine in and of herself; she is heroic in so far as she taps into the strength of something greater. In this case, the power that is lent her

---

13　　Stanisław Brzozowski, "Stanisław Wyspiański," from *Legenda Młodej Polski*, collected in *Eseje i studia o literaturze* (Wrocław: Ossolineum, 1990), Vol. II, p. 1025.

by the nature goddess, and, later, by the water-folk in their "bequest" of the fatal Vistulan crown, is the power of Polish ethnicity. This is the main "idea" that Wyspiański develops in the first of his Wawel plays. In this, the heroism of Wanda is seen, not in the startling effects that her sacrificial choice wins for her, but in the freely-willed choice she makes, of trusting herself, and the fate of her nation, to the ancient ethnic wellsprings of that nation's identity.[14]

Rather ingeniously, Wyspiański makes Wanda's heroism most apparent by contrasting it to her father's unheroic character. Where she embraced her nation's traditions, her father had previously — for reasons that are nowhere explicitly seen — abandoned them, attacked them. During her prayer to the goddess neglected by her father, she states that, if only she were to receive the requisite power from Żywia to save her people, she would destroy her father's castle (as strong a symbol as one may find for "out with the old, in with the new," or, rather, vice versa):

> And on its place I'll raise a fane
> To you, and renew your sacrifice.
> I choose death, that my folk retain
> Their freedom. I am yours by right.

For Krak, for some unexplained reason, destroyed the ancient altars raised on Wawel Hill, where from time immemorial sacrifices were made to the "sacred reptiles" — no doubt the poet's dramatisation of the ancient Cracovian myth of the dragon, whose lair at the foot of the castle hill can still be visited by the curious today. So, *Wanda* is a play about returning to roots, about restoration. Wanda contextualises her sacrifice as reparation to the offended goddess for her father's forbidding of the ancient rites. Because of this act of his, the gods have cursed his house; Wyspiański toys here with the Greek idea of a family curse, by initialising the theme of a brothers' feud stoked by the gods, so as to ruin the offending royal dynasty.

---

14   Wanda is transformed, and so is her people. At the end of Act I, when they run up to the sound of her horn, they are called *narodek* — a strange diminutive of *naród*, meaning nation. The "little nation," with all that term denotes of pettiness and docility, becomes the *naród*, the Nation, in Act II, after their routing of the Germans.

> You slew my father in his sons'
> Quarrels, leaving the sword to me.
> Who am I? — That I should be the one
> Chosen to try such fearsome deeds?

For one thing, she truly is "chosen." Such was the role destined to her, according to ancient prophecy, twice referenced in the short play. In the first instance, in one of the ballads he addresses to the corpse on the bier during Krak's wake, the singer Chuckle [Śmiech] foretells the rising of a mysterious saviour:

> A leader from the dead shall rise
> To lead you on to victory —
> You and your men are sent to die
> Among the spears, the darts that fly,
> The swords' clash — thus your duty,
> The pyre — and there the beauty
> Of your child will share your fate;
> A mighty king comes, of power great,
> Above the pyre's ashes to soar!

This reference, so Christian and eschatological, is odd in the pagan context of the play. Whatever Wyspiański intended to mean by it — whether it is a promise of final felicity for the dead Krak or not — it shows him as a cardinal figure: between the pagan, snake-worshipping past (which he did away with) and the new Christian civilisation of St. Stanisław, which the Cracovians owe in the first instance to the Slavic rite of the Great Moravian Empire (yet to come). The important thing to note here, however, is that Krak is not a stage in the spiritual development of his people from superstition to Christianity. He is a destroyer, not a builder. In moving backwards, Wanda is actually advancing. The spirit is important, yet Krak would deny the spirit in favour of the material. A faulty acknowledgement of the spiritual realm is better than a misguided denial of the same, throwing out the baby with the bath water, as it were. We will find the same theme in *Bishop, King. Bishop*. But more of this later.

Krak's identity as a cardinal, or liminal, figure is emphasised in Act II, where he appears as an undead being, hung up between existence and the dissolution he pines for. He has even been deprived of his name: from here on out, he is known as the Corpse. His words, which open the act, are Dantean in their presentation of his posthumous punishment. Compared with similar scenes from *Forefathers' Eve*, such as the story of the sadistic landowner now torn apart by the souls of the serfs he had tormented during life, it is the one place in the play where Wyspiański imitates his great predecessor in Monumental Drama, Adam Mickiewicz:

> Snakes slither to me from the water,
> Reptiles tear my flesh;
> When will these my torments cease?
> Bound are my wrists, and my feet,
> So harshly bound, my wrists!
>
> The water flees me on the strand;
> The earth my corpse will not receive.
> Through long cold windy nights I stand,
> Cursing, and praying, for relief.
>
> When will this torment reach its end?
> Who'll nourish me with bread?
> Who'll slit the thongs that bind my hands?
> Abandoned am I, left for dead.
>
> And Death so near, Death is so near!
> But, endless are my torments;
> Am I for all ages to stand here,
> With bound, and helpless hands?

Given that the word employed by Wyspiański for Krak's new designation — *martwica* — is grammatically of feminine gender, one might also venture the proposal that he has been deprived of his masculinity. This could conceivably be part of his punishment, for one of the reasons given for his degradation at the hands of the water-folk is for dying not in battle, but in bed:

> The water-nymphs' feast is at hand —
> They dress a festive scarecrow, damned:
> Let us help them with the clothes,

> Since he's put aside a warrior's robes
> And jokish, croaked —
> By sickness, not by battle, broke.

But although he will be mocked and derided, dragged down into the river-weeds and left there in that penumbral existence, it is noteworthy how they dress him, once they despoil him of his royal insignias. He is wrapped in homespun cloth, like a peasant, and around his neck is hung a simple leather bag, filled with seed. In short, he is dressed as a symbol of the Cincinnatian ideal of the Polish royal house of Piast, which was raised to the glory of rule, from the people, of the people. While the Shaman who directs the disrobing speaks in comforting terms at this point, later on it becomes clear that the return to peasant symbolism is an eloquent constituent element of Krak's penance. During his riverside shaming by the water-folk, the Corpse pleads:

> Take some seeds here from my pouch
> And spread them here, there, round about;
> And watch them sprout
> Green seedlings gay,
> To greet the green month of May.
>
> I beg you — take into your hand
> From out my pouch some seed;
> Spread it and see how blooms the land.
> The snakes will have something to eat!
>
> Hey! The seeds will go to waste!
> As I go down, so do the seeds!
> Take but a handful! Take them, please,
> And see the meadows bloom with May.
> One handful save, as down I go,
> Or there'll be nothing left to sow!
>
> Along with me the seeds are lost,
> Never to be in furrow tossed,
> And here I sink, all noosed and bound,
> Near Wawel's cliff I sink, I drown!

In short, Krak is dealt with harshly by Wyspiański as a king who buried his talents. He had been given seeds to sow, which he neglected to do when it would have mattered, and now it is too late. The same is not true for Wanda. She turns away from her father's neglect of the ancient traditions of his folk, and finds salvific power there. Where he, the warrior who dies abed, is most remembered for having done war on snakes and spirits, she allies herself with spirits, with the sacred, to overcome the existential threat to her people on an actual battlefield. And so, whether we choose to consider Krak's abasement as a "passion" or not, he is not to be the resurrected, Christlike hero. That role is reserved to the invigorated Wanda, the androgynous warrior "king:"

> BURDOCK
> *Shouts.*
> The king's been taken by the sprites,
> This holy eve, this holy night ! — — —
>
> CHUCKLE.
> The trees flap in the wind like flags.
>
> BURDOCK.
> As if they were glad —
> A new man rises, a new chief,
> A strong leader, to bring relief!

The king who has been stolen here is Krak. Burdock [Łopuch] cries out when he notices that the prince's body is missing from the bier. But when he goes on to interpret the behaviour of the waving trees, as if the earth itself were celebrating the imminent coming of the "new chief," that reference is made to Wanda.

As we have noted, Krak's character in the play goes from stateliness to farce, from a seemingly heroic past to the grotesque. We come across this clownish Krak in Act II, where he bobs about in the river's current, acting like a kind of sidekick to the Werewolf who drowned his body in the Vistula. It is a very undignified prince we see here. As the Werewolf "smacks his lips" and lasciviously tempts some maidens to enter the water and "embrace his cold breast," Krak chuckles on, seconding the Werewolf's temptations, chortling "take off your shirt!" to the girls, like some drunk undergraduate at a bar on Ocean Drive during spring break. It is an odd scene, and in the context of staging, must have seemed as incongruous to the story as it is difficult to imagine in performance. And yet, it makes ideological sense in this play of ideas. *Wanda* is a play about sacrifice; about giving up one thing, in order to gain another. In his coaxing of the girls, the Werewolf promises them the power to charm others — but first, they must give him something in exchange:

> Come warm my breast. —
> It's cold and chill;
> Your lips I'd kiss;
> O how they swell
>
> With blood! And from then on
> You'd rule with charms
> Whomever you wish
> But first, these arms
>
> Must take you, and teach
> You love, and passion's spurt!

As seemingly comical as this scene is, in a real way it echoes the deal that Wanda makes with Żywia: give me power and rule, in exchange for my life. Krak, on the contrary, is punished for not making a sacrificial deal with the spiritual realm. Instead of holding true to his national faith, he chose to assert his will, unilaterally, on the forces of the spirit, by destroying the sacred altar, and raising in its place a monument to man's rule: his palace.

Here, we may look forward for a moment and consider how this same Monumental theme will be repeated in *Bishop, King. Bishop*. Krak is not just a liminal figure, he is a prefiguration of Bolesław the Bold, who lost his crown because he would not respect the spiritual world represented by St. Stanisław. He too would challenge the Bishop: "It's me that knocks down idols," as he will assert at one point in that drama. But if he does so, he replaces the old with nothing but his own human power. The bishop, just as destructive toward the old religion, is still on the side of the angels: he replaces the old pagan faith with the new religion of Christ, not the sterile material system of earthly kingship.

Sacrifice, in order to achieve a higher goal. The self-sacrifice of Wanda, the heroine, is a high price, but she pays it. And although, as we've said before, we can't be completely certain from the text that she's not mad, her own claims (confirmed earlier by Burdock, who remembers the deal) cannot be lightly dismissed. She feels that she has saved the nation by her actions, and dies victorious, at least in her own mind:

CHORUS
From the riverbank.
The waters upon the land advance!
Throw away that wreath! Your people drown!
The dikes are melting from the banks —
The boat is sinking! It pulls you down!

WANDA.
Through me Fame calls to you.
Fame speaks to you through my lips!
By this arm, victory I grip.
The spirits are my aid, my help.
My knights are in the river's depths!

CHORUS.
She's casting spells upon her own kind —
Enchantment — ah, beware the witch! —
The planks beneath her feet now split.
That wreath is cursed! Unwind, unwind,
Toss it away!

WANDA.
        In it is my life!
This wreath my fame! This wreath, it gives
Me victory!
You — cease your shouts, put by your ire,
My realm — my glory!

RUSALKI.
The wreath you wore beneath your helm:
That wreath is of our water's realm.

> Restore it now, the waters thrum,
> As you into the waters come!

They disappear beneath the waves;
The current takes hold of the boat.

CHORUS
From the riverbank.
The waters seize the boat, it spins,
The oars split, undone are the pins.
Her armour is shining in the sun —
She goes, the mad, enchanted one!
Look there!
By the current sped,
The wreath! Held high in the air
At sword's point! High above her head!
She's chased by Death! Queen of the Dead!

Mad or far-seeing, she is at least a hundred times more tragic, more heroic, than that farcical straw figure that her father has become. And that's the point, really: something for something. Wyspiański himself understood the need for sacrifice, and was willing to deprive himself of personal advantages and comfort, for the advancement of the greater good. In 1919, the writer Stefan Żeromski wrote of a visit he had made to Wyspiański some fifteen years earlier, on behalf of Józef Piłsudski, who was seeking the support of various Polish notables for his scheme of raising a Polish Army during the revolutionary year of 1905:

> He sat there for a long time gazing into my eyes, without speaking a word. At last, he pulled toward himself a few pages of yellow paper from a pile that lay before him on the table, and he began writing something that looked like an application, or some sort of official request. I thought that he was disdainfully disregarding what I had set before him, and thus in reply had turned back to his own concerns.
>
> After a while, it seemed to me that this writing of his was going on far too long. So I asked him directly, what he thought about my proposal.

"I've just written my letter of resignation," he replied.
"Resignation? From what?"
"From the Academy of Fine Arts, where I am a professor."
"But why?"
"Well, obviously, I can't sign an appeal calling on people to donate money for the purchase of arms, and thus inciting them to rebellion, while remaining in the employ of an institution overseen by the Austrian Ministry of Education..."[15]

IN SUM: THE LEGENDS BEHIND THE PLAY, AND THE IMPORTANCE OF MYTH TODAY.

So, again, why the degradation of Krak? The answer is provided by the water-folk themselves. Their animus against Krak stems from his overthrowing the altars of the "sacred snakes." This is the first in a series of overturned temples, a leitmotiv that runs throughout the Wawel plays, including the destruction of the pagan fane at Skałka by Archbishop Stanisław in *Bishop, King. Bishop,* and continuing on to the apocalyptic destruction of the Catholic cathedral on Wawel at the conclusion of *Acropolis*. Why the pagan king Krak should determine to overthrow the pagan altars of the sacred snakes and forbid the pagan rites to the water-folk is unclear, and never explained. After all, he does not introduce Christianity to his people, as in the case of the Archbishop. He dies a pagan warrior; his funeral rites are pagan, attended by his shamans.[16] The only rational explanation is that Wyspiański presents him as a destroyer of ethnic traditions: a traitor to the religious and cultural sensibility of his people. It is in this context that Wanda's death appears as a quasi-religious act. In vowing herself to the goddess Żywia and holding true to her bargain, she delivers her people from the foreign invaders by submerging herself in ethnicity — in "Polishness." And Polishness, for the poets of the Young Poland period, Wyspiański included, means the idealised folk, the peasantry, seen (rightly or wrongly)

---

15   Stefan Żeromski, "Na broń…" (1919) quoted by Płoszewski, Vol. II, p. 222.
16   Thus we translate the Polish term *guślarz*, which connotes not only spiritual power, but a power and authority derived from a bardic office (the term derives from the word *gęśle* — a rebec, or stringed instrument). Because the word *guślarz* is so famously associated with *Forefathers' Eve*, we eschew its use here, so as to avoid allusions to Mickiewicz unintended by the poet.

as the repository of a pure spring of ethnicity, uncorrupted by the overlay of a seemingly foreign Western culture. Artur Sandauer describes this Rousseauish (and somewhat condescending) fashion for peasant nobility:

> In their search for something that they might oppose to [bourgeois culture], the intellectuals of the time turn to the peasantry. They ascribe to the peasants all of the characteristics foreign to the bourgeoisie: as an antithesis to middle-class prudery, they see in the peasants — quite wrongly as it is — the incarnation of moral liberty; as an antithesis to bourgeois parvenu culture they see the peasant as the representative of the timeless laws of nature; as an antithesis to the platitudes of bourgeois rationalism they see in the peasant the symbol of an irrational, elemental force. Parallel to their cult of the peasantry, the writers of Young Poland are nourished by their cult of everything "ancient," everything unspoiled with bourgeois modernity. And thus, in their imagination, folklore is associated with antiquity. The most typical example of this combination is Wyspiański's peasant classicism [*chłopski antyk*].[17]

While there does remain that unresolved matter of her madness, introduced at the end of the play, the fact remains that Wanda is transformed from a trembling little girl into a victorious Amazon, as soon as she vows the sacrifice. She saves her people from the foreign forces that threatened to engulf and enslave them. If she is mad, it is a heroic madness, like that of Hamlet, to whom Wyspiański was strongly attracted. Mad or not, she sets everything right at the end of her play. One of Wyspiański's important prose works is a consideration of how to stage, properly, Shakespeare's *Hamlet* — set on Wawel, of course! — in *Wanda,* he writes his own, Polish, version of the English classic.

Wanda returns to, reaffirms, her ethnic identity, while Krak — again, for reasons unexplained — abdicates them, becoming somehow "unPolish" in doing so. It is worth noting that when his corpse is denuded from the accoutrements of the warrrior-king by the (indigenous, Polish) water-folk of the Vistula, they dress him in homespun, and hang around his neck, in place of a weapon, a leather pouch filled with seed. Here again Wyspiański

---

17 Artur Sandauer, "Od estetyzmu do realizmu," collected in his *Pisma zebrane* (Warszawa: Czytelnik, 1985), Vol. 1, p 137.

reaffirms a legend: that of the peaceful, bucolic Slavic people, whose kingly line — that of Piast — arises from a simple man who tended his fields and his beehives. In those enigmatic scenes in which pity and opprobrium are alternately heaped upon his corpse, a Shaman reaffirms the idea that Krak, in being dressed in this simple way, is being returned to the station and appearance proper to a popular Polish king. Krak seems to realise this himself in his "crucifixion" scene among the reeds at the start of Act II, when he reflects upon the seeds in his pouch, lamenting that "I should have sown them," but did not — i.e., I should have remained true to my ethnic, national nature, but did not. *Modern day Austrian Poles,* one almost hears the poet admonishing, *take note.*

THE SACRED SNAKES

Even today a large limestone cave is found in the cliff below Wawel Hill. Tradition has it that this is the ancient lair of a dragon, who, like his Greek prototype in the Andromeda myth, exacted a harsh tribute from Krak's people until an enterprising peasant named Szewczyk slew the beast with an Odyssean ruse. He filled the carcasses of sheep with sulphur and placed them about the cave opening. The dragon dutifully consumed them, and the sulphur provoked such a thirst in the reptile, that he waded into the Vistula and drank, and drank, and drank, until he burst. Over the years, this dragon has been accepted by the Cracovian people as a symbol of their city. Is Krak, as the "killer of the sacred snakes" a reference to the demise of this beast, whose bones (so legend has it) are among the huge fossils which still hang today above the entrance to Wawel Cathedral? At any rate, the Dragon of Kraków is present in *Wanda*, in one of the songs intoned by the singers Chuckle and Burdock, at that point in her drama when Wanda ascends the bier by her father's side, mournfully, yet dutifully, anticipating her promised *sati* on the morrow.

Oddly enough, the song that is sung has little to do with the Cracovian myth. We have a very Germanic dragon in Wyspiański's song, who, like his cousin in *Beowulf,* guards a treasure-trove. This, and the fact that the helmet that both Krak and Wanda place on their heads is that of a Viking, are paradoxical Germanic infixes in a play, the ostensible purpose of which is a rejection of things Germanic as oppressive, insidious foreign intrusions. One possible explanation of this paradox may be found in Wyspiański's fascination with Richard Wagner, and his desire, like that of the German composer, to create a synaesthetic artistic experience melding poetry, drama, the plastic arts and music. It is a Nibelungan nod to the master — odd, perhaps, but little more than that.

THE LAJKONIK

Several references to Polish culture in *Wanda* are more anachronistic than dragons and snake-worship. During the scenes of the mocking of the corpse near the end of Act I, when the body of Krak is fastened to the back of the Horned Beast (Turoń), and the latter begins to prance about the chamber, the chorus eggs him on with a song which begins *Laj konikiem, laj, / obejdź cały kraj*. This might be roughly translated as "On the broad road, by horse, be off on your wide travels / ride through the entire country." The Polish ear, and especially that of the residents of Kraków, cannot but hear in this line a reference to the Lajkonik. The progress of the Lajkonik is a particularly Cracovian event, which takes place each June, on the octave of Corpus Christi. It is then that a person dressed in a fantastical "Turkish" or oriental style, with a long fake beard, a tall pointed cap, and a gaudy hobby-horse fixed around his waist, dances and prances from the Zwierzyniec section of the city to the Main Market Square. Attended by song, he skips through the crowds, striking people left and right with his staff of office (the *buława*).[18] (Whomever he strikes is glad to be tapped: it brings good luck). The reference is widely anachronistic, as the Lajkonik procession, which has its basis in the frequent conflicts between Catholic Poland and the Muslim East (Turkey, the Tatars, etc.) dates from the thirteenth century — far in the future of the times depicted by Wyspiański in *Wanda*.

"KING" JADWIGA

Similarly, it might strike the non-Polish reader as odd that, when Wanda is chosen by the people to rule over them, they elect her "King" rather than "Queen." This too is an anachronistic reference, to one of the most popular people who ever sat on the Polish throne: Jadwiga [Hedwig] of Anjou. The history of the Polish kingdom — more or less, and for ill as well as good — is

---

18   The etymology of the noun *lajkonik* is uncertain. *Konik* means "little horse, pony." As for *laj*, some linguists take this as an alternative pronunciation for the imperative *lej*, meaning "strike, beat."

the history of an elective monarchy, rather than a strictly hereditary one. In 1382, Jadwiga was elected to the throne of Poland by the aristocracy assembled at Radom. For obscure legal reasons, her election would not have been valid unless she had been elected "King" — for that was the title of the office that needed to be filled. Although Latin documents regularly refer to her as *Regina serenissima,* her elective title was "King of Poland."[19] This historical oddity is well known to those familiar with Polish history, and when Wanda is proclaimed "King" in Wyspiański's play, the Polish auditory will immediately make the connection to St. Jadwiga. It was she who in 1400 reinvigorated the University of Kraków (originally founded in 1364 by her grandfather, King Kazimierz the Great) by donating her jewels for its upkeep. In a dynastic sense, though, it is clear why Wyspiański is making the anachronistic reference.

Jadwiga was first betrothed to the Austrian prince, Wilhelm of Habsburg. However, the powers at the time looked askance at the Western-facing alliance, and for reasons of power and finance they sought rather to pair her with the Grand Duke Jagiełło of Lithuania. Wilhelm was chased from Wawel by force of arms before the marriage could be solemnised, and with the new betrothal of "King" Jadwiga to the Lithuanian prince, the fortunes of Poland were turned toward the Baltic, Slavic, East.

Now, with his Lajkonik reference, Wyspiański is rather innocently restating and reaffirming the antiquity (or at least the sanctity) of Polish traditions which must not be forgotten. With the Wanda-Jadwiga reference, however, he is making a much more daring political statement: the rejection of the Germanic Habsburg partner for the ethnic, Slavic essence by which (correctly or not) nineteenth century Poles wished to define their mythic Polishness.

THE SOURCES OF THE PLAY

Three mediaeval sources speak of Wanda: the *Kronika wielkopolska* [Greater Polish Chronicle, 1271-1273], the earlier *Chronicle* of Wincenty Kadłubek (1190-1208) and that of Jan Długosz (c. 1455). Wyspiański seems to have consulted all three. Almost all of the aspects of Wanda's story found in Wyspiański's play can be located in one or more of these chronicles;

---

19 Cf. Adam Zamoyski, *The Polish Way. A Thousand-Year History of the Poles and their Culture* (New York: Franklin Watts, 1988), p. 43.

Wyspiański even deftly handles potentially contradictory accounts. For example, it is to Długosz that we owe the story of Rytygier, and the famous, patriotic (or xenophobic, depending on your perspective) story of Wanda's choosing death rather than a marriage with the German knight Rytygier — which, supposedly, would put an end to the autonomy of her land, and subject it to the German state from which her husband hailed. The other chroniclers offer the story of Wanda standing at the head of her troops to face the invaders. When the leader of the foreigners catches sight of Wanda's great beauty and valour, he steps back from the invasion, and commits suicide himself. In a clever fashion, Wyspiański determines not to choose between these options, but employs them both. At the start of the play, Wanda's realm is on its heels, about to be overrun by the invading "raiders." On behalf of her people (and at the suggestion of the singer Chuckle), she determines to avail herself of the powers of the indigenous, Slavic gods by vowing herself to them, as a freely-willed offering on behalf of her nation ("See, father!" She cries near the end of the play, as she is about to enter into the waves, "I have liberated your Wawel!"). Then comes the familiar suicide by drowning, although the motif of the German suitor is completely absent from Wyspiański's retelling — perhaps consciously stifled by the poet, as potentially humanising the German invader too much.

Wyspiański found the theme of Wanda's two brothers, and their fratricidal, almost Sophoclean, struggle for the throne, in the *Kronika wielkopolska*. The motif of the brothers' rivalry for her love — saved, at least partially, from the creepy theme of incest by the fact of her being their half-sister, born of the union of Krak and the water-nymph "Wiślanka" — is Wyspiański's own invention (as is the rather realistically painted psychology of the witnesses of her final sacrifice. Is she heroic, or utterly mad?)

This motif of Wanda's generation from one of the water-folk is itself very interesting. Once more it sets before the reader's mind the ontological challenge: Who are you, really? How do you define yourself? — which is a very pertinent challenge indeed in a play that vaunts the (outmoded today, one would hope, though perhaps resurgent) ideas of ethnicity as a defining characteristic of personhood. Most interesting is the identification of Wanda's mother as a Wiślanka. Although this term can be understood to mean "a nymph of the river Wisła [Vistula]," it is also the feminine form of the proper noun indicating a member of the indigenous tribe that inhabited the area around Kraków. For although at her apotheosis near the end of the play Wanda is promised a fame that will stretch throughout the lands of the Polanie, here Wyspiański is being both anachronistic, and inclusive. The Polanie, from whom Poland derives its name, were from farther north and west, centred around the area of today's Poznań. It was the Wiślanie, rather, that inhabited the area around Krak's seat of power. By identifying Wanda with her mother, a Wiślanka, Wyspiański is further binding identity with local generation, and by a clear association underscoring a patriotism centred on Wawel — not on far-off Vienna. In the person of the Wiślanka Krasawica, this nativist understanding of belonging will play a similar role in the historical drama *Bishop, King. Bishop,* to which we now turn our attention.

Bishop, King. Bishop.

Of the two plays that make up our composite drama *Bishop, King. Bishop,* the first one to be written was *Bolesław Śmiały* [Bolesław the Bold] which took shape between September 1902 and April 1903. It was staged for the first time in May of the latter year. Wyspiański was intrigued by the conflict between the Polish King Bolesław and the Bishop of Kraków, Stanisław Szczepanowski, who represented the universal Church of Rome, and whom Bolesław suspected of collusion with the Czechs. Which of these was "more right?" According to Alicja Okońska, from whom we derive much of our information, Wyspiański first sided with his namesake. Then, after having read Tadeusz Wojciechowski's controversial historical account *Szkice historyczne jedenastego wieku* [Historical Sketches of the Eleventh Century, 1904], he began to rethink his position, and sympathised more with the King's accusations of treason.

Whatever the case may be — and the reader of the plays given here in translation can make up his or her own mind as to which of these characters is right — the binary opposition of Bolesław's royal castle of Wawel and the church of St. Michael on the nearby river hillock called Skałka [the "little rock," or "little cliff"] representing Stanisław's headquarters, certainly appealed to his dramatic understanding of conflict. So in 1904 he began work on the second play, *Skałka,* which he did not finish until 1906, shortly before his death.

The two plays fit remarkably well together. According to Okońska, it was Wyspiański's unfulfilled desire that they be presented together, in the manner in which we give them here:

The two works differ artistically, and philosophically. Yet *Skałka* was written as a planned conclusion to the earlier work, an elaboration of the thoughts it expresses, a commentary, an addition of a heretofore missing interpretational element. Both dramas constitute therefore a two-part composition, and, according to the wishes of the poet (confirmed by Stanisław Lack and Leopold Staff), they were to be played together, in the following fashion: the acts of *Skałka* were to be interwoven with those of *Bolesław*, with the production beginning with Act I of *Skałka*.[20]

WYSPIAŃSKI'S PLAYS AND HISTORICAL TRUTH

To what extent is the plot of *Bishop, King. Bishop* based on historical truth? To the extent that Bolesław the Bold reigned as King of Poland from 1076 until 1079, and Stanisław Szczepanowski was Bishop of Kraków from 1072 until 1079, when he was murdered. It seems certain that he came into serious conflict with the king, and most people, since the event happened, have laid the blame for his death at the feet of the king. After the murder, which took place in April of 1079, Bolesław was forced to leave the country. He died in exile in Hungary in 1082. His brother, Władysław Herman, ascended the throne in his place, and ruled until his own death in 1102.

So much we can say for certain. Stanisław, who was canonised a martyr in 1253 (he is honoured in the Catholic Church on the traditional date of his death, April 11; in Kraków, May 8 is an especial feast day, on which a lavish procession transfers his relics from Wawel Cathedral to St. Michael's Church at Skałka), is mentioned in the *Chronicles* of Jan Długosz and Wincenty Kadłubek, as well as that of the so-called Gallus Anonimus, which was composed in the half century immediately following the martyrdom. Three hagiographical works (the earliest two by Wincenty z Kielczy date from the thirteenth century) also offer information. However, for reasons of their political slant as well as the scepticism of historians in relation to hagiography, none of these works is considered to be perfectly objective.

Not that this matters at all, because Wyspiański, as passionate as he may have been about the history of his city and its greatest patron saint, was

---

20   Alicja Okońska, *Stanisław Wyspiański* (Warszawa: Wiedza Powszechna, 1971), p. 349.

not writing history himself. He was creating a dramatic work, a fiction, an interpretation of characters built up from his own imagination — based of course on two men who actually once did live. As far as faithfulness to his sources is concerned, there is hardly anything in either *Bolesław the Bold* or *Skałka* which cannot be found in these mediaeval works, except, of course, the fantastic water-folk, of whom Wyspiański was so fond. Supporters of St. Stanisław emphasise his quarrel with the king as the ethical opposition of a churchman standing up to a cruel tyrant. The motifs of Bolesław's penchant for long, arduous warmaking and cruel punishments (the sadistic sentencing of the unfaithful wives of his knights) are found in Wyspiański's play. On the other hand, those who see the matter from the standpoint of Polish autonomy accuse the Bishop of collusion with the nearby Czech kingdom, and the Holy Roman Empire to the west. This too Wyspiański introduces into his plays. Even the King's direct participation in the murder of the Bishop, when the knights he sent to do the deed for him refused, may be found in the early records. However, as we have previously mentioned, the two plays that make up *Bishop, King. Bishop* are creative works based on a familiar Cracovian story. In this they are similar to *Wanda,* the factual basis of which is incomparably more difficult to establish.

Although he was not writing history, by all accounts, Wyspiański was deeply interested in historical fact, and worked up his dramas from meticulous historical research. According to Okońska, Wojciechowski's 1904 *Historical Sketches of the Eleventh Century* was an important event in the composition of *Skałka*, to which Wyspiański is said to have set his hand directly after having finished the book. Yet whether or not that book can have had a decisive influence on the poet's understanding of the conflict, Okońska's assessment of the philosophy expressed in the first play can be taken as descriptive of both:

> Seeing in Bolesław a politician governing according to reasons of state, he described in his play the conflict of the two historical missions in their maximum tension. For in their antagonistic struggle, both the representative of the spiritual government, and that of the state, had to lose.[21]

---

21   Okońska, p. 348.

It might be suggested that Bolesław "lost more" in the poet's telling. After all, there is that surreal scene with which the composite drama comes to an end, in which the animated silver tomb of the martyred Bishop corners the killer-King in his castle, and crushes him — all the while Bolesław is cursing God. It's hard to imagine a more definitive end to the story, which in its symbolic power goes past even the damnation scene of Don Giovanni at the hands of the Commendatore's statue. For in the Mozart/DaPonte opera, the wronged statue gives the rake a chance to confess his sins and avoid Hell before dragging him off to eternal punishment. Wyspiański's tomb enters the castle like Fate, and puts an end to the King's arguments, once and for all.[22]

And yet, Bolesław is no less a tragic figure for all that. Like many Poles of his day, and afterwards, Wyspiański saw the almost anarchistic democracy of mediaeval and early modern Poland as a constituent element in its gradual decline into triple partition (beginning in 1795). If Poland had developed a strong, centralised monarchy, perhaps the nation might have grown as powerful as France, Spain, or England. Near the end of the play, when the frustrated King berates his retainers concerning loyalty, and lays out a catalogue of his triumphant warring in the East, it is not difficult to catch a heroic note in his boast:

> Three castles I shall grind beneath my feet,
> Then I'll return, with three crowns on my head!

Surely, this was the daydream of all patriotic Poles during the period of Partitions. Whatever lands the angry Bolesław may have had in mind,

---

22   It is a very weird scene, and difficult to take seriously. Leopold Staff (cited in Płoszewski, II, 205) reports that the poet's first idea was to have the tomb carried into the King's presence by the four angels who serve as props to it in the central nave of Wawel Cathedral, and to have them toss it upon Bolesław. Yet, although this might seem more "believable," Wyspiański may have abandoned the idea for good reasons. The Bishop is the King's antagonist, and the victory is his. This is affirmed by the scene of the "walking tomb" as Staff, with a wince, refers to it. If the angels were to carry in the tomb and hurl it upon the King, the Martyr would be reduced to a passive object. At any rate, Wyspiański was not the first Polish poet to bring inanimate objects to life on stage. In the Romantic poet Cyprian Kamil Norwid's *Krakus, książę nieznany* [Krakus, Unknown Prince, 1851], we come across a talking threshold. In any case, the surreal, as something that speaks to spiritual reality, fits in quite well with Polish Monumental Drama.

the audience of Wyspiański's day would certainly, and immediately, have imagined "castles" in Vienna, Berlin, and Saint Petersburg ground beneath the heel of a victorious Polish king.[23] The threat of foreign dominance, and the responsibility of a strong monarch to help the country avoid subordination, is something we often find in Wyspiański's plays. In one of the more curious scenes of the drama, there occurs the following dialogue between Bolesław and his mistress, Krasawica:[24]

> KRASAWICA.
> At you they point the swords they wield!
> Call out your men, before they harm you.
> And I myself shall arm you.
>
> KING.
> Say rather, "with love's wiles I'll charm you…"
>
> KRASAWICA.
> You must kill your brother.
>
> KING.
> My brother I shall never kill.
> I'd rather bend to God's harsh will.
>
> KRASAWICA.
> And spread wide your gates to foreign lords?!
>
> KING.
> Love here lies chambered with a sword,
> And envy's blade hacks at the door…
> Yet I'll arise, by God above:
> My soul shall envy crush, and love!

---

23 This itself is an image borrowed from the vision of Fr. Piotr in Part III of Mickiewicz's *Forefathers' Eve*. In that play, the priestly mystic foresees a warlike Saviour of partitioned Poland eventually triumphing over the three Empires that swallowed the nation.

24 The name, or term, derives from a common Slavic root meaning "beauty." Krasawica is, of course, not a human, but a "Wiślanka," one of the Vistulan waterfolk.

The love-scene between the King and his mistress is a strange one. Operatic in nature, it counterpoints the claims of romantic love with those of duty. Although Krasawica finds it difficult to tear herself from her royal lover's arms at other times in the scene, here she wishes to stir him to action, to rouse him to defend himself from his brother, and the "foreign lords" who stand to gain from the collusion of the Bishop and the King's Brother against him. At the conclusion of the cited passage, it is clear that, although the King will not have his own brother slain, he will go as far towards that as his conscience will allow him — in self-defence, and in defence of his kingdom.

Bolesław, warts and all (and he has quite a few of them) is a heroic character in Wyspiański's play. His tragedy is not that he is a tyrant, per se, but rather that for whatever reason — pressure from without, treason from within, or because of his own personal flaws — he will not be allowed to establish his strong, monarchical rule, and in doing so, set Poland on firm, unshakable bases.

As for Bishop Stanisław, he — and the King's Brother — seem to confirm Bolesław's suspicions of their treasonous intent, and that is evident from the very first scenes of the play:

WŁODZISŁAW.
To raise my sword against my clan,
That ancient legacy? I don't dare.

BISHOP.
And yet you stand here, and you stare.
Your eyes betray your smouldering soul.
You'd split what he would conserve whole,
Your brother, and I ask — why not?
The whole world's so divided; God
Allots each portion in accord
With the given soul's greatness. To each
His own — all that's in his reach
If he dare grasp it. Each is lord
Of his own fortune. Be on guard —
If trust fraternal's to be marred
By rivalry unto bloodletting,
Better for you to cease your fretting

And split away now. You don't dare?
Thus I your tender feelings spare.

He lifts his hand above the cake.

WŁODZISŁAW
To the Bishop.
Wait — if you break that circle, know:
You break the peace with me, as well.
Points at the round cake.
From hand to hand it must go, whole.
Blest as of old, by song and spell.

BISHOP.
It's true that he rules the nation —
 By virtue of my anointing.
Let him remember my station:
 I rule, by God, a second king.
That crown of his, by God bestowed,
 Set on his brow by this my hand,
Is sacred — no mere golden band.
 And as he treads his Royal road,
Thrusting aside my holy will,
 Closing his ears against my word,
Let him know: I'm a monarch still,
 Who holds his sceptre of the Lord!

It is hard to imagine a stronger delineation of protagonist-antagonist than this. It is just as difficult to imagine a stronger affirmation of the thesis that spiritual governance is equal to, or even surpasses, the might of earthly monarchy. Of course, however treasonous the Bishop's words may sound, his contextualising of them against the nefarious behaviour of the King, his grounding them in the immutable moral authority of God, goes a long way toward convincing us that he is no mere plotter. Włodzisław (Władysław Herman) comes off a little less impressive in this regard...

It is difficult to see the King's Brother, or Sieciech, as anything other than traitors, in this play where questions of treason play so important a role. But the King himself does not respect any golden rule. He considers treachery towards his own person a capital offence, yet breaks his faith with man and God without a second thought. He freely admits his infidelity in the very opening scene of his drama (Act II of *Bishop, King. Bishop*), when, despite the mounting tension of uncertainty as the crowd led by the Bishop approaches the castle, he cannot bear to part from Krasawica:

> Come then, once more before we part —
> My lovely one, my love, my life!
> For you I spurn my wedded wife;
> For you I shun her, and my son.

As the play develops, so too does the theme of the King's own "treason." From the accusations brought to him by his angry wife, we see that the King is outfitted with a healthy double standard:

> KING'S WIFE.
> One of your servant girls, I'm told
> Has spread the news, you make so bold
> As to pull her into your bed,
> Tired of my charms — it seems you've said —
> What good are your marriage vows?
>
> KING.
> I made a vow, I made a vow!
> And if I broke it? What's the crime?
> A king can't keep a concubine?
> [...]
> It's jealousy poisons your heart,
> Because I've dandled with that tart.
> You say my oaths I thus foreswear.
> You are my love. My only care
> Is to find favour in your eye —
> To bring you glory, or to die.

For most of us, there is no such distinction to be made between sex and love; the vow pronounced by man to wife (and vice-versa) does not merely refer to contractual exclusivity, i.e. remaining an inseparable pair as far as finances or progeny is concerned; it also enjoins exclusivity of the marriage bed. For King Bolesław, fleeting sexual encounters with servant girls, or even an almost bigamous relationship with a preferred mistress, has nothing to do with the vow given to his wife. It is an arrogant thing he suggests here, and the courtesy of the champion that he appends to his words at the end are nothing but empty sentimentalism.

Worst of all, though, is the sense of being a law to himself, which the above-quoted lines suggest, and which Bolesław explicitly states in the presence of Stanisław a bit further on. As the two giants measure one another across the space of the castle chamber, Bolesław calls the Bishop, and the folk he's led there, to order, to obedience. In a surprising act of humility, Stanisław kneels — to the King? or to God? — willing to have the justice of his cause heard. Bolesław (perhaps correctly) interprets this gesture as an acknowledgement of his authority, and, while inclined to step away, this time, from avenging himself on the affront measured at him by his potentially rebellious people, reminds them of his ruthlessness, as a warning:

> But know this: grovelling wins no clemency!
> Whom I condemn to Death, Night shuts his eyes,
> With no appeal — however sharp his scythe!
> The King decrees, the Lord God shares his crimes!

What a strong, inexcusably prideful attitude that is. More than once, Bolesław refers to the spiritual legacy of his coronation. He, like Stanisław, has been anointed, and he too derives his power and sanction from on high. The Erastian direction this argument takes can be, and has been, debated at great length. What is important here is that God is not referenced as a sanctioning Power, a wellspring from which the King's own authority flows and according to which it is measured, but rather as a passive agent, subject to the King's will. *Żem król — każę! — Bóg ze mną zbrodnie dźwiga!* the line reads in the original, literally: "Because I am a King — I command! — and God bears the crime along with me!" In plays in which the lightning appears so frequently, it's rather miraculous that no thunderbolts appear over the King's head at this moment...

As the play continues, it doesn't get much better. The strange figure of Krasawica — who will be discussed in a moment — switches her own loyalties from the King, to those who would destroy him. She seduces Sieciech, and binds him to an unholy bargain: kill a man and win my love.

Sieciech reveals this to Bolesław, and it is the reaction of the latter that should be noted:

> SIECIECH.
> Eternal love to me she vowed,
> But I may only win her hand
> If first, for her, I kill a man.
>
> KING.
> All right, old friend. So, kill away,
> If you so love the crazy maid.
> As long as you're up to the trade,
> With stout, resolved arms, kill you may
> Whomever she desires, your fair.
> By God in Heaven, this I swear,
> Kill whom you will.

Nothing more needs to be said about the arbitrariness of the King's moral compass. Might is right, and as long as he holds power, he will do whatever he wishes, sanction whatever action is convenient to him, or which does not concern him, without reflection on right, wrong, good, evil, or the consequences for others. Despite his words concerning his anointing, Bolesław really acknowledges no authority but that of his own will. Just as Krak in *Wanda* is a cardinal figure, who destroys the pagan past without raising upon its ruins anything more than his own palace, so King Bolesław in his play(s) repeats the sterile act of cult-destruction. Among the other charges he brings against Stanisław in the early acts of the play, is Stanisław's destruction of the pagan temple, upon the foundations of which he raises the Catholic church of St. Michael. The King fulminates:

> Hear this, Bishop. As long as I wear the crown,
> Nor you, nor anybody else shall lead
> My subjects. As for knocking idols down,
> That is my task. Your help I do not need!

That is a rather odd statement for a Christian king to make.[25] Why should he be angry with the Bishop for suppressing a pagan cult in which he has no interest, from which he derives no advantage? After all, he does not appear in these lines as a defender of the repressed faith, toward which he too is oriented destructively. Instead of allowing the Church to do Caesar's work in eradicating the old faith and shoring up the new, which also legitimises his throne, Bolesław sees the question in terms of a rival authority. His is the task of renewal, and his alone. But, as in the case of Krak, he can destroy the pagan temple, but with what will he replace it? If he is jealous of the Bishop's destruction of the temple as a bid for authority among the people, surely he is not interested in constructing, for the Bishop, a splendid church in its place? And so, like Krak, he will destroy an ancient nexus of power, to replace it only with his own. He will raze the monuments of an ancient spiritual power, preparing the ground for the construction, or rather extension, of his own, temporal authority.

And thus we are led again to the central concern of spirituality. Writing in 1932, the Kraków physician and politician Julian Nowak speaks of the religiosity of the Wyspiański he knew:

> Wyspiański was a deeply pious person, and punctilious in his observation of the commandment to Keep Holy the Lord's Day. On Sundays and holy days he did not work, but rested, and was happy when those he considered his friends would visit him then. He observed the holy day of St. Stanisław with special devotion, and participated in the services on Skałka.[26]

Nowak was a conservative politician, who in independent Poland once served as Minister for Religious and Educational Affairs. That said, there is no reason to doubt his assessment of Wyspiański's personal beliefs, although, judging from the poet's output, he would probably describe himself as the film director Krzysztof Zanussi once did, saying: "I am an artist who happens to be a Catholic, rather than a Catholic artist." It would be a stretch to call Wyspiański any sort of "religious" or confessional poet,

---

25   In *Wanda*, we have a pagan king attacking pagan rites. In *Bishop, King. Bishop* we have a Christian king flouting Christianity. Perhaps in this way the poet underscores the bankruptcy of the very idea of a monarch.

26   Julian Nowak, "W świecie wielkiej legendy," cited by Płoszewski, II, p. 180.

although, as we have frequently repeated, Polish Monumental Drama cannot exist without a positive acknowledgement of the spiritual realm.

In Wyspiański's plays, eternity is broader than the traditional Christian culture of Poland. In *Bishop, King. Bishop,* the spiritual realm is represented not only by Bishop Stanisław, but also by the same fantastic water-folk that we first came across in *Wanda*. Krasawica is as front and centre in the play, in this regard, as Stanisław himself. Although, at the beginning of the story, she allies herself to her lover the King, she reveals herself as an antagonistic spiritual power when attacked by the King's Wife, and the Bishop:

> King, as you've taken love of me
> In the dark night — night after night! —
> Make use now of my mystery.
> Like thunderbolts, my secret might;
> Just say the word, unloose my tongue,
> And by my spells I'll strike them dumb!
>
> SIECIECH.
> Your wife, king! Look — how pale the queen!
>
> KING
> *Rising and moving towards Krasawica.*
> You pagan asp — you thing unclean —
> *Looks to his wife*
> She pales — spell-struck —
> *Pointing at Krasawica*
>   Bind her in chains!
> *To Krasawica*
> Begone! And never come again!
>
> KRASAWICA
> *Frees herself from the Knights.*
> Spawn of Rycheza — bind me yourself.
> I gave you power, I gave you love;
> With lightning's might I burn, the wealth
> Of the once-charmed, now plundered grove.
> I'm called by everlasting Fame —
> A thunderous voice, not like the lame

> Mewling that fills his treacherous church!
> Bind me. Let's see what your strength's worth.
> I'll burst your chains as if they're straw!
> Upon my brow shines forth a star —
> Ruler of floods, sprite, water-maid,
> I stand among you, unafraid!

Why is it that the King does not take advantage of her magical power? Is it because of his loving concern for his wife? Or is it because he is afraid of her power which, even if it be allied to him, is still a rival power, which he cannot fully control? That the latter may be the case, we may judge from the palpable role that Krasawica plays in the unfolding of Bolesław's tragedy as the interwoven acts of the composite drama move on to their conclusion. What is striking, though, is how the pagan maiden, who is at first inimical to the Christian tradition of St. Stanisław, later crouches at his feet in a scene highly reminiscent of the adulteress before Christ in the Gospel of John and acknowledges his authority as genuine:

> KRASAWICA.
> At your feet, trembling, I bow my head
> As once, trembling, I sought his bed.
> It's true, I strove to cause you grief
> By the fire that through the heavens runs;
> Now have I fallen, a trembling leaf —
> For you are of our holy ones.
> In you there glows the lightning's might
> And thus I proffer homage, brash,
> For you illuminate our night,
> Your embers glowing in this ash.
> Before the people, father, raise
> Your immaculate hand;
> Touch me, and free me from all stains
> Of the ancient, sinful man,
> So that my youth might, for all time
> As it in my two eyes plays,
> Sing out the spring-hope of my prime
> Amidst the Vistula's waves;
> So that above the river floods

> My virgin song may resound,
> As you offer your holy blood
> Which to the Spirit redounds;
> So ever about this riverside cliff
> Should echo this your story;
> For this I take of you this gift,
> My Lord, for your eternal glory.

In his book *Wyspiański's Antiquity*, Tadeusz Sinko expresses surprise that "Krasawica too, a pagan goddess, humbles herself before the bishop and begs him for absolution:"

> [...] And she receives it. But one mustn't forget that, from the very start, the bishop asserted that his God is the God of the sun, who gave into his power "all the earthly elements." His God is — a pantheistic God, as He is identified with "fire and water, wind and earth." Krasawica had this in mind when she said to the bishop "you are one of our holy ones."[27]

Perhaps because Sinko's fascinating book interprets Wyspiański through the lens of the classics, and the solid classical education that the poet received, it is excusable that he should understand St. Stanisław's views here as "pantheistic." Yet that really cannot be squared with Catholicism, which posits a God who created all things, but is not, Himself, all things.[28] Rather, the Bishop's words throughout the play indicate the submission of all nature, and all religiosity ("every spirit") to Christ, and his seemingly strange alliance with the pagan agents in the play looks more like syncretism. He comes out, swinging violently, against the pagan tradition. Once it has been laid low, he does not deliver the final coup de grace to the moribund tradition, but is willing to let it die out on its own. And while it lives, he will not refuse its aid against the godless king.

While never questioning the propriety of the supersession, and suppression, of the pagan cult by the true religion of Christ (note the

---

27   Tadeusz Sinko, *Antyk Wyspiańskiego* (Warszawa: Instytut Wydawniczy Biblioteka Polska, 1922), p. 217.

28   In our translation, the lines in question read "Fire and water, earth and air / Are Thine alone by right."

touching lament of the rusalkas for the passing of the sun-god that precedes the Rhapsode's nostalgic dialogue with Pandora), Wyspiański, and his Bishop Stanisław, display a striking inclusiveness in this regard. The Bishop does not deny the pagan entities; from the beginning, he recognises their existence, though demanding their subjection to Christ with his device that "all spirits must serve the Lord." If there is a conflict in the play, it is not so much one between Christianity and Paganism, as it is between the nihilistic earthly authority of the King, and the supernatural, which is represented by both Stanisław and Krasawica. Alicia Okońska is quite right in her assessment of the scene of conciliation between the Bishop and the Rhapsode (during which the former restores the sacred lyre to the latter):

> The bridge leading from the pagan temple, destroyed by the lightning bolt, over which strides the Bishop, returning from Wawel, becomes a bridge of sorts between the old faith and the new. This Christianising of paganism is effected on the basis of an alliance against the King: both old and new ethical systems unite against crime. Even Krasawica, who wanted to burn down the church, humbles herself at the feet of the Bishop.[29]

Even at the very beginning of the play, when the latter is none too positively disposed in regard to the former, the Wiślanka is aghast at Bolesław's determination to do battle with Skałka:

KRASAWICA.
A war — with Skałka! Tread with care —
Charmed is that place with ancient spells.
The sacred grove chants nearby, where
Stands the temple, the holy well...
Both simple folk and runic sage
Honour Skałka with song, holy from age on age —
This wreath of holy leaves I wear
First grew upon the branches there,
The sacred grove, where is jasmine...
And my home, toppled in ruin.

---

29   Okońska, p. 360.

Even before what can be termed her conversion scene, while still lamenting the Bishop's destruction of her ancient home and the suppression of the pagan rites, she acknowledges the legitimacy of his spiritual authority. It is the same with the Rhapsode, the pagan bard, the keeper of the old ways. At the beginning of the story, Wyspiański seems to set him up as an antagonist to the Bishop. He is the only one among those gathered who does not kneel in the Bishop's presence, but glares at him. He is strong enough in his own authority to challenge the Bishop's warlike intentions, reminding him of how a "shaman" should approach civil disobedience. Toward the end of his story, when his lyre has been restored to him and, through it, he is once more able to contact the future in vision, he recognises the Bishop as a spiritual brother:

> RHAPSODE:
> *Looks toward Bishop.*
> Sower of souls, accept my thanks.
> Imperial will, whose nod is deed;
> Shaman, I stand in the same ranks
> As you — whom yet I must precede.
>
> After me, Spirit, shall you fly,
> O man in the might of God;
> You I bequeath these flaming eyes
> Before I wash this path with blood.
>
> BISHOP
> *Makes the Sign of the Cross over him.*

It is worth noting that at the very beginning of the play, when the Rhapsode makes his first appearance, the Bishop acknowledges him as a man of faith[30] — even if that faith belongs to a past, never to return. And

---

30   Very effective in this sense is the antiphonal ritual in which the Bishop engages at the end of Act III. With its rhythmic, rhymed chanting and, especially, the repetitive antiphonal response of the Chorus, the scene is consciously reminiscent of Mickiewicz's *Forefathers' Eve*. That ceremony was a folk-mélange of pagan and Christian rites, which even in Mickiewicz's own day the Church struggled against, as something superstitious. One of the great ideological thrusts of Mickiewicz's masterpiece is a plea for tolerance in this regard. Bishop

here, Stanisław blesses the retreating Rhapsode, even though the latter did not explicitly accede to the Bishop's demand that he now enlist in the ranks of the Triune God.

In short, the sacred is one. As we have already noted, it is the spiritually-sensitive (Stanisław, Rhapsode, rusalkas) against the spiritually-empty (the King). When the Rhapsode moves away, having been blessed by the Bishop, he goes off to make the first salvo of the holy war against Bolesław, which will be conducted to its successful conclusion by the Bishop. When asked by the King how he might be repaid for the lay he has just sung, he replies:

> RHAPSODE.
> I want to die —
> But first, to kill him, who killed fame.
> Rycheza's grand-whelp, I curse thee
> And these thy bloody hands.
> Thou'st murdered many, now kill me!
> And then, eternally be damned!
>
> KING.
> You'll die for that!
>
> RHAPSODE.
> Kill me — alone
> Of all men you. No one else dares.
> In the ruined temple is my home —
> God's sentinel, sacrosanct seer!

It is a request which the goaded, amoral king promptly grants. In a foreshadowing of his murder of Stanisław, the spiritually-dead King first slays the priest of the Old Order, revealing to our eyes, once again, his villainy as well as his arbitrariness.

For all of these reasons, it is difficult not to see the Bishop — like the Rhapsode and even Krasawica — as the hero of *Bishop, King. Bishop.* Certainly, the poet hints at his regret that a strong King was unable to found the type of stable monarchy that would have helped Poland to

---

Stanisław's ritual here is itself open-ended, inclusive, tolerant — an implied rallying of believers of all sorts to the same flag.

avoid the troubles that were later to beset her, and with which Poles of Wyspiański's generation were still coming to grips. Even though the Partitions were not to occur for another six-plus centuries, the reader familiar with Polish history smells the rot already setting in with Bolesław's ouster. After all, Władysław Herman, the King's Brother, kept the crown united only for his own lifetime, after which, in Lear-like fashion which prefigures the Partitions of 1795, he divided the land between his two sons: something which lends an ironic tinge to his reluctance to split the crown "which should be passed on whole, from father to son."

It is an open question whether or not the King is as strong as we make him out to be. After the crime, like Shakespeare's Macbeth, he loses a great deal of his manly stature. Just as he and Krasawica open the play in uncertainty — is that a shepherd's horn? or an enemy's bugle? — so at the end he seems uncertain as to what those sounds are, that are borne to him across the waters from Skałka:

> RUMOUR 3.
> At Skałka — your wife, your son,
> Mourning, sobbing,
> Hear them crying — — ?
>
> KING.
> The rain is plashing — winds are sighing —
> The roof-tiles drum —
> The gutters
> With water
> Are throbbing.

But perhaps we are being too kind to him here, giving him the benefit of the doubt. No, he knows exactly what he hears, and his desire to hear "winds sighing and rain plashing" rather than the laments of his wife and the tears of his child is a sad attempt to fool himself. For but two scenes on, with the entry of the Lieutenant and the Sexton, he is forced to relive the murder he has just committed. In a manner that recalls the congregational reading of the Passion during Holy Week, Bolesław — whose lines are enclosed in quotation marks in the original — replays his role in the murder:

SEXTON.
All for candles broken!

LIEUTENANT.
Look — he stands at the altar!
His eyes, his eyes are on you!

KING.
"Have you no swords?"

LIEUTENANT.
They measured with their swords,
But — see: they've checked their haste.

KING.
"Cowards!"

LIEUTENANT.
Support them with your right hand!

KING.
"Now!"

Whether this role of his was reenacted "in public" or not (as the two other characters disappear from the stage immediately, and we cannot be sure that they were even aware of the King's presence), it is plain that the King cannot say that he is not conscious of what he's just done.

And then, ungainly or not, the "walking tomb" of St. Stanisław falls on the King, crushing him, rendering him now irrelevant. This is true no matter what sympathy the poet may have felt for him, no matter how he may have striven to defend him in the "Argumentum" (see: Appendix), which was probably written for one reason and one reason only: as a last attempt on Wyspiański's part to effect what he was unable to do during the play itself — to justify King Bolesław the Bold.

Acropolis

THE PLAY

The tomb which brings *Bishop, King. Bishop* to an end opens the action of the final play of our Wawel series: *Acropolis*. If, as Adam Chmiel states, Wyspiański was "madly in love with Wawel,"[31] none of the Wawel plays proves this more clearly than *Acropolis*. In a play that is unusual for the number of fantastic characters it contains[32] — nearly all of the characters are magically enlivened statues and tapestries from the Cathedral — Wyspiański gives a dramatic expression to the sentiments expressed in his lyric poem "O, I love Kraków," with which we began our introduction. What is most interesting, however, is that Wyspiański does not enliven the statues and arrases so that they should enunciate the feelings and desires of people, his nation, or even himself. Wyspiański so empathises with the stone that he is able to imagine its feelings. They speak for themselves, these statues, or, rather, in Wyspiański's enchanted cathedral, they speak how one imagines they might speak, had they the consciousness to do so. At the very beginning of the play, when the four angels that serve as props to the silver casket of St. Stanisław group together, they express some surprising sentiments:

> ANGEL 1.
> And thus are gathered we four bards.
> Ah, oh! The freedom!
> And look: our figures are still young!
> My arms, stretch out!
> Stretch out, my wings!
> — That tomb!
> I'm fed up with that gruesome thing!

The main reliquary of the city's most revered patron saint, not only a burden, but a "gruesome thing?" One can imagine the murmurs that spread through the audience at the première, when the casket is described as "full

---

31   Cited by Płoszewski, II. 88.
32   As Milosz notes on p. 357 of his *History*, "nowhere in Wyspiański did an invasion of the fantastic reach such proportions as in *Acropolis*."

of dust and grave worms," unceremoniously tossed onto the altar slab, and then spoken of in this fashion. And yet, above and beyond Wyspiański's understandable sensitivity to artworks[33] these lines make perfect sense. Statues are not Christians; the saints and martyrs do not intercede on their behalf; what is the casket of the venerated bishop and martyr to them but an oppressive weight that they are made to bear through the ages, with only one brief respite, on this Easter vigil?

An even stronger passus may be found in the words of the Angel spoken in reference to one of the most sacred monuments in the cathedral: the large black crucifix in the sanctuary, before which St. Jadwiga herself was said to pray:

> No, no, I can't move from this place.
> His black chest, bruised, his sooty face,
> The blood! Oh, all that blood, the veil
> So black, too black! His panting torso,
> So cruelly... No! I cannot look
> Each day upon His death. O crime
> Beyond all crimes, and all the more so
> Recalled each day upon this altar!
> I won't go! — He's dying up there,
> A crown of thorns pierces His hair! —

Very strong words, expressive of the horror felt by the Angel at the depiction of the Crucifixion — a source of solace to the pious Christian — and even at the recollection, the reenactment, of the same during Mass. But these are the words of a statue: not the words of a human; the silver Angel cannot understand salvation history in the same away as a man or a woman, for that history does not apply to him. It is most important to note here that the Angel is not rejecting Christ, Whom he/she pities to tears. Rather, it is a rejection of the cruelty that led Him to the Cross; it is a reflection on the cruelty of men, who would consider doing such a thing to a sentient

---

33 Writing of the "last moments of Stanisław Wyspiański," Konstantyn Srokowski reports him saying to Wilhelm Feldman, that "his inability to paint weighed down upon him, as if someone had placed one of the towers of St. Mary's Basilica on his chest, and that however much he was suffering, he would agree to suffer ten times worse, if only he could still paint." Cited by Płoszewski, II. 467.

Being. Once more, those words of Wyspiański about the kindness of stone, as greater than that of man, are made strikingly apparent.[34]

And yet, despite the gulf that separates us men and women from Wyspiański's animated monuments and tapestries, this is not to say that we cannot learn from these beings, so unlike us. The words they say about their fate, their roles in life, can excite us to reflect on our own behaviour. This is part of the dialogue between Angels 3 and 4 and the Lady from the Skotnicki Monument:

> LADY.
> It's not worth the trouble.
> This grave encloses me.
> This slab's imposed on me.
>
> ANGEL 3.
> You were his wife?
>
> LADY.
> I don't recall. No, not his wife.
>
> ANGEL 4.
> You knew him?
>
> LADY.
> I don't know — I prayed,

---

34   The American poet, Robinson Jeffers (twenty years Wyspiański's junior, though Czesław Miłosz sees them as kindred in their philosophy), a great advocate for the nobility and rights of animals, was angered when people would describe acts of barbarity as "inhuman." On the contrary, he would argue, they are quite quintessentially human, as sadism and barbarity do not exist in the animal kingdom. He created a philosophical outlook called Inhumanism — it might not be inappropriate to compare Wyspiański's preference for art as a more moral thing than humanity, with Jeffers' opinions. The connections between Wyspiański and Jeffers, as early twentieth century poets, is worth exploring. Miłosz finds a common "Nietzschean instigation" among Jeffers and the poets of Young Poland, and offers, "Even [Jeffers'] long narrative-poem/tragedies of incest and murder might be effectively compared to Przybyszewski and Wyspiański." See Miłosz, „Punkt widzenia, czyli o tak zwanej drugiej awangardzie," collected in *Zaczynając od moich ulic* (Kraków: Znak, 2006), p. 178.

And took my lyre,
And on my lyre I played,
And had my two arms splayed
In despair.

ANGEL 3.
    Your hands — unbind.
LADY.
Unbind…

ANGEL 4.
    Your fingers untwine.

LADY.
And the pain, that I bear in my breast?

ANGEL 3.
Here, wipe your brow. Now put to rest
Your pain. What else do you recall?

ANGEL 4.
Were you ever happy?

LADY.
You ask me was I ever happy?
I don't know. I know that I grew sad.

ANGEL 3.
Why?

LADY.
I stood on that slab.

ANGEL 4.
And now you've stepped down from that grave.

The monuments in Wawel Cathedral have been set in their positions of mourning, piety, or service by the hands that created them. The Lady mourns a person she does not know, because that is what is expected of her. Extrapolating from her sentiments, liberated in this hour of enchantment and led on to their surprising conclusion by the kind Angels, we might ourselves reflect upon our own true feelings. Expressions of love, hatred, patriotism, tolerance or judgement — how often are these behaviours of ours, free agents though we be, expressions of what we truly think and feel? And on the contrary, how often are they nothing but learned expressions, opinions and statements repeated at the dictation of our society, our church, our family or our nation, because we know that that is what we are supposed to feel? Decades before the existentialists, Wyspiański is subtly exploring matters of individual authenticity — no simple, straightforward notion for a citizen of early twentieth-century Austrian Kraków. Conditioned by recent history to be ethnic patriots, striving toward the re-establishment of Polish independence, how many Cracovians of Wyspiański's day would have been brave enough to wear a yellow and black ribbon on a Habsburg holiday, or state out loud, "Well, independence may be fine and good, but, really, I have a good life in this multinational Austro-Hungarian conglomerate, and why should I wish to rock the boat?"

We know, not only from this play, that the archly Polish Wyspiański had little, if anything, in common with our hypothetical conservative. Yet he certainly seems to raise the question, again and again in *Acropolis*, of truthfulness to nature, as opposed to acquiescence to what the majority enjoin. One of the most poignant such passages, reflective of the tyrannical pressure of the group, can be found in Act IV:

> CHORUS OF EUMENIDES.
> 1. Mother, dear mother, the perfume
> Of roses! Ah, close not the tomb!
>
> 2. The scent of living roses pours
> Upon us! Ah, one moment more!
>
> NIGHT.
> No, daughters, turn away the face;
> Treacherous beams — that hateful stench!
> The votive lamp shows you our place:
> Below, with bones, on the grave bench.

CHORUS OF EUMENIDES.
That kneeling man's harp — how it rings!
Allow us but to hear him sing!

NIGHT.
Daughters, the sun nips at our feet.
Soon you will feel his searing heat!
CHORUS OF EUMENIDES.
Mother! A bird rests on my palm!
He throbs, just like the heart of man!

NIGHT.
Cover your eyes before the dawn
That wakes the roses, dews the land!
Quick! Into the depths with me to hide:
The heavy doors creak open wide!

Everything is relative: the scent of roses, which invigorates and delights the Eumenides, is described as a "stench" by their Mother Night. Our place is in the tomb, she reminds her daughters; descend, and now! It would be too much to suggest that in pointing at Wawel, which he so loved, Wyspiański was pointing at the beautiful, exterior sarcophagus, for example, of Władysław Jagiełło, as signpost to a greater, brighter future, while castigating those patriotic historians who constantly harp on the past, as necrophiliacs stirring about the unwholesome dust it contains. And yet, would we be so wrong to suggest that Wyspiański gently probes, in *Acropolis*, a polemic with patriotic fanaticism? Something of the sort is hinted at in the words of the Maiden from the Sołtyk Monument directed at her partner, Clio:

> Many long hours have I sat
> In deep thought of myself, and you,
> Wondering: what on earth have we to do
> With brooding, weeping, and with mourning,
> Slaves to a sorrow vain, and scorning
> Freshness, and joy! Come, sister, friend,
> Bring book and mourning to an end.
> We'll live our own lives!

Clio, of course, is the muse of History. To suggest, as the Maiden does in these far-seeing lines, that too much brooding over a book, over the past, is a noxious thing, an obstacle to "freshness and joy, and life" must have sounded like heresy to some of the people seated in the theatre when they were first pronounced.

Wyspiański himself does not go this far, but he might have: Why must the present, youthful generations sacrifice their lives to rectify the mistakes of their grandparents, their great-great grandparents, their antecedents from the corrupt eighteenth century? In his *History of Polish Literature*, Czesław Miłosz offers a list of eight "factors" toward an understanding of Wyspiański's dramas. The very first one speaks somewhat to the issue at hand:

> His native city, Kraków, was one solid museum, preserving the glory of Poland's past. It was also subject to the inertia typical of provincial towns of the Habsburg Empire. Wyspiański both loved the museum and revolted against it.[35]

At any rate, this "internally independent" artist, who "never acknowledged the partitioning powers,"[36] felt independent enough from the pressures of majority groupthink to look at the claims of patriotic history with a critical eye. This provocative Maiden is one of the more interesting characters in Wyspiański's fantastic drama. She puts forward this very argument in her delightful love-scene with the statue of the soldier from the tomb of Włodzimierz Potocki:

MAIDEN.
Unbuckle, and lay aside your sword,
And set it down by your breastplate.
Come down.

WŁODZIMIERZ.
    Where are my boys? My mates?!

---

35   Miłosz, *History*, p. 353.
36   Thus, with a bit of exaggeration, suggest Płoszewski, et al. in the critical apparatus to vol. 14 of the collected works.

MAIDEN.
What boys? Only you and I are here.
I've come, because I love you, dear.
And you? —

WŁODZIMIERZ.
I need to save the nation from
A tyrant!

MAIDEN.
What tyrant? There's no such one
Here about. — You're mistaken.
Lean down — and when you've taken
A look around, you'll see:
There's no one else here but me,
Eyes locked on you. Come down.

WŁODZIMIERZ.
You, love me?

What tyrant, indeed? one might ask. Franz Josef, who was to return Wawel to "the Polish nation" and contribute a sizeable sum from his personal treasure for its restoration? Franz Ferdinand, his heir to the throne, perhaps the most pro-Slavic of the Habsburgs, whose ironic assassination at the hands of Slavic nationalists in Sarajevo sparked the process of European decomposition into ethnic enclaves and racist ideologies with which we are still dealing in the twenty-first century? Or perhaps Blessed Karl I, the last of the Emperors, currently on the path to canonisation in the Catholic Church? Political or not, Wyspiański's Maiden is a very modern sort of girl, who prefers love, youth, and the future built on a peace and prosperity that really exists, over an idealistic, brooding devotion to battles long settled.

The most original writing to be found in *Acropolis* is at the beginning of the work, in Act I, with the vivification of the monuments, and in Act IV, when the sculpture of David descends from the organ loft and begins his psalm-like hymning. Between these two sections we have Act II, in which the embroidered figures depicting scenes from the Trojan War take life, and Act III, in which the figures from the tapestries illustrating the story of Jacob are given voice. Wyspiański brings little of idiosyncrasy to these acts;

in Act II, the play is a paraphrase of themes from Homer, foreshadowing the sacrificial patriotism of the hero Hector as contrasted to the selfish eroticism of Paris and Helen. Act III is simply a dramatic presentation of the Jacob passages from the Old Testament, lifted *in toto* from the classic, sixteenth-century Polish translation of Scripture by Jakub Wujek.

It has been traditional in some Polish art to use Troy as a metaphor for Poland, and sometimes to see in Jewish history parallels to contemporary Polish times. The nineteenth century painter Wojciech Korneli Stattler, for example, created a famous canvas depicting the heroic Maccabees, in which, of course, the steadfast Jews are meant to stand for the unbowed Poles, and their sadistic Roman oppressors, for the Russian or Prussian partitioning governments. Such allusions are hinted at in *Acropolis,* with the Wisła (Vistula) River now being termed the Skamander, now the Jordan. Yet this is as far as Wyspiański goes. Hebrew and Greek themes are included in the play, but only so as to include more of the artworks on display in the Cathedral. This is no patriotic appropriation of the past; it is, if anything, an acknowledgement of the two cultural traditions from which Poland springs: the Hebrew, and the Classical. Such an acknowledgement might be made by any poet, from any European or Atlantic tradition. Yet there is a brief nod toward politics in Act II. In the conversation between Paris and Helen, the latter fluctuates between dim-witted eroticism and political scheming. At one point, she castigates Paris with his lack of ambition for the throne of Troy. He replies:

> PARIS.
> Did you see? Today I bear the fleece.
>
> HELEN.
> The golden fleece! But the sceptre — when?
>
> PARIS.
> Patience.

In an Austrian context, the Golden Fleece was the most prized decoration that one might receive from the hands of the Habsburg emperor. It was said to make one "part of the Imperial household." Can Wyspiański be making a political statement at this point, associating the conservative, subservient Poles with the generally despised, effeminate character of Paris? The scene is made all the more poignant when one recalls that one of the Cracovians who most lusted after the Golden Fleece was Stanisław Tarnowski, rector of Jagiellonian University, and a person none too positively inclined towards Wyspiański. So incensed was he by the depiction of an historical character in the poet's play *The Wedding Feast*, which, according to him, set his wife's family in a poor light, that he agitated to have the production of the play stopped, and future performances banned. So, the Golden Fleece, as a symbol of subjection to Vienna, is derided as an unimportant shiny thing. That said, nothing is ever straightforward in truly great works of art. Rebellion? Usurpation of government? "Patience," Paris suggests, in perhaps the only passage in which he is shown in a serious light. *Patience*. If this word meets the poet's approval, we see him here as more on the side of the aforementioned young Maiden, than on that of the warlike Włodzimierz Potocki.

Act IV brings us another surprising destruction of a temple. In this case, Wyspiański imagines the apocalyptic Second Coming of Christ/Apollo, in which the glorious destruction of Wawel Cathedral is described, leading to the renewal of the people. The Harpist — David from the organ loft — urges on the coming End Times:

> 6. Come Lord, before my people, bright;
> They call to Thee, my nation.
> Rise to us, as Thou rose Easter night,
> Make tremble this fane's foundations.
>
> 7. Before Thee, this grand church shall fall
> Upon my people's necks;
> Yet after three days, at Thy call
> It shall stand new, erect,
>
> 8. Of ancient crimes and sins made clean,
> Its slavery forgot;
> Renewed shall stand, eternal, serene
> At Thy Word, Holy God.
>
> 9. Tear through the vault, push down the walls,
> Tumble down altar, throne;

Come, sweet Redeemer! Thus we call
In the rosy-fingered dawn.

10. I hear a rumble from afar —
Hoofbeats — Here comes the Sun!
Thus rush the hosts of Thy centaurs,
Smashing pillar and column!

11. The mortar cracks, the blocks down slide,
Walls pavements now bestrew.
Thy golden cart majestic rides
Triumphant over the tomb.

12. Thy golden face shines brilliantly,
Thy robes, like golden fleece.
Thine eyes sparkle with victory,
Night's mysteries now cease.

13. Thy wheels roll over the silver tomb.
O Saviour, crush our chains!
Speak, Dawning Lord "I am with you"
Great One, Lord of this fane.

14. Say, Lord: "I come, as God I come"
And on these cold stones write:
"God am I, there is no other one,
None equal to my might.

15. "By the fires which about me play,
By this my Holy Word,
A new cathedral shall stand today,
Where I shall be your Lord."

When we speak of Wyspiański, the so-called "fourth bard," in reference to the great Romantics who preceded him, it is most often in the context of Adam Mickiewicz. After all, he is the national bard *ne plus ultra*, whose *Forefathers' Eve* Wyspiański staged in Kraków to continuing acclaim, and whose character Konrad he borrowed for his own *Wyzwolenie* [Liberation].

Yet in this surprising, apocalyptic razing of the temple he so loved, we see, rather, a reference to another of the Romantic bards: Zygmunt Krasiński. In that poet's most recognisable work, the Monumental Drama *Nieboska komedia* [Undivine Comedy], basic matters, both aesthetic and social, are discussed. As far as the latter is concerned, the old, aristocratic system (from which Krasiński himself came) is confronted with its revolutionary antithesis: a revolt of the people, which both looks back to Robespierre's Reign of Terror and forward, to Marxist totalitarianism. Devotees of Hegel will be disappointed at the clash of thesis and antithesis: the poet could see no human synthesis arising to return harmony through progress. In one of the boldest strokes of the Monumental stage, the final scene of the drama depicts the triumph of Christ, who arrives with His Kingdom of peace, at the Second Coming. Here Wyspiański reaches for the same solution, or, at least, a similar one: beyond the politics of the day. In so doing, he elevates his great drama from the parochial into the universal.[37] This does not mean to suggest complacency, or a tergiversation in regards to the realia of the world in which he himself was born. The last words of the play are directed at the reader:

> *9. With sonorous voice sings Zygmunt's bell —*
> *Its hammer strikes with might.*
> *Trumpets resound over hill and dell,*
> *Joining his regal flight.*
>
> *10. Trumpets like cannon-fire resound*
> *As once, on these same leas;*
> *As if all Poland had risen now*
> *From off her bended knees.*
>
> *11. As if she'd now good fortune won*
> *After so many years,*

---

[37] Tadeusz Sinko points out, perceptively, that the entirety of the drama plays out in eternity: "Because Tempus set aside his scythe and went off on his nighttime stroll, the wheel of time was brought to a standstill, and the histories embroidered on the Wawel arrases became — contemporary events." Vide Sinko, p. 195.

And faded in oblivion
Were all her toils and tears.

12. High over the peoples, through the air,
The sacred song takes flight;
Over bloodied Poland, Acropolis, where
Her kings sleep, as does their right.
13. I'll wake the centuries one day;
I've stood before God's face,
Whose Living Word conquered the fray —
His victory I praise.

14. The song is finished, Wawel's rune,
Her deathless fame re-told.
God's finger hovers above these stones,
Once, and again, His scroll.

While refusing to present a political solution to his play, the poet does not reject a Polish one. Okońska sums up her understanding of Act IV thus:

> The poet's foundational idea is that Poland will never arrive at freedom unless she first bid farewell to even the most beloved symbols of her past. For this reason, Wawel crumbles to the dust in the last act of the play; Wawel, that treasury of the nation's memories — is useless in the new age. [38]

And so, the apocalyptic razing of Wawel Cathedral can also be seen as the preparation of the ground for a new, and better, temple to be erected by a renewed, bettered, people. And this is something that — in a more prosaic sense — Wyspiański was able to envision, and which he formulated in his

---

38   Okońska, p. 380. The twentieth century poet Zbigniew Herbert is thus ungenerous in his criticism of Wyspiański's attachment to Wawel. In his poem "Wawel" (from the volume *Struna światła*) Herbert mocks Wyspiański for having "patriotic cataracts" on his eyes, which cause him to overvalue this "silly jumble of brick / the royal apple of the Renaissance / foregrounded against Austrian barracks." Compared to the general Polish tendency toward national hagiography, it is rather astounding, the fresh, one might almost say iconoclastic, way that Wyspiański approaches things Polish — and not only in *Acropolis*.

discussions with Władysław Ekielski concerning the renovation of the Castle.

THE ARCHITECTURAL PROJECT

According to Jan Adamczewski, the name Wawel comes from an old word, *wąwel,* which in the Polish of the XIIth century signified "an elevated place surrounded by marshes."[39] A stone palace, and a cathedral, have stood here since the tenth century; archaeologists have found traces of human occupation dating to 50,000 BC. Kraków, and the surrounding lands of the Wiślanie, first found themselves within the sway of the Great Moravian Empire. With the decline of that Czecho-Slovak entity and the rise of the young Polish state, led by the Polanie tribe emanating from the north-west, Wawel and its surroundings entered into Polish history. As the royal seat in the (second) capital of Poland, it found itself at the centre of Polish government until the transfer of the capital to Warsaw at the turn of the seventeenth century, though it continued to be an official royal residence. Wawel Cathedral (which witnesses to the ancient Czecho-Slovak pedigree of Kraków in its dedication to St. Václav)[40] was the main coronation church of Polish kings throughout the existence of the monarchy, and its crypts contain the tombs of nearly all the kings and queens of Poland.

It has had military significance, in the ages of siege warfare that preceded heavy artillery and aerial bombardment, and when the city fell into the hands of the Austrians during the partitions of the late eighteenth century, it became a military garrison complex, with barracks and hospitals.

At the turn of the twentieth century, plans were drawn up for its purchase from the central government. Emperor Franz Josef acceded to the requests of the regional parliament, donated to the subscription fund himself, and saw to the withdrawal of the army from the hill. This process began in 1903, and was completed only in 1911.

As noted by the architect Władysław Ekielski, he and Wyspiański began to discuss the ways in which the castle and its surrounding buildings might be renovated, and utilised by the Polish people. It is important to note that neither of the two had any doubt that Kraków would one day

---

39   Jan Adamczewski, *Kraków od A do Z* (Kraków: Krajowa agencja wydawnicza, 1986), p. 189.

40   The Cathedral is officially dedicated to both St. Václav and St. Stanisław.

revert to an independent Poland. From their stipulation that the Castle would serve, at least partially, as a "residence of the King," we can assume that they believed that the regenerated Polish State would be a monarchy, and that the capital of the state would revert from Warsaw to Kraków. This too is a measure of the "piety to the past" shared by both men, frequently underscored in Ekielski's text.[41]

The castle had been modified, through the ages, in a practical fashion according to military exigencies (without much regard for historical preservation). Likewise, "restorations" had been carried out in the nineteenth century that were no less destructive of historical truth. And so, when Wyspiański and Ekielski set out to re-imagine the future of this "Polish Acropolis," they approached it in the spirit of men with a *carte blanche*. There was, in short, a lot to repair, and a lot to destroy. To their credit, as both of them had previously participated in historical renovations,[42] this would be done with care and respect. Ekielski often points out their disdain for ahistorical reconstructions. Their plan would leave the Castle itself untouched (save for returning it, where necessary, to its former state). In the case of reconstructed buildings, like the two small churches they wished to rebuild, these would be set within their original mediaeval footprints.

In their plans, Wawel is imagined as a seat of both the Church hierarchy and the political powers — as if to finally bring accord to the conflict described in *Bishop, King. Bishop*. The architectural model worked up from the plans, on permanent display at the National Museum on 3rd of May St., is a sweeping and elegant design. It preserves the main silhouette of the Royal Castle familiar to all who have ever visited Kraków, and its

---

41   Who was to be this "King of Poland?" Was the new Poland to remain in a personal union with the Habsburgs, the Emperor to be crowned "King of Poland" in the same way as he wore the crowns of Hungary and Bohemia? Neither Ekielski nor Wyspiański are precise on this point.

42   Wyspiański had wide experience in this regard under the direction of Jan Matejko, especially at St. Mary's Basilica on the Main Market Square, near which he lived for a number of years. Ekielski was a main architect overseeing the renovation of the mediaeval Franciscan church near the Bishop's palace (the Archbishop of Kraków's residence remains there today — plans for a Bishop's palace on Wawel, like most of the plan itself, were never realised). Wyspiański also worked at the church; it is from this project that his friendship with Ekielski dates.

additions — such as the subtly Baroque dome that crowns the never-built Polish Parliament, are beautiful, and fitting.

There is a preciousness, perhaps, to the fanciful additions that the two men proposed. A wooden replica of the legendary palatial structures of Kraków's past — surely an idea of the same Wyspiański who created *Wanda* — is a little too cute for our present tastes; it seems of the same order as dressing up a mastiff as the legendary dragon. The sports complex, and the Greek theatre, are also unnecessary touches, although understandable, both according to the spirit of the age, and the drive of the authors to include a piece of everything in this "Valhalla" of Polish culture.

In conclusion, considering these architectural grace-notes, one might wonder whether it was Poland and her culture that were foremost in Wyspiański's mind when drawing up these plans, or his own vision of Poland, and his own artistic legacy. In one of his less noble moments, the poet Jan Kasprowicz was reported to have suggested that "Wyspiański dealt with national themes only to appeal all the more to the public."[43] Ekielski disagrees with that sentiment entirely. Passing over the incongruity of an open-air, Greek-inspired theatre cut into the side of a Polish hillock, he describes it as a fitting monument to the dramatic genius of his friend, who "possessed all the gifts necessary to bring to life the tragic figures of our history and legends, addressing the soul with concise words and stirring it with tragic speech and dramatic complications." Whether the reader of these translations will agree with that assessment or not is not for us to say. It certainly is the viewpoint of the majority of those familiar with the works in the original Polish; if Wyspiański's words in our English fail to hint at the breadth and grandeur of his original verse, it is our fault, not his, for which we tender our sincere apologies in advance, to you, Reader, and to Him, the poet.

THE TRANSLATION

At the presentation of my translation of Adam Mickiewicz's *Forefathers' Eve* in London earlier this year, one of the persons in the audience asked why I chose to translate the plays in rhyme, instead of blank verse. The short answer to that question is, because Mickiewicz wrote the play in rhymed

---

43   Vide Płoszewski, II, 210.

verse. To translate *Forefathers' Eve* into blank verse would be to falsify the text.

Of course, there is no lack of people who hold that all translation is falsification anyway, so what's wrong with one more? Although an adept versifier himself, Wyspiański's contemporary, Tadeusz Boy-Żeleński, was an advocate of the prose translation of verse. The poet's thought is what matters, he felt; form was a secondary concern, and irrelevant to the purpose of an English reader, for example, who just wants to know what Mickiewicz or Wyspiański has to say.

There is nothing inherently abhorrent to this approach; by translating into prose, Boy-Żeleński brought over into Polish an impressive number of French classics, from *Roland* to Proust. I, however, ascribe to the contrary view that form is content too. To give just a few quick examples familiar to the English reader, I would suggest the following. While a prose translation of Shakespeare's *King Lear* or Pope's *Rape of the Lock* might be satisfactory for a Pole who wants to familiarise himself with the flow of the stories presented in these narrative-heavy, and regular, traditionally-conceived works of art, can anyone suggest that a prose rendering of the poems of Gerard Manley Hopkins, or E.E. Cummings, might serve as an adequate introduction to these two demanding, formally-conscious artists? In the case of Hopkins, poetic form plays a crucial role in the reader's appreciation of the poems, while in the case of Cummings, there is often no other content presented but poetic form.

In reading my translations of Mickiewicz or Wyspiański, in which I have striven to approximate the form of the works as closely as I was able, I hope that the reader will get some inkling of how the originals sound in the ear of a Pole. As far as Wyspiański's works are concerned, Czesław Miłosz, among others, has perceptively suggested that what we are reading are not so much stage-plays, as "librettos."[44] While the poet was not writing operas, it is clear that music was never far from his mind. The actors' scripts are broken down into lines of almost folkloric compression: the balladic four-foot line preponderates, and these lines are often grouped into regularly rhyming stanzas, frequently of four lines each.

Besides the dialogues, which make up the majority of the texts, Wyspiański is inordinately fond of songs. His plays are more frequently interwoven with "arias" than, for example, those of Shakespeare. These

---

44   Miłosz, *History*, p. 354.

songs would be set to folk melodies that he would sing to his patient directors, such as Solski, or have his peasant-born wife or housemaid intone. It is for this reason especially that a prose translation of Wyspiański, or a translation eschewing rhyme, would not suffice to convey the experience of the original to an English-speaking audience.

Polish is an inflected language, English is not. For this reason, the Polish language has a power of compression, of compactness, that English, based on word order and clause, lacks. Immediacy is often necessarily sacrificed to periphrasis. The bilingual reader may find more enjambments in my translation than in the original. Inversions are also used — I hope, without too much exaggeration — as is assonance. Hopefully, as both of these can be found in traditional folk poetry, they will not detract from the experience overmuch, and add at least somewhat to the folkish feel of the verse, which is endemic to the Polish originals.

Except for these peculiarities, I have striven to render the plays in modern English speech. The Young Poland period was an era of linguistic abandon, with sometimes overwrought coinages abounding, and, on the other end of the scale, a devotion to a strained rendition of peasant speech. These characteristics give Wyspiański's works a peculiar tang which dates them to the Young Poland period, and have made generations of Poles, beginning as early as the 1930s, wince. Although these characteristics are identifying markers of Wyspiański's style, they are irritants, and better not attempted by the translator. Though this may seem like a contradiction to my earlier statements concerning the importance of form, let it rather be the exception that proves the rule. There is no way, for me at least, to effect a recreation of Wyspiański's (rather infrequent) neologisms, or his (all too present) peasant speech patterns, without falling into parody.

As George Steiner reminds us, translations are a curious type of literary endeavour. The translation would not exist without an original, to which it ought to point. It is my hope that, having read Wyspiański's work in my translation, the reader will be intrigued enough to reach for the originals, especially if that means having to learn a new language in order to do so. If that should happen, the power which impels him or her will be the residue of Wyspiański in these English pages. Conversely, whatever in them is unclear, poorly phrased, or downright wrong is entirely my responsibility.

ACKNOWLEDGEMENTS

I consider myself extremely fortunate to work with the people at Glagoslav, especially Ksenia Papazova, my editor. I would like to thank her, and the publishers Maxim Hodak and Max Mendor, for the privilege of bringing Adam Mickiewicz and Stanisław Wyspiański to the attention of the English reading public. Everyone at Glagoslav, including the patient copy editors, deserve my deepest thanks for their aid and support.

I would like to acknowledge the Book Institute of Poland for their generous financial support of the publication of this book, and the National Museum in Kraków for their permission to reproduce the illustrations included in it. The reader will find the visual materials associated with the Wyspiański/Ekielski plan for the renovation of Wawel an immense aid to their understanding of that document.

Finally, I acknowledge the patience and support of my wife Ola, to whom everything I do is dedicated.

Miami Beach
May 15, 2017

WANDA

(Legenda II)

PERSONS OF THE TRAGEDY

Krak, the Prince
Wanda
Chuckle (singer)
Burdock (singer)
Chorus

THE ACTION OF THE DRAMA TAKES PLACE ON WAWEL HILL.

ACT I

*Ages ago, on this very hill
An old king lived, famous in arms,
Whose clothes were of a peasant cut,
Whose sceptre was a gnarled crook.
Mighty he was, swift, invincible,
A club of oak in his right hand.
Around him he gathered shamans wise,
Learned in simples and in song.
The seat of power he built himself:
Cross-wise the plan of the courtyards.
A palisade of pointed logs
With sentry-gates at intervals.
The walls were faced with planks of fir,
Around stood pillars clever-carved:
The runes and figures of his gods.
And from the shaded battlements
The Vistula — broad stream — was seen,
Upon which bobbed many a barge.*

Farther on met the old man's eyes
Dark woods, for the Bielańska hill
And that of Bronisława too
Were thickly wooded, evergreen —
From which he had those planks of fir.
The fragrant river scents, the calls
Of watermen would waft to him,
And at the castle's foot, a cave
Scraped in the limestone by the floods
Where was (they say) a spring, a freshet —
There a fierce dragon once had his lair.
Because all snakes were holy then,
An altar slab — perhaps a temple —
Was raised there, till the knightly Krak
Threw down the stones and ploughed the land,
And now the ridge about was spiked
With bastion, gate and battlement.

But now the sick king lies abed,
With years as well as mortal ills,
For which no simple may be found
To cure him. All those offered now
By witch and warlock, of no use
To ease his pains as death draws near.

The morning star of his last day
Is now grown pale before the sun,
And all his folk await the passing
Of their beloved lord. To him
They come to sing, and gently strum
Farewells — this with the undertone
Of mourning their own prompt demise:
For bandits now attack the state,
Shattering doors and murdering,
Looting and raping; these demand
For ransom Krak's daughter beloved:
A wonder of a peerless girl,
Beauteous, strong of mind, and just:

Wanda, her name. Her shame they sought,
Reducing her to a slave's lot.

Now look: the old man's just expired
A moment past — his faithful folk
Fall to their knees around the corpse —
Shamans and wizards there abound,
Shepherds and horsemen and courtiers,
Servants who've kept him through the years.
And now his daughter, flaxen-haired,
With eyes as blue as heaven's expanse,
His daughter draws close, stained with tears,
For near at hand a great fir pile
Waits, raised on timber, bound with green
Rope knotted — this a funeral pyre
For king and princess. Once set alight,
The wooden castle will be fired,
Then let the bandits have the char!
Yet still Krak's men defend it, fiercely.
Thunder and screams invade the halls
As the foemen tighten the ring,
Advancing on the royal keep.
Sand is spilled down from battlements
To blind the raiders; rubble, stone,
Arrows and spears greet the axe-men
Who boldly climb up the siege-ladders,
Turrets are prised upon their heads.

The westing sun glares angry, red.
The bards await, with harp in hand,
The holy night that is to come.

Still they defend the castle walls.
See? How they all, with fading might
Fight on:

CHORUS.
>They've overcome the battlements!
>They're in the lower court!
>They're over the abatis!
>Hear them laugh! Like the lynx
>In the hencoop! Spears!
>Archers, here!
>Tumble them down with a spar!
>Topple them from that wall!
>Company, halt! Fire at will,
>Archers! Support the pikemen. Kill!
>Look — he's fallen!
>He fell from the wall —
>Sappers, pickets, in! All!
>Pass the stones for the sling —
>Just look at that white-haired animal,
>And after him, his soldiers, all
>Racing through the upper galleries —
>Their armour flashing in the gloom.
>Hold fast! Protect the inner room!
>Come on, young fellows, lend a hand!
>Look how he laughs! His face, how bright!
>Cast down the rubble from the height!
>Push back, crush the bandit forces
>With stones tilted from the upper courses.
>Now, open a path, nice and clear —
>Tempt them in here...
>Now, fire the buildings! Topple the posts!
>Surrounded by flame, may they choke and roast!
>Fling down the torches on their heads!
>Ready the tar-pots!
>Come on, men!
>Shoulders, together —
>Now, dump them!

BURDOCK.
>Night falls, the heavens are black.
>Clouds speed, like hordes wind-chidden;

The distant trees moan, and crack —
The castle is in darkness hidden.

CHUCKLE.
That's a storm for sure, a storm!
Such a black cloud in the sky!
Soon there'll be a downpour.
Rains come, and then mudslides —
So shall it be with us.
The pressure builds in the heights,
Then down the cliff the boulders rush!
O, look! — the darkness clots
And sinks the hall in black.
Come on, lads, there's still lots
Of us here! Bar and spar! Push them back!

BURDOCK.
Quickly, before they see:
Hang up some heavy gear —
Roll down the door-logs, quickly!
That will chase them away from here.
Block the inner room...
Come, raise the portcullis logs —
Hey there now boys! Heave, ho!

*Several peasants grab ropes and pull.
Among them:*

CHUCKLE.
I can't hold longer! I'm not able!

BURDOCK.
Now! Cut the cables!

CHORUS.
Look! The Germans — here they come!

CHUCKLE
> *Bending over Wanda.*
> Your house, princess, now is gone.
> Your future shall be: slavery, shame.
> You're not disgusted by the chain?
> You — bound and dragged through the street,
> And your father: dog and crow meat!

CHORUS.
> Run! Escape!

WANDA.
> Cowards! Cowards!

> *As the ropes are cut through with an axe,*
> *The portcullis falls with the logs,*
> *Cutting off both the invaders and the defenders.*
> *The defenders have no hope of retreat,*
> *And are left to their fate.*

CHUCKLE
> *Behind Wanda.*
> Look — there's only one hope left you now.
> Bind yourself fast with a vow,
> And you'll be granted a man's strength.
> All your weakness shall vanish hence...
> You are young and beautiful.
> Her part the goddess shall fulfil.
> Speak to the goddess Żywia now;
> She'll hear you out, respect your vow —
> From Burdock, who knows spells, I've heard:
> Whom to the goddess gives his word
> Is given in return...

WANDA.
> And you advise me — ?
> I give my vow to Her, who stands
> In naked beauty? in whose hands

An apple shines, and on her brow
A wreath of simples, herbs, is wound?
To Her, from the sacred wood,
Where the sun stains the firs with blood
At evening? She — calls me?
It's me she desires
From her shrine among the spires
Of fir?
And I — am I worthy of her?
You stun me. My hackles rise — I shiver!

CHUCKLE
Speaking from behind her, close to her ear.
      ...power omnipotent,
To her who swears a testament
To Żywia, so Burdock states;
Great her powers, so great
As to chase the enemy from our land,
Hurl him from the walls
And all our people — safe under her hand,
Who the lightning calls
Down at will — her holy blood
Vowed in virgin flood
Is the cost;
Otherwise, all is lost!
The king defamed,
Denuded, shamed!

WANDA.
What shall I do? The fight
Goes on — and neither side
Quite overcoming yet — Those screams —
The castle's funeral pyre it seems —
Moans from sacrificial victims, weak
As I am. Dare I speak
To Żywia, queen of this land,
Who holds a quiver of lightnings in her hand?

She of the shining eyes?
Shall I not be despised?

CHUCKLE.
Speak, and she'll hear you. You are pure,
A virgin; call the thunder down!
Kindle the conquering flame!

WANDA.
My eyes — aswim in sparks...
She's here! And her lovely face is dark
With blood...

CHUCKLE.
              You hear that sound?
They're in the inner court, for sure!

WANDA.
Is it the Germans who cry out so?
Or my own countrymen?
I'm caught in the coils of necessity.
Necessity binds me; I can't see —
Who is that, who through the courtyard goes?

CHUCKLE.
When they axe down these doors,
You are no longer yours.

WANDA.
Better the lightning strike me! Lest
I be their slave...! My knife, my breast —
My choice to die rather than to bow.
I'll make the oath to Żywia! Now!!

CHUCKLE
Backs away from her in fear, while she is speaking.
You're choosing death?

WANDA.
A sacrifice!
Death, rather than chains!
She prays:
Żywia, goddess, bright one,
Zezula, beauteous maid,
Golden one,
Cloaked in the sun,
Of milk-rosy cheeks,
Goddess mighty in power!

She kneels on the ground like a voiceless killer,
An agent of doom,
Then grabs with both arms a tame doe
Which she forces to the ground,
Holds helpless, and stabs with her knife.
A stream of hot blood spurts forth.
She raises aloft the polluted blade,
Wipes it in her hands,
And smears the blood on her face.
The voiceless killer,
The agent of doom,
Kneels with her arms crossed
Over her chest.
Around her, lightning flashes.
Lightning crowns her head.
She traces runes with the animal's blood,
And forms the oath with her lips.

BURDOCK.
What's going on? Is she possessed?
Or mad? Whom does she address?
God? Through the lightning?
Did she pronounce the curse?
O, Death will take her first!

To Chuckle:
And you, brother, Death's harbinger!

WANDA.
    I kneel before Your altars.
    I shall leap into the waters,
    Into their stone-lined depths,
    And keep my vow.
    It's me you want — I am young;
    My beauty you will not disdain.
    It is a price I gladly pay;
    This life I hold as naught.
    Give but what I beg of you,
    And grant it me now.
    Pour your strength into me;
    Make me your weapon.
    My hands are weak and sexless —
    See how those vultures gather!
    My father's palace shall be overrun.
    Grant me the strength of your might,
    Your ninefold power
    For this one night
    Alone — and who I aim at,
    Let me annihilate
    At will — then shall you claim
    What is yours,
    According to the ancient rites.

    My father banned your rites,
    Killed the sacred reptiles,
    Forbid your bloody sacrifice,
    And the sacred groves defiled.

    And so you've sent catastrophe
    Upon us; now, restrain your hand.
    Allow me this brief victory,
    To rule, as he did, this land.

    Sick, long on his cot he lay —
    Your vengeance so you sate.

He's dead now. Death took him away
And left me, unfortunate.

Not for myself I ask this now —
O, my poor people save!
Not for myself I seek a crown —
Let not your folk be enslaved!

Let me perform his obsequies,
His passing song, let me intone.
After tomorrow's victory,
I'll smash his castle, wood from stone,

And on its place I'll raise a fane
To you, and renew your sacrifice.
I choose death, that my folk retain
Their freedom. I am yours by right.

You slew my father in his sons'
Quarrels, leaving the sword to me.
Who am I? — That I should be the one
Chosen to try such fearsome deeds?

If it be true, I am your daughter,
And powers great are to be mine,
I conjure earth, and fire, and water —
Send forth your lightning as a sign.

A distant peal of thunder is heard.

Crush then my flesh, with fire consume,
But grant victory to my soul!
Let my spirit conquer the tomb,
And Fate's triumph shall be whole!

Another peal of thunder.

Do not allow the dogs to tear
The body of my warlike father,
Nor stain their chaps with his cold gore.
Take me in exchange for him —
Set lightnings round his bier
As funeral tallows.
Do not abandon his soul to the gloom;
Put an end to his torments.
I conjure you — seal your power
By hurling down the living fire,
Tearing through the clouds!

Lightning.

And now, these vulture bandits banish,
Who iron-tipped halberds brandish
To drink deep of my people's gore;

Vanquish their rapine-hungry hordes
Who take their axes to our doors.
Send down your flame! Make them no more!

Lightning.

As a wolf in a netted enclosure,
Spinning around the periphery,
Seeking a weak point in the net, thus Rytigier,
The white-shocked warrior rages, weapons bearing
In both his hands. He speeds to the gate,
While round their leader, like a pack
Of lupine thieves, spin frothing
The iron men he leads, invading;
Their axe blows thunder on the fir posts,
Sending chips flying, bursting bolts;
They kill the castle dwellers
With quick blows
Cutting a pathway through the people
Who die in Wanda's defence; they rush

To take the inner chamber,
To take the witch within,
Around whose crown the lightning plays.

WANDA.
    Today the lightning is on my side;
    Today the storm and I, allied,
    Will cut you down, and chase you hence.
    Before my Word you've no defence!

    Stoop, vultures, crash from out the sky,
    Broken, upon the dust to lie —
    The words I speak, the tears I cry
    Sap all your strength! And now you die!

    Bow down before me in the dust!
    I and the goddess now do thrust
    The weapons from your arms unkind —
    Now look your last! I charm you blind!

    Throw down your swords, cast down your knives!
    Let fall your axes — lose your lives!
    With spells Divine I make you quake —
    Now, beasts divine, I call you! Awake!

    I conjure you. Gaze in my eyes!
    My beauty is alive, today!
    Both Fame and Death walk at my side —
    For this one hour behold me gay!

As if blinded by the heat and light
Of a thunderbolt, they fall;
Even Rytigier, their chief, is stunned,
As his iron retainers
Heeding the spells she sings,
Faint away in terror
As if struck in the breast
By a sledgehammer blow.

So he lifts his horn to his lips
And sounds retreat.

The gates are cleared.

Slowly, the terror ebbs.
The rains continue their downpour,
Harried again and again
By strong gusts of wind.
The tempest races through the palace
Until it pushes off to fall upon the woods of fir.
The storm lessens, and dies.
And the air smells fresh
In the nostrils of the reprieved;
The foes have retreated;
They melt away in the shadows.
The foes have retreated;
The nightmare has passed,
And the late hours of the night come on.
Wanda stands like a woman spellbound.
Like a shaman in the grip of the prophetic spirit,
Gripping her knife soiled with blood,
With the slaughtered doe at her feet.
Her nation tastes peace instead of terror.
Her spell has laid the nightmare.
They begin to move from the corners in which they'd crouched
Toward the courtyard gates.
At the battlements, they gaze upon the fallen,
And keen and wail and mourn.
Funeral and ritual feasts:
The stoves are laden with bread and slaughtered beasts.
A shaman leads the ritual
And all respond antiphonally.
They lament in song their lord expired,
Whose body has been meetly prepared,
Wrapped in royal robes, with sword in his cold hand,
And set on the straw-filled funeral pyre
Along with some sheaves of wheat.

The dead prince sits upon his pyre;
Around him: jars with honey and milk,
And smaller vases, holding tears.
For his house is forbidden to weep,
Because their tears would burden his soul.
Keeners are set apart to mourn
Beside the pyre:
Chuckle and Burdock take their place
At the dead prince's feet;
They rest their hands upon their rebecs.

SHAMAN.
 Pour the blood into the horns.
 Sprinkle the pyre.
 Dip in the fir branches.

CHORUS.
 Sing prophecy.

SHAMAN.
 I won't — — —
 Laughter I hear, and mockery.

CHORUS.
 What? How —?

SHAMAN.
 Laughter I hear upon the winds.
 You hear the bitter voices?
 Evil is riding on that wind,
 Beckoning, and seducing.

CHORUS.
 Send it away!

SHAMAN.
>   I lack the might.
>   A soul's been sold into its power.
>   Evil is triumphing tonight.

CHORUS.
>   Who has been sold?

SHAMAN
>   *Points at Wanda.*
>   Her!

WANDA.
>   The foe's been driven off. Farewell!
>   I'll sing my father's funeral song.
>   Tonight preside the hounds of hell,
>   And it is these I take my seat among
>
>   Here on the bier. So bind my arms
>   And help me now to mount the pyre.
>   Tomorrow, before the new sun dawns
>   You'll see us both consumed in fire.
>
>   Father and daughter both shall burn.
>   Then, set alight the castle keep.
>   The ashes, to the four winds spurn;
>   The wind, if it so choose, may weep.
>
>   Only bare ruins shall remain
>   Where once a lofty palace stood.
>   What good is Legend? What good, Fame?
>   Once done, flee this burnt ground for good.
>
>   More beautiful than castles grand
>   Your humble cottages, your life;
>   No suitor's ever sought my hand
>   To barter for; to take as wife.

None sought my hand; none ever dared
To climb so high — to wed a princess!
Today I have this one last care,
Tomorrow — I'll have one the less.

On your behalf, this sacrifice —
To shunt from you Żywia's curse.
My death is your redemption's price,
And so I'm sworn to die the first.

The daughter of a water maid,
Stolen from where I ought to be,
It was my most unhappy fate
To cause such grief and misery.

The blood that stained a brother's hand —
By spilling his, I vengeance wrought;
My beauty then tempted to our land
A foe — the scourge of a vengeful god.

Tonight I'll sit among your ring,
One final night, before I die.
I'll face the stake in the morning.
Now, come close, these two wrists to tie.

Farewell, farewell, this one last night
Shall be my final night of song.
Death waits the coming of the light;
Sing with me, till the break of dawn.

This last night I remain with you;
The last time I look on this world.
The dying stars fade in the blue;
My future fades, while yet a girl.

I have for you one final kiss.
Once more to you my lips I incline,

My faithful girls, my friends, my bliss:
At sunrise, I am sworn to die.

Hurry the sun-up! Let it rise!
My Death shall be my wedding day.
Night from her lover keeps the bride —
Her forehead garlanded with fame!

Fame, speed your feet! Be you not late!
Off-spring of my curse, by name
I conjure you — hurry to my gate;
Hasten to me, O holy Fame!

And now her handmaids bind her wrists.
They set her at her father's side,
Crowding round her tenderly themselves.
As if warbling songs of comfort,
They kiss their beloved mistress goodbye.
All the people take their seats
And partake of the funeral repast.
Now is the time for the rebecs to sound,
To cheer on the souls of the departing.

CHUCKLE
   Takes up the rebec.[45]
   Passed now troubles, passed now pain,
   Embraced by an eternal peace,
   As you set out for the dark bourn
   Of death, where, once crossed, you must remain,
   Hear the rebecs as now they mourn.
   Moan, my rebec, and tremble, strings,
   And of your weeping do not cease,
   Like mournful winds among the trees,
   For they set out for the dark bourn

---

45   The term used by Wyspiański is *gęśle*. Like the rebec, it was a mediaeval stringed instrument. Although often played with a bow, it seems that some were operated by a crank — which is what the original stage directions call for here.

Of death, into eternal peace,
Across the waves of death, no more
To come again. Like men at war,
Howl, rebec — weep and ever mourn.
Passed now troubles, passed now pain,
Hear the rebecs as they complain.

BURDOCK
Takes up the rebec.
Where leads the path my lord shall tread?
Where shall he rest among the dead?
Where warriors grip, bathed in blood,
And gore is like a stream in flood.
What knights, what arms will, in his train
Accompany their lord to the strains
Of battle drums and clashing swords?
And cries of Victory! And Fame!

CHUCKLE
Takes up the rebec.
To death, to death, to restoring sleep.
Passed now trouble, passed now pain,
Endless and peaceful the sweet night;
Laved by the black waters deep
In endless comfort's sweet embrace,
Hear the rebec's lamenting plaints.
A Leader from the dead shall rise
To lead you on to victory —
You and your men are sent to die
Among the spears, the darts that fly,
The swords' clash — thus your duty,
The pyre — and there the beauty
Of your child will share your fate;
A mighty king comes, of power great,
Above the pyre's ashes to soar!

BURDOCK
> *Takes up the rebec.*
> Hear the rebecs' lament —
> Hear their sad mourning call
> As on your journey sent,
> The black waves lap your pall.

CHUCKLE.
> Passed now trouble, passed now pain,
> Journeying to an endless peace,
> As you set out for the dark bourn
> Of death, hear as the lyres mourn.
> You set off for the night's embrace,
> Eternal fame to chase, to chase —
> You warrior-prince, your ship awaits!

BURDOCK.
> You leave behind your palace gates,
> To endless peace you are to sail.
> Ah, warrior-prince, your ship awaits!
> Hear the rebecs' lamenting wail...
> *Takes up the rebec.*

CHUCKLE
> *Takes up the rebec.*
> 1.
> In times past, in times past,
> Songs were, and laughs,
>   And feasting;
> As birds take flight,
> So speeds the night
> Gay daylight
> Ceasing.

BURDOCK
> *Takes up the rebec.*
>
> 2.
> As the Dawn, as the Dawn
> Comes, and is gone,
> Though never in sadness sunk,
>> Now past
> Is your laughter
> And like the rain water
> By the parched earth drunk.

CHUCKLE
> *Takes up the rebec.*
>
> 3.
> Water flows, Water flows,
> Decrepit grows
> The beauty of the Maytime.
> The stormwinds blow,
> The wrinkles grow,
> Deep night harries the daytime.

BURDOCK
> *Takes up the rebec.*
>
> 4.
> Now dried are the blooms
> And the earth now consumes
> All beautiful things, like the dawn.
> To the brave young who play,
> Endless seems holiday
> But sun, laughter and warmth soon are gone.

CHUCKLE
> *Takes up the rebec.*
>
> 5.
> Just so: they, like the birds
> Who fly over the surge
> Of the sea in the fall bid farewell,
> They're soon off —

Look aloft:
See the eaglets soar in the wind's swell!

BURDOCK
Takes up the rebec.

CHUCKLE
Hey ha, ha hey!
In the thick woods at play,
Leszy rumbles through brush, bursting branches,
Through the bogs and the wastes,
Leszy tumbles a-chase,
While quick Whistle one step before, dances.
Hey ha, ha hey!
And behind him, hear Afterwhistle play,
Makes the rebec sound.
While the peasant boys chase him,
Makes up the rebec sound.
And long ago, you could outface him!

BURDOCK
Takes up the rebec.
1.
Do you know that you're right,
When a prophetic fright
Plants you firmly in eternity's demesne,
And your heart pounds like thunder,
You suddenly wonder
Has everything, then, been in vain?

2.
With the portcullis gained
As the roofs rage in flames,
And the rams start to batter doors, walls,
Then your prophetic fright
Moans midst laughter and pain —
What else evil is there yet to befall?

Do you know that you're right,
Or has all of your life been in vain?

CHUCKLE.
   1.
Sadness grips you, sadness raves.
Come, I know that field well.
Buttercups trampled in fresh graves,
Willows hang their tresses pale
Above the clods of dirt;
Gay buttercups, after a spell
To must and mud revert.

   2.
But I know joys; the heart can race —
Come, I know that sunny mead;
Your horse awaits. Off, to the chase!
On Jarowit's white steed —
The pines and firs sing, hey!
And gaily shall I play!

BURDOCK
   Takes up the rebec.

CHUCKLE.
   1.
Jarowit's stallion,
With hooves like golden medallions,
Gold-braided mane waving bold,
With his saddle of gold,
Saddle-cloth, bridle, and bit
Wrought of gold by the smith.

   2.
He trots up in the night
All of smoothness, and bright,
Neighs with laughter; his bridle it rings.
As he thunders his hooves

The sound rings through the roofs —
He needs fodder, then onward he swings!

BURDOCK
Takes up the rebec.
1.
The brand awaits, the flame, to char.
The fire does obeisance.
The wind speeds hither from afar
And makes the gold leaves dance —
The brand awaits, the brand awaits,
    Gaily rejoice! The flame!

2.
The heart awaits, the feast awaits,
The people humbly bow.
Although their feasting's gay and great,
Still tears of sorrow flow.
Feasting awaits with dance and song,
With cake and mead and hops,
But soon the feasting stops.
And ah, the road, how long!

BALLAD 1.

CHUCKLE
Takes up the rebec.

1.
"A brother's lost his life,
And the knife
Is found beneath your robes.
Around the bier she goes,
Mourning and bowed, with tear-stained eye;
You mourn your brother — and you lie."

BURDOCK
   Takes up the rebec.

   2.
   "Oh, lovely maid,
   You pushed the blade
   Between the brothers!
   One slew the other.
   For, one's love respecting,
   The other you spurned, rejecting."

CHUCKLE
   Takes up the rebec.

   3.
   "I was his delight,
   And the cause of the fight
   That saw him killed —
   Now vengeance must be fulfilled."

BURDOCK
   Takes up the rebec.

   4.
   "That sword is sharp, sister —
   Why do you unsheathe it?
   Why is it you need it?
   Your eye clouds — just like a vulture's."

CHUCKLE
   Takes up the rebec.

   5.
   "Your eyes will dim cloudy,
   As I stain this sword bloody!
   You struck down your brother;
   Here — take you another!

From the sword that was smithed
Near the old dragon's cliff."

BURDOCK
Takes up the rebec.

6.
"So I die, but recall —
Young, beloved of all,
You're a foundling, a child of the waves,
Whom our mother found
Where the Vistula laves
The reed-bearing marsh ground.
You're a Rusalka's spawn —
The waves shall claim their own."

CHUCKLE
Takes up the rebec.

BALLAD 2.

BURDOCK.
1.
Each night,
Each moonlit night,
Under the cliff, those moans —
The cliff of limestone groans,
The dried mud cakes and cracks,
The river waters hiss
Into an abyss,
Then, sun melts the mists
When morning dawns
And look! Those beastly tracks!

CHUCKLE
Takes up the rebec.

2.
"I'll go there myself,
And bring you great wealth:
Bracelets and necklaces,
A gold band for your tresses,
Brooches and earrings
And all sorts of costly things;
For in the cliff a dragon has his lair,
And jealously he guards the hoard hidden there."

BURDOCK.

3.
To the riverside
Goes the peasant lad
To hide
Among the reeds.
He waits and waits
And then he sees
The dragon pad
From out his lair into the night.
The moon is bright —
He sees it go
Where the waters flow;
His eyes
Are like a man's
With lashes;
Greedily, he splashes
In the water, till he satisfies
His thirst, and then
He bathes
In the cool waves.
Then he returns to land;
Near the cliff he stands
On his many paws.
There, where flowers abound,
Hanging down from the mound,
Honey-sweet mallow,

Nettle stalks sallow;
With careful eye
He glances thither and nigh,
Then he tears the cliff-face with his claws.

CHUCKLE
Takes up the rebec.

4.
"Alas! The grave
He guards does not have
Treasures for you, my lass;
All that I found
When I picked around
In the silt
Was a sword with a hilt
Of coral — bitten
By rust — so long it lay hidden.
So I'll take
The sword of that snake
With the coral hilt
And on the grindstone I'll mill it,
On the limestone and quartz,
Till it's clean and nice,
And can cut and slice
Better than a hundred swords!"

BALLAD 3.

BURDOCK
Takes up the rebec.

I.
Wiślan
The water king
To his oldest daughter did bring
A broadsword

And spoke such words:
"Take this sword and clean
Off the rust, that the sheen
May be bright —
Grind it,
Golden-haired princess,
That I may find it
Sharp, brilliant in brightness."
"Weles," she crooned,
"Shine bright,
Weles, tonight
My father gave to me this sword
And I to him have given my word
To cleanse it from rust,
So cleanse it I must —
I shall not rest
Once I've begun,
Until in brightness
It rivals the sun."

CHUCKLE
Takes up the rebec.

II.
Wiślan
The water king,
To his eldest daughter did bring
A broadsword
With these words:
"Take the sword and clean
Off the rust, till the sheen
Flush from tip to hilt of coral."
There, where Wawel bathes
Its shoulders in the swirl
Of the Vistula's waves,
"O Weles, shine bright
For tonight
My father gave his sword

And I've given my word,
To cleanse it from rust,
So cleanse it I must.
I'll shine it
I'll grind it
Until it's sharp and nice
For thrust and slice.
Flow river, flow,
As I sing here below,
Shine down, O moon
As I grind and I croon,
Whetting it sharp, whetting it nice
For thrust and slice."

BURDOCK
Takes up the rebec.

III.
Ah, before long
Someone heard her song —
A knight in armour gold
Came down the hill to hold
Wiślana in his embrace,
And kiss her lovely face
As she sat on the sand
Whetting the sword she held in her hand.
"Weles, Weles, don't descend —
Your reign of darkness pray extend!
All the night long
I to Krak shall belong —
Tomorrow I'll resume
My tune;
Tomorrow I shall grind.
Tonight, Krak is mine!
Tonight no more of this —
Tonight, I shall kiss, and kiss…"

Here the old songsters fell asleep;
Upon their fiddles rest their chins.
Something appears to them in dream:
Night visions' great deceit begins.

Something appears to them in dreams:
Visions from sleeping heads are grown.
They drowse, they sleep, their lyres seem
As if they had been made of stone.

They see a troop of warriors come
In shining robes to where sits
The corpse of Krak. They bend down upon
Him, settling over him like a mist.

Now from out their sacks they pull
Fresh apples — and the scent expands
Throughout the room, rich, sweet and full,
As when the harvest is at hand.

Their staves above the sleeping heads
Of the funeral guests they now extend,
And as they've come, so soon they're fled,
And night and darkness reign again.

The tired old songsters droop asleep,
Upon their instruments they rest their chins;
New things appear to them in dream:
Night's visions still their web they spin.
They drowse, they sleep, and flesh and bone
Seem to be made of heavy stone.

WANDA.
    They sleep, but when they wake, alas!
    The whole assembly will see me.
    I must get out, I must — O, chains!
    Have I been charmed so utterly?
    With rasping ropes my wrists are bound:

They cut my flesh — right to the bone!
And I want life! I want to live!
I want to love, and to be gay!
Feasting and joy is what I want,
Not to be fed to the joyless tomb.
I've got to leave — this Nemesis
That wants my sacrifice — how cruel!
How can I save myself? They'll kill me!
O, my river Vistula, my waves,
You who loudly rush on below,
Come here, and rescue me, beloved!
Yet Death's there too! Death's at all hands —
How to get out, get out!? My strength fails me —
They'll kill me!

Fettered, as if genuflecting
Among the sleepers all around,
She crawls into a dark corner
Among the shadows of the night.
Beneath the stove she crouches, scared,
And there she drowses, spent, worn out.

All of the banqueters are asleep;
Fallen about the floor: the singers,
The feasters, the keeners, all enwrapped
In the soft mantle of the night.

But look — the old dead prince now blinks,
And with surprise surveys the room.
His heart again beats in his breast,
A few last beats before it stills
Forever in the peace of death.

Blood flushes his wan cheeks anew.
His senses once again are sharp;
Still in his ears ring the rebecs,
Still echoes in them the song now fled.

The old man listens, harkens, thinks.
His soul is chasing after the echo.
His voice — has it returned as well?
The echo drifts away, is lost.

He looks about, and notices
The courtiers all submerged in sleep.
The crowd of people, underneath
The thick aromas of the feast,

Which rise from out the bowls and platters
And make the old man smile. But — there —
A pipe resounds, far in the fields —
Again the echo reawakes.

KRAK.
    Someone's been winding funeral wreaths.
    The celebration must be grand
    To merit such a wealthy feast.
    In whose honour? At whose command?

    It must have been a fair repast —
    Their heads are lolling on their necks
    Asleep; and how many are here! Vast
    Their number — shamans, two with rebecs...

    And still I hear faint music ringing — —
    Rebecs, responding to a breeze?
    Are those my people I hear singing?
    Or just cicadas in the trees?

    The battle — does it still rage on
    About the harried castle gates?
    Shall I again behold the sun?
    So soon am I regenerate?

    Is this that other world, of wonder,
    Since war has fully passed away?

My people all about me, slumber
Like children lulled by a soft lay.

Who was it that repulsed the raiders
Who fell on us — catastrophe! —
Leading away, enslaved, our maidens
And mocking us triumphantly?

Hey! — How silent — People! Fellows!
To me, lads! — Nothing. They're stone deaf.
The shepherd's piping in the meadows!
All snore on, still, in the night's depths...

Granddaughter, hey! Open your eyes! —
You recognise me, no? Young lass?
My nation round me sleeping lies...
Is this a funeral repast?

My children! Servants! Hey, courtiers!
None heeds request, none hears my chiding.
Wake up, you sleepers! Open your ears!
Men! Guards! Where are you hiding?

A funeral this? Or a wedding feast?
A long procession nears,
Their foreheads cinct with rosy wreaths,
And harpists lead them here.

Who's getting married? My daughter?
Who takes her for his own?
Harpists lead the procession here
That winds before my throne...

The ground yawns open at his side
And three old hags emerge,
Each with a veiled countenance;
Two of them are spinning yarn.
A golden thread unravelled is

By one; her sister takes it up
— The thread — upon her spindle, while
The third stands by, intent, musing.
The old man sees them, stands, and spits,
Retreating to the rear.
He gazes on while they travail,
Then, timorously asks:

KRAK.
    Whose golden thread is it you spin?
    One of my daughter's maids?
    I see your fingers trembling, dim...
    Who can you be?

CHORUS.
                The Fates.

KRAK.
    I can see nothing... Where's the loom?
    Your faces — undo their coverings!
    When will you finish? And for whom?
    What comes of your labour?

CHORUS.
                      Nothing.

KRAK.
    Why do you speed so? What's the haste?
    Why do your fingers flutter?
    One of you slips the golden lace
    And she — winds it around a shuttle?

    Hey, hey! — When I was still a child
    The women spun, my cradle nigh.
    Come closer. Here — work at my side,
    And one of you, a torch lift high.

Show me — give it here into my hand.
Let me a while delight my eye.
Old memories the heart expand
With times past — O, how swift they fly!

The gates now open on their own,
The portcullis draws up, by itself.
Once more one sees the broad expanse
Beyond the river, beyond the woods,
All shining in the bright moonlight.

What is that crowd of people nearing?
What maiden chorus rings them round?
Wreathed for a wedding, they come singing
And wind a wreath around the king,

The ploughman-king. Strange are their robes,
Celebratory their attire.
Blooms round their midriffs; in their hair
And fresh bouquets they bear in hand.

Hey! From the Vistula they come,
Singing and dancing somnolent,
A shaman's wand directs their steps,
The chosen chief of water maids.

Where his staff points, they turn their eyes,
And dance with lazy, graceful tread.
The hour of charms gives him this power,
The hour of charms holds them spellbound.

The moon's their lamp, its bluish shine
Lights up their way, and pales their hue;
They shine in pools of light, in shade
They darken, nearly disappear.

At their head goes an aged shepherd,
His sun-bronzed face shines bright with flame.

A plain grey pouch hangs from his neck;
It's he who plays upon the reed.
And after him come the strange pairs:
Half-naked nymphs, the Rusalkas,
Their charms hidden with flowers, leaves.
Behind them shamble the werewolves,
Shaggy and various, clothed in skins.
Fauns next, and ram-headed men, upright,
And other wonders: all the children
Of the Rusalka-haunted waves
— The drowned — come. Sadly plays the reed
A dim-remembered, lovely tune
Weft, so it seems, of low birdsong.

SHAMAN.
    As waters ebb, troubles subside
    And after war comes peace.
    Then shall you list, O happy bride,
    Sweet wedding harmonies.

WITCH.
    1.
    Above the Vistula Wawel thrusts;
    There were you abandoned, daughter.
    It's time that you returned to us,
    To your Vistula's waters.

OLD MAN.
    2.
    The while your spirit slept inside
    You might be where men gather.
    But now, your soul's eyes open wide:
    Return now to the water.

    3.
    One day, and you'll be filled with strength.
    You'll win past adversity, and bother;

Keep you fast, though, to your intent,
And return to the water.

WITCH.
1.
Oy, you would like to taste the joys
Of living, maiden sad!
Your gloom would pass — more than one boy
Would gladly see to that!

2.
Oy, love and yearning fill your head,
You'll have your wedding soon:
For Death shall make your bridal bed,
Wherein you'll join your groom!

CHORUS.
As waters ebb, troubles subside
And after war comes peace.
Then shall you list, O happy bride,
Sweet wedding harmonies.

Enter the wedding party.

WEDDING PARTY.
1.
The groomsmen knock upon your gates
To call you forth. Your bridesmaids —
What is the wreath they weave? You think
It's sweet, strong mead they drink?

2.
Who are the guests that form a ring
You from your bridegroom's arms defending?
Who are the musicians at play
When the wreath at your feet they lay?

3.
Who are the groomsmen who regale?
Who are the bridesmaids, sad and pale
As they climb the wagons to depart,
Singing those tunes that break the heart?

4.
Who were the groomsmen, whirling, flinging?
Who were the bridesmaids gaily singing
When all came to the wedding feast
For song and dancing, mead and treats?

KRAK.
1.
Play on! I long for zithers playing!
I'll feast and sing with you.
Death can wait! My death I'm delaying —
I wish to die...
   ho hee hoo!

2.
Just you play on! Hey there, my girl —
Come stand here at my side.
It calls to me, the fiddle's skirl;
In dreams my pains subside!

3.
Just play on, fiddlers, play the reel;
Ah youth, how quickly spent —
Play on, you fiddlers, play the reel!
And back youth comes again!
   heoo hey, heoo hey!

4.
They've dressed me up in festive robes,
In dancing shoes I'm shod —
There, where the music's stormwind blows,
I'll whirl and jump and trot!

5.
The mountain wind — hear how it grows!
The mountain wind roars loud;
Death's wind about the castle blows
And flutters the grave shroud!
     heoo hey, heoo hayo ho!

6.
I had my years of youth and health,
O summer times! hoo ha, hoo ha!
Cottage and orchard for my wealth,
Such wealth was mine!
     Hoo ha! Hoo ha!

The weft grows beneath the spinners' hands,
The shuttle speeds the warp;
A spinning trinity they, and crepe,
Black crepe falls from their brows.
The old man now grows cold with fear,
Fixes his eyes on them,
As warp and weft grow fuller still,
Both broad and wide.
Their brows are bound with crepe of black;
Their gloomy and ancient faces
Can just be glimpsed beneath their veils.
The old man starts now, anxiously,
And then he turns to them,
The horrid spectres spinning still
The precious golden thread:

KRAK.
 Whose warp are you weaving there, old wife?

HAG 1.
 That of your life.

HAG 2.
   That of your life.

KRAK.
>   There in your hands, old woman,
>   The thread makes golden braids...

HAG 1.
>   This is your childhood faith,
>   Long before you were summoned
>   To labour and to pain;
>   While you yet remained
>   At your father's hearth.

KRAK.
>   I don't recall — show it me here.
>   Why did your hand just start?

HAG 2.
>   What started was your heart,
>   Shot through by love — as by a spear.

KRAK.
>   A happy love was it? Or a sad?
>   I don't remember how it was.
>   Remain there yet a little while!
>   It's pleasant to recall past loves.
>   Why do you jerk it with your hand,
>   The thread?! — Wherefore, this nervy bile?

HAG 2.
>   Love is pain and misery.
>   Your love is passed — is history.
>   Begone, now! As we swiftly spin
>   Before you, many a victory.
>   Before you, many the armed forays
>   Before we count out all your days;
>   Struggles and gambits,
>   Your fate, knightly bandit —
>   Hey, swiftly now, swiftly we spin!

KRAK.
>Give the thread here into my hand —
>Let it sweep here across my palm.
>Let me with my own fingers feel
>Again my destiny as man,
>As it flows on, like a calm
>Eternal river...

HAG 2.
>   Off! Begone!

HAG 1.
>He's playing with it, like a toy!

HAG 2.
>He's a cunning one! It's a ploy
>To slow us down, make our spinning stand.
>Hey, swiftly, swiftly spin, my sisters!

KRAK.
>You'll tear it — — What's that in your hand!?

HAG 3.
>Scissors.

CHORUS.
>He's stopped it!

HAGS 1 and 2.
>   Sister, snip the span!!!

Here the old witch cuts through the thread,
And, fainting, the old man's head falls
Upon his chest, like ripe wheat stalks.
Again his heart has ceased to beat.
The witches three, their labours done,
Again disappear through the earth.
The shaman, who the chorus leads,

Has caught sight of what just befell.
His train now rounds the chief about
And, everything that they must do,
He shows them with his staff of rule,
And his commands they're swift to fulfil.

SHAMAN.
    Drag here the corpse from the embankment.
    Enchantment
    Shall make him warm.

CHORUS.
    The water's charms.

DROWNED HERDBOY.
    Breathless I entered the reeds
    That night,
    My feet
    Stumbling after those lights.

WEREWOLF.
    And the reeds, they lashed your chops?

DROWNED HERDBOY.
    When I halt, the light stops.
    Then it goes, and someone pushes
    Me down among the rushes.
    I fall on all fours
    There, where the bullfrog snores,
    My hands — all muddy brown...

RUSAL.
    He's remembering when he drowned.

DROWNED HERDBOY.
   I flail at a birch-tree braid,
   And above me, those maids
   Laughing, and pursing their lips…

WEREWOLF.
   From those lips honey drips!

DROWNED HERDBOY.
   'Twas the devil I kissed!

RUSALKA.
   Jasiu, Jasiu, darling boy —
   I would be a living maid;
   You would all my charms enjoy
   If only you kissed my lips,
   And pulled me close to you, by the hips…

CHORUS.
   Jasiu, Jasiu, grab our hands
   As we braid our limbs, as we dance,
   And whichever one you choose,
   She shall be yours; she shan't refuse!

   There's oh so many of us here,
   And only one man — you, are near.
   Come, inspect us while we twirl,
   Choose from among us for your girl,
   And whichever one you choose,
   She shall be yours; she shan't refuse!

WIŚLANKA.
   Jasiu, Jasiu, turn around —
   Jasiu, if you shall be drowned,
   Whatever shall become of me?
   If you drown, I soon will follow
   And choke myself among the mallows!

Jasiu, if you leave your girl,
What shall I do in this cold world?

DROWNED HERDBOY.
Shh — the old shaman nods his head...

SHAMAN.
Take him up upon your shoulders,
And bear him to his muddy bed,
There by the boulders
Where the ford is marked with sand.
The water-nymphs' feast is at hand —
They dress a festive scarecrow, damned:
Let us help them with the clothes,
Since he's put aside a warrior's robes
And jokish, croaked —
By sickness, not by battle, broke.

WEREWOLF.
Up at the castle, I smell food!
You see? — a fresh corpse. I smell blood!
Look — up by the gate.
They met their fate
Lightly — felled by the axe:
One or two hacks!
Their gore makes puddles in the mud.
I'd like to lap and suck that blood!

RUSALKA.
Look, look — up there by the grates —
A boy worth an embrace!
So honey-sweet his charms;
I'd take him in these arms
If he would lead me into the wood...

WATER SPRITE.
At evenfall, when the air is good,
Fresh breeze, and dew.

RUSALKA.
    If he just wished it too.
    His juice would slake me,
    O, naked let him take me!

WEREWOLF.
    It's blood, it's blood! You smell the grave.

DROWNED HERDBOY.
    Shh! The shaman nods his stave.

SHAMAN.
    Strip him of armour, shield and sword,
    Battle-axe, sceptre and crown.
    With homespun now be he adorned,
    And wind pea-blossom his head around.

CHORUS.
    Bring forth your gifts.

SHAMAN.
                            Bring forth your gifts.

WATER SPRITE.
    In consternation, the corpse lifts
    His brows! He's listening? — — —

WEREWOLF.
    The castle's silent. Not a thing
    Stirs in the chambers there —
    Blood's dripping only. Blood to spare — — —

WATER SPRITE.
    Shh!

WITCH.
    They're sleeping side by side.

WEREWOLF.
                    Live men!!

WATER SPRITE.
                    Asleep!

SHAMAN.
　　Before a new day dawns again,
　　Dress up the corpse in simple garb.
　　Undo his fingers, from his grip
　　Take away his weapon, dress him plain,
　　As if he tended bees again.
　　Simple for beauty's sake,
　　When he should re-awake.

　　Take off the axe, take away the blade,
　　Undo the thong that holds the sword.
　　With blood it's stained — — —
　　Loop round his shoulder leather cords
　　And hang therefrom an earthen jar:
　　With seeds and simples, orchard-
　　Cuttings, fill it, so
　　He'll look like when he used to go
　　About his fields to plant and sow...
　　Simple for beauty's sake,
　　When he should re-awake.

WEREWOLF.
　　And we're to shoulder that dead beast
　　And bear him off at mourner's pace?

GOAT-HEAD.
　　They cook the meal, but will they feast?
　　Both root and leaf have a sweet taste!

WEREWOLF.
　　Both flesh and bones we'll toss away.
　　We'll suck the blood dry,

All night, all night,
While the moon is bright!
Drag him thither, drag him nigh,
As long as the blood lasts.

GOAT-HEAD

To the corpse of Krak.
You banned the rites, you made us fast!
You slaughtered all the sacred snakes;
For all times hence you shall be pent,
Curst, bound, in torment!

Wait the summer, wait the spring,
And if you can, delay your death.
Wait until all the corn turns green:
We'll laugh until we have no breath!

CHORUS.

Set him upon the Horned Beast!
He'll bear him hence like lightning, greased!

HORNED BEAST.

He rides, he rides, the lavish lord,
His full jug hanging from a cord...

CHORUS.

The Horned Beast pulls such a dray!
Ring round him, dance, sprightly and gay!
They clap their hands.

HORNED BEAST

Dances, turning round and round;
He bows to the corpse,
And stops.

CHORUS
Sets the corpse on the back of the Horned Beast
Like a rider.
They clap.

SONG.

1.
Course, course,
Hobby-horse,
Course through night and day,
Course the country, long and broad.
Course through mountain, stream and wood,
And on your fiddle play.

2.
This hobby never lolls in the glade;
This hobby chases his own shade.
Winter, summer, through all climes,
Promising new golden times,
Promising the May.

3.
Course, course,
Hobby-horse,
Leap and frolic at your sports.
The Horned Beast
Performs such feats!
And you, old fellow, as he flies,
Let go the reins and close your eyes!
Just hold on tight and grit your teeth!

4.
O haunted hobby horse,
Restrain your course
And stay!
My eyes are bound closed.

He stays? He goes?
When does it come, your May?

HORNED BEAST
Halts in mid-road
As he was circling the chamber.

WITCH.
In the corner, near the stove,
She's fallen fast asleep.

OLD MAN.
Knackered with the wars.

DEAD HERDBOY.
She doesn't know — the crown is hers —?

RUSALKA.
Shh!

WATER SPRITE.
She blinks her eyes.

WEREWOLF.
Shh!

SHAMAN.
Tomorrow, at sunrise...

WITCH.
Shh! She can hear in her dreams.

SHAMAN.
The sky's still shrouded by the night.
At morning, when the beams
Of sunlight clear it,
She'll come to know her might,
And the power of her spirit.

WEREWOLF.
   How?

WATER SPRITE.
   Half-open, her eyes.

WITCH.
   Avaunt —

RUSALKA.
   Shh! Shh...!

DROWNED HERDBOY.
   She sighs.

RUSALKA.
   She sleeps.

DROWNED HERDBOY.
   Shh.

SHAMAN.
   She ascends the steeps
   In spirit.

WITCH.
         Before the dawn
   She'll leave the castle, and once gone,
   She never shall return.
   She'll leave, but she shall call to her
   The peasants, whom she'll arm —
   From past the rivers and the hills
   She'll call them from afar —
   And how they'll mow, and slash, and kill!

OLD MAN.
   And tomorrow that huge thing
   Named the folk, will name her king!

WITCH.
 Shh.

DROWNED HERDBOY.
 Her sleeping hand frets.

WITCH.
 It's her swelling, tormented breast.

OLD MAN.
 O, her breast is filled with pain.

WITCH.
 It rages inside her, the flame!

OLD MAN.
 Let her dream.

WEREWOLF.
 Let her dream.

CHORUS.
 Let her dream.

HANCYN'S SONG

I
1.
Heya, heya, see the staff
I made myself, I hold —
Soon it shall be a royal sceptre
Flourishing with gold.

2.
A golden staff with blooms of gold
And leaves of brightest green.
And more — there's apples on my wand,
The brightest ever seen.

3.
I bound these apples to my staff,
All night, by candle pale.
All the night long I kept my watch
At feverish travail.

4.
Take it, king, this masterwork,
Take it in your hand;
And may the golden sceptre lead
You to a fortune grand.

II
1.
Hey there crown, you kingly band
That I from roses wove;
On whose forehead shall you be placed?
Seek out the one I love.

2.
Brush back the hair from the forehead
And smooth the face so bright;
Above her hover sacred flames —
She's lit with holy light.

3.
And there they play — rose-intricate,
Twining and brightly flashing:
From them beat calm and happiness
And youth forever lasting.

4.
And there I've sown three rosy tears,
Dew of a weeping heart;
For you, they foretell happiness,
Joy that shall never depart.

SHAMAN.
    Her breast is torn with weeping.

DROWNED HERDBOY.
    She sobs while sleeping.

RUSALKA.
    She sobs while sleeping.

WITCH.
    Leave her a dowry, a bequest.

WATER SPRITE.
    What's that, mother, that you suggest?

WITCH.
    A dowry she must take.
    Tomorrow, when she wakes —
    Blood will thirst for blood.

DROWNED HERDBOY.
    Her wrists are bound.

OLD MAN.
                She's bound for the wood —
    The stake,
    When she awakes.

WEREWOLF.
    What sort of bequest, now?

RUSALKA.
    The Vistula's crown.
    The bloody blossoms of the river.

WATER SPRITE.
    And this — who will give her?

WITCH.
>The dowry must be paid
>By a virgin maid.
>It can be no other.

RUSALKA.
>What did you say, old mother — ?

WITCH.
>You — give her your wreath of maidenhead.

RUSALKA.
>Old mother, what's that you said?
>So sorry you'd make me
>To part with that sum!
>My beauty would forsake me,
>My youth would be done —
>I've only got one
>Such chaplet — that wreath,
>Which my own hands did weave!
>O my spray, my maidenhead —
>Old mother — what was it you said?

WITCH.
>Give her your chaplet of virginity.

RUSALKA.
>Take pity on me!
>O, the pain!
>Once gone, never to come again,
>The flowers, the blooms —
>And that chaplet spells doom,
>Death to whoever wears it!

CHORUS.
>Take it off, bear it
>To her.

OLD MAN
> *Stretches his hands above Wanda's head.*
> Fetters, bonds — hence!

SHAMAN
> *Stretches his hands above Wanda's head.*
> Arise strong, confident!

WITCH
> *To Rusalka.*
> The wreath — bring it nigh!

CHORUS
> *To Rusalka.*
> Through the wreath, prophesy!

RUSALKA.
> Little wreath of virgin leaves,
> Give to her all that she desires.
> So young, alas, I part with thee —
> Someone else thee now requires.
> Overruled is my own will;
> Now, her wishes deign fulfil.
> Serve her well, my maiden wreath,
> What she desires, do thou bequeath,
> Long be her rule, strong be her skill.

WANDA
> *Dreaming, struggles with Rusalka over the wreath,*
> *Until she succeeds in pulling it from her.*

RUSALKA.
> Take it, take it away,
> Take it hence;
> Haste: in that wreath is strength.
> You shall be gay
> But one day — — —
> Hey, my maiden wreath, hey.

CHORUS.
>Today, today you shall walk wreathed
>In the dread power that we've bequeathed.

WITCH.
>You shall have whatever you please
>As long as you possess that wreath;
>Even be it half the whole world's breadth,
>Even be it love, even be it death;
>Desire it, and it shall be at hand
>At your mere command.
>But do not forget:
>You're in our debt
>And must return hither,
>Ere its fresh leaves wither.

WANDA
>*Places the wreath on her head.*

WIŚLANKA.
>In the water's depths
>Many such blooms are kept.
>Shining, bright and fair,
>Freshly ringed pairs.

CHORUS.
>In a wreath blossoming
>Stately adorned: the changeling!

WIŚLANKA.
>Recall your given vow,
>Which you have freely sworn.
>By it you wear the crown.
>Take care — be not foresworn.
>In charms you placed your trust
>When you had need of us,
>You were victorious.
>You must not disown us now.

Recall your given vow.
Take care — be not foresworn.
Guard well the chaplet fair;
In private dress your hair —
Let the sun never see
That you're a maid of conjury,
Who gives the lie to beauty.

CHORUS.
Hey, in a wreath fresh blossoming
Adorned is the changeling!

WIŚLANKA.
In the water's depths
Many such blooms are kept.
But keep hidden the wreath,
And in secret you must bathe;
Let the sun never see
That you're a maid of conjury,
Nor that you owe that wreath to me.

CHORUS.
Hey, in a wreath fresh blossoming
Adorned is the changeling!

WIŚLANKA.
In secret your robes don,
And fear, O fear the sun.
Let the sun never guess
That you're one of ours
And the wreath round your tresses,
That wreath is not yours.

CHORUS.
Remember well your vow;
Be you not foresworn now!
In the water's depths
Many such oaths are kept.

The train passes toward the portcullis.

SHAMAN.
    Wring not your hands, smite not your brows,
    Soon he'll return from the meadows,
    Against the grates his poll to clang,
    To roar with laughter and bared fang.

CHORUS.
    Wring not your hands, smite not your brows,
    Soon he'll return from the meadows,
    And with his head he'll strike a blow
    Against the gates, and laugh like a crow,
    And out to him you'll gladly go.

    Farewell to you. Let no man hear
    Foul words from you; before your tears
    We bow in homage. You'll be done
    With weeping when you shall become
    The king; the first your folk among.

HORNED BEAST.
    Farewell
    Speak well
    Of us, who venerate.
    Cease now the while
    To sob, and smile —
    I'll meet you at the gate.

He bows in homage before Wanda.

CHORUS.
    He rides, he rides, the lavish lord;
    His full jug dangling from a cord.
    The Horned Beast pulls such a dray —
    Dance and be glad round him, and gay!

*The train exits the chamber and moves off along the corridor,
Into the castle arcades, taking with them the festively dressed
Body of the prince.*

WANDA
*Pushes her way through the departing train, quick and lithe
In her movements, yet still as if in the grips of a somnolent spell.
She collects some of the armour scattered on the floor,
As well as the sword belt and the sword, and the horn,
Which she drapes over her shoulder.
She takes up the head covering
And places it on her head.*

BURDOCK
*Half wakens at the clang of armour, as Wanda loops
The sword belt round her hips. He watches as she dresses,
And a strange music meets his ears.
He hardly can believe his eyes:
There, where the dead knight had his seat,
The space is empty — someone stole the king!
The Vistulans took him off by force;
Their song retreating faintly sounds.*

CHORUS.
   Hail, sire, hail!
   Eternal praise
   To the heroic knight.

BURDOCK
*Now understands: the king's been stolen.
The Vistulans have taken him off by force;
Their song retreating faintly sounds.
He starts up, cries out, wakes Chuckle —
And harkens to the echoes from the field.
He starts again and shakes Chuckle.*
   Hey, ha! Hey ha!
   Get up! Get up!

CHUCKLE.
   Where's the old man —?

BURDOCK
   Whispers.
                        Among the rocks
   Down by the river banks, among the reeds
   All silver — there the water-folk
   Are bearing him away, with song!

CHORUS.
   Swell, river, swell!
   Foam the cliffs with your waves.
   Bear him swift in your flight!

BURDOCK
   Shouts.
   The king's been taken by the sprites,
   This holy eve, this holy night! — — —

CHUCKLE.
   The trees flap in the wind like flags.

BURDOCK.
   As if they were glad —
   A new man rises, a new chief,
   A strong leader, to bring relief!

CHUCKLE.
   Jarowit is the cause —
   On this, the vigil of the water gods'
   Holiday —
   Corpse and scarecrow are at play:
   The corn is gone from the bier,
   And instead of the maid, here
   We have a mighty chief
   In her place!

Shouts
>Get up! Arise from your sleep!

WANDA
Who until this moment had stood motionless
Now gathers her thoughts
And sounds her horn.

CHUCKLE and BURDOCK
Look on, listening.

THE LITTLE NATION
Awakens.

THE PEASANTS
Gather round, at a run.

BURDOCK.
Have they lost all their fear
Now the trumpet strikes their ears?
Now they hold terror in scorn
At the blast of that horn?
Those who ran from the fight
Run toward it tonight —
From the alleyways of hell!

WANDA
Speaks lively, sharply.
They're asleep
Down in their trenches, exhausted.
Take up the weapons all,
From the armoury;
Take all the iron
And all the wooden shafts,
And follow me! While it's still dark!

She opens wide the chamber door
And reveals all kinds of weapons:

Blades, battle-axes, helmets and shields;
She arms herself anew, while the peasants take out
The rest of the arms.

WANDA.
    We'll rush down from the battlements
    And get ourselves into the woods
    Beyond the river.
    There, all who are men
    Will stand to the task:
    Each with a weapon in his hand,
    Each with a buckler for defence,
    Fastened tight with thongs.
    And then: To horse!
    We'll thunder through their camp
    Where they pen our stolen cattle.
    We'll hammer them in battle!
    Make sure your pouches are filled with stone,
    The rocks that lie below the cliff.
    Tell this to the slingsmen —
    Denude the shore of shingle!
    And when I'm gathered together,
    When I'm fully armed,
    Then, my hearts, I'll slice your rye bread!

    To Burdock:

    You! My harness.
    Now!

BURDOCK
    Runs to her, then suddenly stops, as if charmed; unnerved at her expression and behaviour.

WANDA.
    Come on then, quickly, man!
    Take the straps in your hand
    And tie them tightly round my hips.

BURDOCK
Does so, eying her carefully.

WANDA
Striking the helmet with her hand.
Songster — this helmet that I wear
With golden wings above the ears —

CHUCKLE.
It is the same one
The waves once flung
At the cliff-foot, upon the mud,
When the stream was in flood;
Too heavy for mere human hands…

WANDA.
And yet I wear it.
I can bear it —
Here I stand.

CHUCKLE.
The Norsemen, who the wild seas dare
Have such helmets; Prince Krak would wear
It, when he called the folk to moot.

WANDA.
And now you'll swear your troth to me!
To listen, and attentive stand —
It's I who now gives the commands!
You both will set aside the lute
And take up axe, and sword, and shield
And come with me — to the battlefield!
We're off to fill the halls of hell!

BURDOCK
Takes her by the hand, halts her progress.
What's that peeks out beneath your helm?

What sort of wreath is that runs round
Your brow — ?

WANDA.
It's just some blooms to fill the marge —
Else the helmet would be overlarge.

CHUCKLE.
The wings upon it seem to be waving:
Like those of falcon, or of raven...

WANDA.
Because it's time for me to fly
Unto the field of battle.

CHUCKLE.
                    But why
Do you set the wings down
Upon your ears? They rustle! Hear it?

WANDA.
What will tomorrow's weather be?
A cloudy sky? Or fair, sunny?

BURDOCK.
Such cares as those beset your spirit?

WANDA.
There will be miracles, no doubt,
When the sun rises anew.

BURDOCK.
Already wonders round us about:
So like a warrior born are you!

WANDA.
> My shield!
> Fashioned of bull's hide seven-fold,
> Hammered fast with nails of gold.

CHUCKLE
> *Giving her the shield.*
> That shield — barely a man might wield!

WANDA.
> You find it heavy? Not I.
> With it in hand, I can fly!

> *Commanding:*

> Tear the bushings from the spears
> And chuck them in the quivers!

CHUCKLE.
> O, wonders! How is it that you
> Are with a warrior's strength renewed?
> You bark your orders just as he,
> Krak, did among the soldiery.
> This strength — comes it from enchantment?
> From spellcasting, this awesome might?!
> Are you the one that was foretold
> By the soothsayers of old?
> "He shall appear upon the heights,
> Endowed with brave Krak's warrior-might."
> Your limbs — like his — You fill his place;
> And yet, you've got his daughter's face!

WANDA.
> Why waste your breath with empty words?
> With me, my lads! Unsheathe your swords!
> Send heralds, quick, from house to house
> The men to gather, the troops to rouse!
> And then we shall renew the fight

While the foe slumbers in the night.
We'll rush upon him like the lynx
Suddenly, and laugh as each man sinks
His blade into a sleeping breast —
And then we'll slaughter all the rest.
Here — you can smell the blood that's dried
Along this metal... take it up!
And rush with me into the fight!
Who wants to fight will find enough
Weapons to hand! None stay, none flee —
After me, lads! To victory!

PEASANTS
    Follow her.

ACT II

    the riverbank below wawel. sand, reeds, woods in the distance. a boat.

CORPSE [of Krak]
    Among the reeds.
    Snakes slither to me from the water,
    Reptiles tear my flesh;
    When will these my torments cease?
    Bound are my wrists, and my feet,
    So harshly bound, my wrists!

    The water flees me on the strand;
    The earth my corpse will not receive.
    Through long cold windy nights I stand,
    Cursing, and praying, for relief.

    When will this torment reach its end?
    Who'll nourish me with bread?
    Who'll slit the thongs that bind my hands?
    Abandoned am I, left for dead.

And death so near, death is so near!
But, endless are my torments;
Am I forever to stand here,
With bound, and helpless hands?

Snakes slither to me from the waves;
Reptiles tear my flesh.
Living, I feed them from my grave,
So harshly bound, my wrists!

The night is windy, cold and grey.
My heart shivers inside.
In the cold wind I bob and sway;
Snakes slither near me from the tide.

I've seeds here in an earthen cup,
Seeds I was meant to sow.
When the reptiles have lapped them up...
I stand, the cold winds blow!

My thick, black fields no more I'll till,
And vacant stands the manor.
Evil the will that holds me here, still;
Cursed am I, and dishonoured!

The times they run, the times they chase,
The night is cold and grey.
The wind above the livid waves
Makes me to bob and sway.

Snakes slither near, dragons, reptiles —
Bugbears, ghosts of the drowned;
I had a castle, a noble pile,
Whence I was stolen, thus bound.

WEREWOLF
Emerges from the water and crawls near the Corpse.
You'd fain retake your royal seat?

You lived there snug, and fine?
With mead to guzzle, soup to eat —
All that, you've left behind!
You'd like to sink beneath the waves?
Well, your bed's being made
By three women,
Three sprightly queens.
By morning, perhaps
It will be spread.
Meanwhile, keep vigil here instead.
Ha, ha, ha...
You're cold? I'll cover you in rushes.
I'll sink you deep — up to your neck,
Your head —
Hey, how's the water?
How's it taste?
Pure Vistula spring water!

He sinks the Corpse in the water.

DROWNED HERDBOY
  Among the reeds, playing his pipe.

SONG

1.
My pipe is sweet, my pipe is thin.
I found it near the strand;
A little branch it once had been,
Now it whistles in my hand.

2.
I play my pipe among the reeds,
My song is sprightly, gay.
O, how it wept hot tears, the tree
When I sliced this away!

3.
Play, little pipe; regale the ear.
I finger you as I wish.
The night is sharp, the leaves are sere,
The river waters swish —

4.
The river waves flash back the stars,
That in the mists expire.
My soul is in the devil's claws;
I'm roasted in hellfire.

Dawn.

MAIDENS
On the boat.

SONG

1.
Misty, misty
Flow the waves
    the river waves.

Kiss me, kiss me
Darling maid
    if you be brave.

2.
River water,
Ever race
    till in the seas you hide.

River daughter,
Kiss his face
    and love him as a bride.

3.
Misty, misty
Flow the waves
  the river waves.

Kiss me, kiss me
Darling maid
  if you be brave.
  Hey ha, ha ho!

WEREWOLF
  Rises out of the water and looks on.
  They're winding wreaths,
  Plaiting, binding,
  Winding them around the trees.

CORPSE
  Swaying beneath the waves.
  What's happening?

WEREWOLF.
  When the sun
  Rises, there will come
  A crowd of men,
  When the fighting ends.

CORPSE.
  They're still fighting?

WEREWOLF.
  They're mopping up.
  It's winding down.
  The stragglers run
  Till they're cut down.

CORPSE.
  I can't see a thing...!

WEREWOLF.
> So lift your head
> Above the water.

CORPSE
> *Lifts his head above the water.*
> You hear that noise?

WEREWOLF.
> I hear the noise,
> But from afar.
> They cut them down
> Near the Rudawa.

> *He catches sight of the girls on their boat,*
> *Begins to coax them.*

CORPSE.
> Why do you smack
> Your lips
> And bare your teeth?

WEREWOLF.
> You see that
> Girl, those hips?
> What a treat!

CORPSE
> *Jesting.*
> Hoo hoo ha!
> Give her a scare —

WEREWOLF
> Shh — she'll hear...
> *Coaxingly:*
> Come here, girl,
> Into the swirl

Of the waters below,
Holla, ha ha ho...

For your sweet tresses
You'll have strings of pearl.
Just put off your dresses
And slip into the swirl.

Come warm my breast. —
It's cold and chill;
Your lips I'd kiss;
O how they swell

With blood! And from then on
You'd rule with charms
Whomever you wish
But first, these arms

Must take you, and teach
You love, and passion's spurt!
Look here — undress! — I reach
For you — toss away your shirt!
Holla ha ha ho!

CORPSE
Jesting.
Hee hoo ha...
Toss off your shirt...

GIRL 2
On the boat.
Look there! Look there!
In the water — that swirl...
Something plays
Something sings...
Something calls...

WEREWOLF.
                      Hey, girl —
  Time for love, my fair!

GIRL 1
  On the boat.
  Something buzzes in my ears,
  O, I feel I'm getting dizzy!
  Someone's there — who is he?

WEREWOLF.
  Undress — dive in! Come now, missy!
      Holla ho ha ho!

CORPSE.
  Take off your shirt...
  Hee... ha... ha...

WEREWOLF
  Disappears beneath the water.

GIRL 2.
  There's evil in these river deeps;
  Chuckles above the waves echo!
  A head bobs out the water, and peeps —
  Straw-stuffed it seems; a scarecrow?

GIRL 1.
  My head spins, swarms
  Of bees buzz through it...

GIRL 2.
  You've been charmed —
  We must undo it!

GIRL 1.
  Something beckons — from the water —
  Something in the water calls me...

WEREWOLF.
    Holla ha ha ho!

RUSALKI
    Emerging from the water
    They creep upon the girls from the rushes.
    Shh, shh, shh — there's two of them.
    They've come to wind some wreaths — — —
    They're ours, good...!

WEREWOLF
    From beneath the water.
    Ho ha ho!

RUSALKI.
                    We'll lap their blood...

GIRLS
    Run off in fear.

RUSALKA.
    Look look — there's someone here,
    Wrapped in a rope, noosed, bound...

WATER FOLK
    Gather round the corpse.

WIŚLANKA.
    Hey! It's the prince!
    The prince called Krak,
    From Wawel's hilltop castle!
    Just a day since,
    His corpse was dragged
    Along the shore, and hassled...

RUSALKA.
    Hey old fellow, how'd you sleep
    All night long
    In the open?

GOAT-HEAD.
    Did you know your daughter
    Will cross the water
    Beneath the cliff so high?
    Against that rock
    Her head she'll knock —
    Did you know that she'll die?

WIŚLANKA.
    Did you know she'll kill
    Whomever she will?
    She'll rise among the stars —
    But she'll curse the hour
    She reached for power,
    And took that wreath of ours!

CHORUS.
    Regretful daughter,
    Dearly you bartered
    For that cruel wreath of ours!

GOAT-HEAD.
    What's that that stirred?
    Him! He seeks his sword —
    The scarecrow
    From his sleep's emerged —
    But his arm is — froze...

CORPSE.
    I've got no blade.

RUSALKA.
>My wreath, my wreath
>Of virgin blooms —
>You soon will totter above the deeps
>And watch it go
>As on it flows,
>The wreath that spelled your doom...

CHORUS.
>The wreath — it spelled your doom.

CORPSE.
>Take some seeds here from my pouch
>And spread them here, there, round about;
>Then watch them sprout,
>Green seedlings gay,
>To greet the green month of May.
>
>I beg you — take into your hand
>From out my pouch some seed;
>Spread it and see how blooms the land.
>The snakes will have something to eat!
>
>Hey! The seeds will go to waste!
>As I go down, so do the seeds!
>Take but a handful! Take them, please,
>And see the meadows bloom with May.
>One handful save, as down I go,
>Or there'll be nothing left to sow!
>
>Along with me the seeds are lost,
>Never to be in furrow tossed,
>And here I sink, all noosed and bound,
>Near Wawel's cliff I sink, I drown!
>
>When shall they end, the tears, the throes?
>When shall they crack and melt, the floes?

When will it pass, tormentful night?
And when return, the blood, the might?

When will it be returned, the sword?
When will I feel it in my grip?
When shall I lead my battle-horde?
Who from my wrists these thongs shall slip?

CHORUS.
Hey viburnum, hey mullein,
Through the rushes breezes blow,
Bearing with them the echo
Of a distant strain
Over hills and trees
And streams and leas.
Hey! Softly sigh the trees.

The woods afire,
The red mounts higher:
It's the blood of the sun.

But now it's set,
The fields grow wet
With dew — the sowing's done.

But dawning brings
The sun — full springs
On all heads — blooming May.

Hey breezes blow!
Hey breezes, flow
Above the blossoms' play.

Two armies struggled on this field,
Knights all about are lain;
Blood trickles from armour and shield:
The knights pant and faint in pain.

The blood that pulses from their wounds
The Vistula drinks, and glows with red;
The white warrior prince goes off alone,
The white warrior prince... is dead.

Hey viburnum, hey mullein,
Breezes weave throughout the wood,
And all these breezes reek of blood...

Upon a steed
The people lead
Another warrior-king.

A horn resounds
And its bright sounds
Through brush and meadow ring.

Hey, through the trees,
Over the leas,
The boastful horn it sings.

The breezes dart,
The rushes part,
The riverside
Is shown;
Again it hides
As the reeds part and close and moan...

Now with a flash
Of armour, past
On a white horse speeds
The king, urging the steed
By the snaffle;

Flashing bright
Her helm delights
The peasants, flush with battle.

The horns resound,
The echoes bound
From wood and lea
And riverside.
There they group,
The happy troop,
In victory
Around the knight.

Hey viburnum, hey mullein,
Through the rushes breezes blow.
Through the trees, over the leas,
Hear the breezes sighing low.

Horns.
Sunrise.

NATION
Descends to the riverside
Gathers near the corpse
Drags down a straw scarecrow
And sinks it in the water.

SONG.

CHORUS.
1.
Scarecrow, scarecrow,
Now it's time for you to go.
You held the field
Now to summer yield:
The sun has strung his bow.

Hey summer, summer, golden time,
Rule the field! You're in your prime!
Swell the stalk, increase the yield,
And grant us labour in the field.

May our wagons creak in time of harvest;
Hear us, O Żywia, golden goddess!

2.
Scarecrow, scarecrow,
Now it's time for you to go.
All winter long you wore your crown,
Now in the river you shall drown.
The sun has strung his bow!

Hey summer, summer, golden time;
Rule the orchards in your prime!
Swell the apples large and bright,
With your ninefold holy might
Bless harvest, bless the cider press,
O Żywia, hear this our request!

3.
Scarecrow, scarecrow,
The sun is high, it's time to go!
Pain filled your rule,
Now you are pulled
To your muddy bed down below!

Summer, summer,
Sun-faced god!

WANDA
Ascends the boat.

PEASANTS
Armed, ascend the boat.

CHUCKLE
With a huge wreath of flowers and sheaves,
He comes before Wanda and bows humbly.
To bid your hand
Gaily, here I stand

And lift my voice now, maiden.
The sun is high,
Heralds haste nigh
With song and sceptre laden.
Both old and young are here:
All the Polanie partake of the cheer!
So happily,
I bend the knee —
Deign grant our plea!

MUSICIANS
Ascend the boat.

CHUCKLE.
They name you king.
To the castle above
This escort brings
You, with praise and love.

CHORUS.
Hoo, ha!

CHUCKLE.
Love! They exclaim —
Their hearts you've won.
Long may you reign
O chosen one!

CHORUS.
Hoo, ha!

CHUCKLE.
Rejoice with us
On this blest morning,
O beauteous —
They name you king!

CHORUS.
    Hoo, ha!

CHUCKLE.
    Though a mere maid,
    A girl barely grown,
    Over us shall you reign,
    From Krak's royal town.

CHORUS.
    A maiden-king
    In a maiden's gown,
    Wears a warrior's crown!

CHUCKLE.
    As custom dictates, royal sire,
    Raise high your helm upon the spear!
    With your crown adorn the May-oak nigh:
    As a sign of victory. King, hear
    Your people murmuring, like a hive
    Of bees...

CHORUS.
    Sire, upon your eyes we'd gladly gaze!
    Pray, doff your helm, your visor raise!

WANDA
    Removes her helmet with both hands.
    As she raises it aloft, the wreath of the Rusalka may be seen on her brow.
    Here is the sign of victory —
    Here is my royal crown.
    Raise the crown high on the May-tree;
    Now, turn this craft around,
    And row me to the other side!

CHUCKLE
    Takes the helmet from Wanda's hand and raises it aloft on the spear.

WANDA
Gladdened, raises aloft her arms.

CHORUS
From the boat.

    1.
Oak of green, green oak of May,
In a crown freshly dight;
The world's four corners slash and slay:
We greet you, holy knight!

    2.
O knight, the world's four corners slay,
In your fresh crown of green.
O oak of green, green oak of May,
Blest sign of amity!

MUSICIANS
Play.

CHUCKLE
From the boat
Hear the fiddles sprightly play,
    Hoy da dana ho,
On the king's coronation day,
    Hoy da dana ho!

CHORUS
From the riverbank.
May the king be in the Spirit's keep!

WANDA.
To the castle now, over the deep!

RUSALKI
From beneath the waters.
The wreath you wore beneath your helm:

That wreath is of our water's realm.
Though gay you be, forget not now
What you have sworn — your sacred vow.

WIŚLANKA

From beneath the waters.
Come to us, leap
Into the waters deep!
He calls, your dreaming father —
Come, come into the water.
In the water's depths
Many such blooms are kept...

CHORUS

From beneath the waters.
The wreath you bore
You must restore,
Mysterious one;
Look: high is the sun.
Unveil your face so pure!

Mysterious maid
You've been gainsaid.
That sun you ought to fear!
The sun your crown will sear —
The wreath that is not yours!

RUSALKA

From beneath the waters.
In the waters' depths
Many such blooms are kept.
It shines in glory,
Celebratory,
Come join us here, bewept!

WANDA

Stiffens, stunned — and slowly lets her arms fall to her brow.
She touches the wreath, and remembers.

RUSALKI
From beneath the waters.
Come, queenly daughter,
Into the palace of the waters.
Silver pulse the waves.
So many blooms we have,
You rosy-gorgeous girl;
Enter the river's swirl!
Come, queenly daughter;
We've flowers in the water,
You've flowers at your brow!
The sun has risen now;
Your father calls his daughter
Into the river water.

RUSAL
From beneath the water.
Snap the oars and hurl the boat —
Crush it against the cliff!

WEREWOLF
From beneath the water.
Hurl the skiff
Against the cliff!
Snap the oars, and spin it round,
Split the beams, and drag it down!

BURDOCK
From the boat.
Charms and spells! The oars are broke —
The rudder splits! The water folk
Now drag our boat down in the depths —
Drag us to our death!

He leans over the gunwale and gazes into the water.

There's wonders in the waters deep:
An old man's face! It seems to peep

From out a coral bush;
An old man's face, with beard of grey
Beneath the current's rush —
On the cold rocks he seems to lay...

RUSALKA
From beneath the waters.
The wreath you bore beneath your helm,
That wreath is of our water's realm.
Return it now — the Vistula calls...

BURDOCK
From the boat.
What do I hear? What's happening?
Odd sounds above the waters ring —
I hear laughter, I hear someone sing,
And then I hear someone groaning!
Hey! It's cursing, then it's moaning;
The voices, recalling
A wreath, calling, calling!

CHORUS
From the shore.
The wreath you bore beneath your helm —
That wreath is of the water's realm!
The river demands its restoration;
At what a cost you've saved the nation!

CHUCKLE
From the boat.
Toss that wreath away!
Becalm the troubled waves
That round about us rave;
Help us! We are afraid!
Get rid of the wreath!
As I foretold,
You — young, beautiful and bold,
Of blushing sadness —

To Żywia promised sacrifice,
And in a trice
She heard your prayer!
She gave the wreath, and thence
There woke in you such strength:
A warrior's soul, a warrior's skill,
And whatever you willed
Took shape!

BURDOCK
From the boat.
Princess — and king! —
Forgive us, poor girl;
It's the charm, tugging
You to the water's swirl,
And depriving
Us of our lord!

CHUCKLE
From the boat.
What might is in you, spell-cast Word!
You seat Death at the wedding feast;
You train bright eyes on the abyss,
And as the whirlpool takes a wreath,
So you too yawn for our princess!
Her life perfected in her deeds:
Her heart now yearns for death, and bleeds...

Gazes into the waters.

There's wonders in the waters deep:
An old man's face, that seems to peep
From out a coral bush;
An old man's face, with beard of grey
Beneath the current's rush —
And on cold stones he seems to lay!

RUSALKI.
>   The wreath you bore beneath your helm:
>   That wreath is of our waters' realm.
>   Restore it now, the waters thrum,
>   And you into the waters, come!

CHUCKLE
>   *From the boat.*
>   Get off the boat! It's sinking!
>   The slats split; water's rushing in!
>   The water-folk have it in hand,
>   Unplugging pin, undoing tack,
>   Escape!

>   *All leap from the boat.*

WANDA
>   *Remains alone on the boat.*

RUSALKI
>   *From beneath the waters.*
>   Join us here in the deep water.
>   There's many such blooms that are kept
>   Flourishing in the river's depths.
>   The sleeping father calls his daughter!

CHUCKLE
>   *From the riverbank.*
>   Look, look! The water maidens take
>   Our king by the hand!
>   And her face — it seems to radiate?
>   Doesn't she understand?
>   She's glad?!
>   Has she gone mad?
>   And she can't utter a single word?
>   What? She can't utter a single word?

BURDOCK
> *From the riverbank.*
> O gods! The river wave
> Above the boat now looms,
> And she smiles at her doom!

CHUCKLE.
> Her eyes search the abyss,
> Rapt, wondering — in bliss!
> She looks toward us, and waves!

BURDOCK.
> She's cursed! Cursed! Stay away from her!
> Will she not regain her senses?

CHUCKLE.
> From the deep river's surge
> Strange creatures, monsters, emerge:
> Ghosts, ghouls, the drowned,
> In the sunlight they crowd around
> And in the sunny hazes
> They warm their wan faces!

BURDOCK.
> Laughing, they splash about,
> In pairs, they laugh, they rout,
> Embracing in the silver waves...

RUSALKA
> *Above the surface of the waters.*
> Guard well the chaplet fair:
> Only in secret dress your hair.
> Let the sun never see
> That you're a maid of conjury...

CHORUS
> *From beneath the waters.*
> Guard you well the chaplet fair...

CHORUS
>   *From the riverbank.*
>   Spells and charms! Spells and charms!

WANDA
>   *Retreats toward the riverbank.*

CHORUS.
>   *From the riverbank.*
>   Move back! Move back! She returns!
>   By enchantment possessed,
>   Her mad eyes glow and burn,
>   And her gaze — so powerful!
>   Avoid it! Lest
>   She draw us into the whirlpool!
>
>   *The water's depths open wide*
>   *And in their rocky depths reveal*
>   *A palace bright: azure and gold*
>   *From turret-spire to foundations.*

WANDA.
>   Look there, and see!
>   My fame — of the water —
>   I have my victory!
>   O, my father,
>   Your Wawel now is free!
>   I won its liberty —
>   And look: where the water lifts,
>   The water-folk, bearing gifts!
>   There is your sacred land.
>   Take your rebecs in hand
>   And gaily for us play —
>   For me and for my gay
>   Court, deep below
>   The rushing river's flow,
>   Beneath the wave.
>   See there: my falcons brave,

    My palace guard
    Who served their lord
    With spear in hand;
    And with them stand
    Fresh maidens, brows
    With wreaths of rose
    Wound, sheaves of wheat;
    Their voices sweet
    As summer birds; they wheel
    In a bee-like dance
    About my father's happy lands!
    My father, king!
    King, of the water!

BURDOCK.
    What does she say? What does she boast?
    The mad girl — summoning the ghosts!
    A sacred flame is shining bright
    In her eyes — is she seeing right?
    Does she not know, that what she espies
    Are but illusions? Lies — — ?!

WANDA.
    He who would have victory,
    Come! Rush here to me!

BURDOCK.
    The wreath! Throw away the wreath!

WANDA.
    Begone! My life is there — beneath
    The waves: my victory!

BURDOCK.
    Tear the wreath from her forehead!

WANDA.
    Who dares touch me will be struck dead!

BURDOCK.
    They herd her back toward the waves!
    O, throw that wreath away, away!
    They're herding her into the deep!

WANDA.
    It is my kingdom that I seek:
    Play, fiddles, play! My realm is here!
    And you there: dry your useless tears.

BURDOCK.
    She is possessed! Grab her!
    Tear the wreath from her brow!
    Surround her!

WANDA.
    A happy king I have become —
    Unhand me, you! Begone, begone!

CHUCKLE.
    She's bared her sword!

CHORUS.
    She won't be stopped!

BURDOCK.
    They're herding her into the depths!

WANDA.
    I take possession of my realm.
    They sing my coronation hymn!

With naked sword she defends the wreath
And will let no one tear it away.
Her own folk press her toward the waves,
While with her sword, she warns them off.
Again she boards the fatal boat.

BURDOCK.
>They're pressing her toward her death!

WANDA.
>My coronation hymn they chant!
>And you there — dry your useless tears.
>My kingdom's here! My kingdom's here!

She sounds her horn.

CHORUS
>*From the riverbank.*
>The waters upon the land advance!
>Throw away that wreath! Your people drown!
>The dikes are melting from the banks —
>The boat is sinking! It pulls you down!

WANDA.
>Through me Fame calls to you.
>Fame speaks to you through my lips!
>By this arm, victory I grip.
>The spirits are my aid, my help.
>My knights are in the river's depths!

CHORUS.
>She's casting spells upon her own kind —
>Enchantment — ah, beware the witch! —
>The planks beneath her feet now split.
>That wreath is cursed! Unwind, unbind,
>Toss it away!

WANDA.
>   In it is my life!
>This wreath my fame! This wreath, it gives
>Me victory!
>You — cease your shouts, put by your ire,
>My realm — my glory!

RUSALKI.
    The wreath you wore beneath your helm:
    That wreath is of our water's realm.
    Restore it now, the waters thrum,
    As you into the waters come!

    They disappear beneath the waves;
    The current takes hold of the boat.

CHORUS
    From the riverbank.
    The waters seize the boat, it spins,
    The oars split, undone are the pins.
    Her armour is shining in the sun —
    She goes, the mad, enchanted one!
    Look there!
    By the current sped,
    The wreath! Held high in the air
    At sword's point! High above her head!
    She's chased by Death! Queen of the Dead!

    The corpse now rises on the wave
    And chases the maiden-knight.
    The boat, pressed on at furious pace
    Is borne quickly on the waves,
    And the straw man gaily rages
    In the sunlight, riding the waves,
    Chasing the maiden-king,
    Until, there where the river bends,
    A horrid crash is heard; the boat
    Is splintered on the cliff and sinks
    Into the turbulent water's depths.

    Long, long the people lined the banks,
    Watching and waiting. Will her corpse
    Return…? And yet the Vistula,
    As it then sped whispering by the banks,
    Still whispers on — the maiden's corpse

Never relinquishing. The folk, mourning,
Gaze sadly at the fatal cliff
Where she was borne, and dashed, by Evil.
They gaze as well toward the woods,
Toward the spires proudly stretching
Toward the heavens from the high
Palace of Wawel, above the flood;
The water bears the corpse afar.
The winds mourn loudly through the woods;
The fir trees bend unto the waves
And willows dip their pale braids
Into the Vistula, all mourning,
Keening with almost human voice.

Hey! On, the river current speeds,
Beating its foam against the cliffs.
The morning dawned with you a queen,
And still that same sun shines aloft
At which you gazed, happy and proud —
But the cold currents hold you fast,
And on the Vistula races, mad.

But there, where she gives up your corpse,
On that riverbank, foison with blooms,
There a kurhan will soon be raised
To you, by your human subjects' hands;
There shall your funeral rites be sung,
And the mournful repast consumed.
For you were liberated from shame
By your great will, victorious,
And for your steadfastness, your courage,
You shall for all time be remembered.

Farewell, O queen; maiden, farewell,
You in your golden diadem;
The Vistula will ever sing
Your name as whispering it flows
Throughout the breadth of Polish lands.

Farewell, queen of an ancient time,
Farewell, O joys of ancient ages;
Come close, black woods of ancient firs,
You royal friends; we by that ancient faith
Can only be cured in such a fane:
The ancient woods, over which you reign.

Hey now, return with song!
And along
With singing,
Heroes be bringing!
May good fortune return to us
Who have been long awaiting her,
Before our golden thread is snipped;
Before the blooming flower dries,
Before the falcon, who now flies
The heavens, falls with broken wing;
Before I cease to sing...

BISHOP, KING. BISHOP

(Skałka / Bolesław Śmiały)

Note on the translation: Both *Skałka* (1904-1906) and *Bolesław Śmiały* (Bolesław the Bold, 1902-1903) are based on the historical conflict between the Polish king at Wawel, and Stanisław Szczepanówski, Archbishop of Kraków. The latter is associated with the "little cliff," a geographical location in Kraków, which gives its name to the title of the first play. It is there that the Bishop was martyred, and it is the centre of his cult. As in the case of the 1170 martyrdom of St. Thomas Beckett, Archbishop of Canterbury, at the orders of the English King Henry II, St. Stanisław was put to death by the Polish King Bolesław, nearly a century earlier (1079). Whereas St. Thomas died defending the autonomy of the Church from the crown, St. Stanisław was accused of treason on behalf of the nearby Czech kingdom. Although the two plays are independent works of art, toward the end of his short life Wyspiański determined that they ought to be performed together. He envisioned a production of alternating acts, beginning with Act I of *Skałka*, followed by Act I of *Bolesław the Bold*, after which Act II of *Skałka* would be performed, and so on. Our translation of the two plays puts the poet's wishes into effect. The resulting play, which we entitle *Bishop, King. Bishop*, is a composite work of six acts. The reader who prefers to read the plays separately will be aided in this by the subtitles. Thus, our Act IV is subtitled "*Bolesław the Bold*, Act II; Act V is "*Skałka*, Act III" and so forth. In the original Polish, the play *Bolesław the Bold* is introduced with a long poem in lieu of didascalia. As this is intended for the reader, and not to be spoken on stage, we have moved it to the Appendix so as not to interrupt the flow of the composite drama.

ACT I

(Act I of *Skałka*)

THE ACTION TAKES PLACE AT SKAŁKA.

Night
Darkness
Stars

BISHOP
Dressed as an Archangel, in armour.
He stands still,
Both hands resting on his sword
Eyes fixed in the direction of the castle.

RUSALKAS
Emerge from the waters of the pond
Ascend the steps
And halt at the temple porch.

RUSALKA 1.
Like a stone — so lost in thought.

RUSALKA 2.
As if — in eternity.

RUSALKA 3.
In his face — an eagle. And God.

RUSALKA 4.
Eaglets as yet unhatched — what do you see?

RUSALKA 1.
Eaglets. The fledglings of his mind.

RUSALKA 2.
>One day, eagles shall gather here.

RUSALKA 3.
>The little reptiles round the water shine,
>Among the lilies of the valley they appear;
>Between the green fronds, they bob and sway.

RUSALKA 4.
>His eyes glow too — two shining flames:
>A blazing terror's sparkling embers.

RUSALKA 1.
>Look — at his feet, bound, knotted, lie
>Those who erstwhile guarded this fane
>With arms entwined and sleepless eye.
>Now, by his hand they lie cast down,
>Their faces humbled to the ground,
>In shameful dust, and void... they die.

RUSALKA 2.
>An eagle proud, he soars the skies;
>Gloomy his eye measures the clouds,
>See? — He scans whole ages with those eyes!

RUSALKA 3.
>He slew them all — he cut them down —
>Furrowing graves with his broad sword.
>An altar once stood on this ground,
>Which sacred flame the gods adored.

RUSALKA 4.
>The fire with water he doused and damned,
>Threw down the temple with his hand;
>Mighty, his evil aim attained...

RUSALKA 1.
>He's mighty.

RUSALKA 2.
> Saintly.

CHORUS.
> He's a saint.

RUSALKA 1.
> Higher then, eagle, in flight,
> Speed thought and soul to the heights.
> Spread wide your wings as you haste,
> Your eyes fast fixed on Wawel's gates —
> Those gates will spread wide in the spring
> And let pass seven men of the king.
> Then a vulture shall grip you, my lord,
> As each one of the seven, his sword!

RUSALKA 2.
> Your blood will flow along the grass
> And stain the lily blossoms red,
> There, where the little reptiles pass
> Among the blooms, with bobbing head.

RUSALKA 3.
> Your soul it longs for martyrdom.

BISHOP
> *Dips his right hand in the font*
> *And, lifting it to his forehead,*
> *Makes the Sign of the Cross.*
> All spirits, who these words can hear
> In the grey silence of the dawn;
> Spirits of water, earth and air,
> This sign I make is a clarion —
> You shall become an instrument,
> Fulfilling the Lord's each commandment.
> And thus, a new life is begun
> In the Name of Father, Ghost, and Son.

RUSALKAS
*Rush away down the steps
And plunge beneath the water to hide.*

*A whistling sound is heard.
Enter, from the right*

WŁODZISŁAW
*Who stops
At the porch.*

Enter, from the left

SIECIECH
*Who stops
At the porch.*

BISHOP
*Turns toward the church;
At last, his face is visible.
At the temple steps kneel, now,
And cross yourselves upon your brow
With water from this holy spring.*

*He dips his hand in the font
And gives water to each.*

WŁODZISŁAW
*Kneels,
Facing the church.*

SIECIECH
*Kneels,
Facing the church.*

Birdsong.

BISHOP.
> Hear as the birds to mattins ring.
> He kneels.

WHISTLE
> *Hidden among the high branches*
> *Of an oak.*
> Flit from branch to branch, my bird;
> Chirp and trill right through the scale.
> Run to the wellspring, pretty girl,
> And bring with you your watering pail.
>
> Attach it to the winch, young lass,
> And drop it down into the well.
> Gaze deep — as if into a glass —
> The water shall your fortune tell.

AFTERWHISTLE
> *Hidden among the high branches*
> *Of an oak.*
> The ripples spread, the water spells
> The future — who can guess
> What the deep pool shall prophesy?
> The first draught, maiden, brings a lie:
> Joy can be found deep in the depths.
> Well, well —

WHISTLE.
> Deep in the depths it lies!

MAIDEN
> *Approaches the pool with her pails,*
> *Pushes aside the winch,*
> *Bends over the water*
> *Pulls out a bucket*
> *And fills her pails.*

I rise up from my bed
With the new dawning light.
When he left me, he said:
"I'll be with you tonight."

But the night becomes day
And I'm here all alone.
To another you stray,
Leaving me on my own.

A new morning's sun warms
— Is that you at the gate? —
No — Bewitched by her charms,
Still you leave me to wait.

Did I see you outside?
Or were my eyes misled?
Ah, my anxious heart lied:
You're still with her, instead.

High the morning sun flew
Over the Vistula's wave;
Here, my heart's split in two,
Dark and cold as the grave.

Exit.

BISHOP
Rises.

WŁODZISŁAW
Rises.

SIECIECH
Rises.
To Włodzisław.
Tell me now, quickly, what you'd like.
You say you have the right, or no?

Might's what makes right. He bows low,
Whose shoulders cannot bear the weight.

WŁODZISŁAW
To Sieciech.
Ah you, who see me through and through —
You'd like a portion of it too?

SIECIECH.
Sure! Did I not keep it safe with you?
Were all my watchings then for nought?
You've not outsoldiered me a jot.
Think on old Lestek, how he waxed,
And he — a shepherd next to me!
My court is grand; it nothing lacks
Compared to yours. In amity,
As equals, I extend my hand.
Take it in yours, and let me aid
You to a brother's just demand:
Your portion. As for me, my blade
Will win what's mine.

WŁODZISŁAW.
                    That's only just,
That you should get what you deserve.
But to divide it, how?
Points at the ceremonial cake that rests on the font.
                    Observe —
A perfect circle, wreathed with staves
Of wheat and ribbons, round and whole,
And dedicated to the Lord.

SIECIECH.
And so? Every perfect circle's made
Of sections stretching from mid-pole
To ambit. And you ask me how
To divvy it? Stand there, near the nave
Points to where the Bishop is standing.

And like old Chrobry at Kiev,
Split it in two halves, with your sword.

WŁODZISŁAW.
To raise my sword against my clan,
That ancient legacy? I don't dare.

BISHOP.
And yet you stand here, and you stare.
Your eyes betray your smouldering soul.
You'd split what he would conserve whole,
Your brother, and I ask — why not?
The whole world's so divided; God
Allots each portion in accord
With the given soul's greatness. To each
His own — all that's in his reach
If he dare grasp it. Each is lord
Of his own fortune. Be on guard —
If trust fraternal's to be marred
By rivalry unto bloodletting,
Better for you to cease your fretting
And split away now. You don't dare?
Thus I your tender feelings spare.

He lifts his sword above the cake.

WŁODZISŁAW
To the Bishop.
Wait — if you break that circle, know:
You break the peace with me, as well.
Points at the round cake.
From hand to hand it must go, whole.
Blest as of old, by song and spell.

BISHOP.
It's true that he rules the nation —
    By virtue of my anointing.
Let him remember my station:

    I rule, by God, a second king.
That crown of his, by God bestowed,
    Set on his brow by this my hand,
Is sacred — no mere golden band.
    And as he treads his Royal road,
Thrusting aside my holy will,
    Closing his ears against my word,
Let him know: I'm a monarch still,
    Who holds his sceptre of the Lord.

WŁODZISŁAW.
    Half of the land is my birthright.
    Nor shall my will brook such a slight.
    I must have something to pass on,
    From my father unto my son.
    Quickly then, for it's nearly dawn.

BISHOP
    Goes off into the vestibule
    Past the font
    Stands over the stairs leading to the pond
    Searches with his eyes.

    A whistling is heard in the copse.

SIECIECH.
    Hey — is someone there?

BISHOP
    Without turning around
    Silences Sieciech with a gesture of his hand.

BISHOP
    Calling toward the path that runs through the copse.
    Hey — hey! —

AFTERWHISTLE.
Hidden among the high branches
Of an oak.
    Hey — hey! —

BISHOP.
      Listen!!

AFTERWHISTLE
Hidden among the high branches
Of an oak.
Hey — hey! —

BISHOP.
    Hey — hey!

AFTERWHISTLE.
      Listen —

In the depths, near the entrance to the copse
Along the path leading from the banks of the Vistula
Comes:

RHAPSODE
 Slowly
 Towards the pond.

WHISTLE.
 Hey ha...

AFTERWHISTLE.
    Hey ha!

WHISTLE.
     People!

AFTERWHISTLE.
　　Hey people — peasants — simple folk!
　　Come here! —

WHISTLE.
　　　　　　　Come here!

AFTERWHISTLE.
　　　　　　　　　Come here!

WŁODZISŁAW.
　　　　　　　　　　　Who's there?

SIECIECH.
　　The runic thrummer.

BISHOP.
　　There in the copse is where he lives.
　　His hovel's there.

SIECIECH.
　　　　　　　With the beehives.
　　He talks to trees. Or to himself.
　　He knows where bides each gnome and elf —
　　They say he tends the fire at night.

WŁODZISŁAW.
　　A shaman?

BISHOP.
　　　　　An old man of faith, all right.
　　But it's these stones that he adores —
　　These ruins. Crouched upon the moss
　　He draws his faith, he feels his might.

　　Pointing at the font:

But let him cast his eyes on that —
His gods are gone — their idols tossed
Into the dust — they are no more.

Points to the church porch.

I've cast the evil down. They lie
Face to the muck, every last one,
Humbled they lie, before the Sun.
My God is heaven's lord. He rules the skies —
Above my head He stretches wide his wings.
Above the mountain summits see Him rise.
This is the Holy Ghost of my preaching.
His sign — the Cross, and when a man is blessed
Upon his brow, upon his lips and breast,
He wins a crown of holy victory,
Order, peace, divine security.

WHISTLE
Calling, drawn out.
Hey ha! — Reapers!

AFTERWHISTLE
Calling, drawn out.
                    Hey, corvée!

WHISTLE.
Draw up, field hands! Gather round! Hey!

BISHOP.
Here come my thighs and shoulders.

From the copse
In a group, come
The Peasants,
With bent scythes over their shoulders.
They stop
At the wooden palisade that circles the pond.

RHAPSODE
Is among them.

WŁODZISŁAW
Looks now at the peasants, now at the Bishop.
What are they come for?

BISHOP.
                      Every dawn,
When they are called into the fields,
They gather here, and stare at the pond.
Their service to the Church they yield,
And since God sends them here to me,
He gives them ought of His bounty.
It's here I offer sacrifice.
I draw some water from the font
And over their heads
When their prayers are said
I bless them in peace with the Sign of the Cross.

He draws some water from the font
In his hand,
And, tossing it in the four directions
He makes the Sign of the Cross over the people.

PEASANTS
Kneel.

RHAPSODE
Stands amidst the kneeling crowd
Glaring at the Bishop.

BISHOP
Calling out to the people.
My people — brothers — I need your aid.
You've come to pray here at the pond
Before your labour in the sun.

I beseech you, by God's holy Word,
My simple folk, stand by your lord.

Fix into spears the scythes you bring;
At dawn we go to see the King.

PEASANTS
> *Arise from their knees.*
> *Murmurs and movement among them.*

BISHOP.
> Come close — here in the vestibule.
> A hard lot's fallen to us all.
> The people's justice now does call
> Us to obey the Spirit's rule.

PEASANTS
> *Begin to move toward the Bishop,*
> *But halt at the Rhapsode's words.*

RHAPSODE
> *In the midst of the peasants*
> *Beyond the pond, from afar,*
> *Calling to the Bishop.*
> Where will you lead these sinless men,
> Unspotted yet with any guilt?
> You know, when you unleash blind strength
> In knightly quarrels, blood is spilt,
> As from the clouds, rain, in torrents.

BISHOP.
> My will has to the hour matured,
> To rouse the souls given to my cure.

RHAPSODE.
> A shaman should battle — with words.

BISHOP.
    The king must now face God's sacred sword.

RHAPSODE.
    You would usurp my rule as here my fane.
    I should go boldly, and in the front ranks
    Since my life is already on the wane,
    Since sister Death I'd greet, with thanks
    As she covers my cold eyes with the sod...
    And spares me the sight of my desecrated gods.

BISHOP.
    As blind as you, those gods of wood!
    They didn't put up much of a fight.
    I toppled them down from where they stood
    And — there they lie.

He points to the toppled wooden idols.

                    Perhaps you might
    Still join them? —

RHAPSODE.
                    O, fret not for me —
    It's you who will be sharing their fate —
    Nor where my song leads, have no fear.
    Only one road leads from there to here,
    From you, to me: through the sacred pond,
    Where stood the temple of my God.
    Though you be called God's emissary,
    You'll never plumb their mystery,
    These waters, whose runes I know well,
    Unless you augment the holy flood
    With libations of your own heart's blood —
    And cross yourself over the swell!

PEASANTS
Cross to the porch and
Come up to the vestibule.

BISHOP
Stands amidst the Peasants.

WHISTLE
From the top of the oak tree, hidden in the branches.
Preach them, teach them what's to be:
Make the simple folk to rise.
Magic words,
Thirsty swords,
Give them knives, and you make them lords!

AFTERWHISTLE.
Have them dip their harvest scythes
In the pond there, nice and deep.
Bend the metal — stun the hordes
With magic words —
Scythes into swords!

WHISTLE.
Lelu, Lelu, work his end,
My toppled ancient friend;
Let the stiff metal bend
Since he so thirsts,
O charmed water, heed his curse!

PEASANTS
Submerge their scythes in the pond
After which they bend the blades in their hands
Making them into straight weapons.
They stand there with the scythes erect.

WŁODZISŁAW.
Brothers, we will begin the siege;
Stay here, while we toward the castle go.

And when we're safely past the bridge,
Well signal, with a trumpet blow.

PEASANTS.
We'll await the signal!

WŁODZISŁAW.
Then, after us! And fiercely run —
In tight formation, all as one!

He departs.

SIECIECH
Follows him.
After a minute, we see them
Rounding the pond,
Moving along the main path through the copse
Toward the Vistula and the bridge
Where
They are met by knights
And they move across the bridge.

BISHOP
Departs
At the head of the Peasants.

PEASANTS
Follow him; loud is their tread.
After a moment, we see them
Rounding the pond,
Moving along the main path through the copse
Toward the Vistula and the bridge.

RHAPSODE
Gazes after the departing throngs.
Once they have gone
He nears the palisade surrounding the pond
Bends down,

And leaning upon a blackened wooden pillar
Gazes into the water.

WHISTLE
From the top of the oak tree, hidden in the branches.
Brother, hey! —

AFTERWHISTLE
From the top of the oak tree, hidden in the branches.
      Hey — what?

WHISTLE.
         See him there?

AFTERWHISTLE.
Where?

WHISTLE.
At the water's edge. He stares
Deep in the pool.

AFTERWHISTLE.
      And there he sees...
What?

WHISTLE.
The church shrouded in grey mists
Reflected on the pool's still pane;
And there — just inside the fane,
Something of olden times remains:
Something of his — high up there! — sits...

RHAPSODE
Deep in thought
Gazing into the water.
At last, he sees it.
My lyre! — —

AFTERWHISTLE.
  Shh!

WHISTLE.
    Shh!

AFTERWHISTLE.
      Shh, hush! Shh!

WHISTLE.
  He sees it! While he's by himself,
  Slip down fast, lynx-like! On your way!
  Lead him to where it hangs, and help
  Him find it! He must take it today!

  Moves down from the oak
  Stands at the grass at the edge of the pond,
  Moves about the pond clockwise,
  Whistles.

RHAPSODE
  Approaches the vestibule
  Circling the pool counter-clockwise.

AFTERWHISTLE
  Moves down from the oak
  Stands at the grass at the edge of the pond,
  Moves about the pond clockwise.

RHAPSODE.
  Enters the vestibule.

WHISTLE
  In the vestibule, past the gates to the left.

AFTERWHISTLE
  In the vestibule, past the gates to the right.

WHISTLE.
  It's here, it's here —

AFTERWHISTLE.
            Just one more step.

RHAPSODE.
  Touches a lily with his hand.

WHISTLE.
  Don't touch!

RHAPSODE.
            That flower — — —

AFTERWHISTLE.
                      Not yours, that bloom.

RHAPSODE
  Lets the flower go
  Moves on a step
  And sets his hand on the font.

WHISTLE.
  Don't touch! —

AFTERWHISTLE.
            That's venom! It spells doom.

RHAPSODE
  Takes his hand away from the font
  And moves on a step.

WHISTLE.
  It's here he'll fall, beneath the sword,
  Who calls himself this temple's lord.

AFTERWHISTLE.
>   Another lord, through seven gates,
>   Will rush in here, with seven blades
>   And slash him down.
>   *He points off into the distance.*
>   There's the castle.

RHAPSODE
>   *Looks up*
>   *And sees the castle*
>   *In the distance*
>   *Beyond the Vistula.*

AFTERWHISTLE
>   *Points to the church.*
>   And here's the church!

RHAPSODE
>   *Turns*
>   *And looks about the church.*

WHISTLE.
>   You see it?
>   *He points at the lyre*
>   *That hangs on a buttress of the church.*

AFTERWHISTLE.
>   You see it now? Good!

RHAPSODE
>   *Sighting the lyre*
>   *Gazes at it from afar.*
>   Pure —

WHISTLE.
>   Not stained with any blood.

AFTERWHISTLE.
　Take it.

WHISTLE.
　　Take it.

AFTERWHISTLE.
　　　　It's yours.

WHISTLE.
　　　　　Now!

AFTERWHISTLE.
　Do you hear her heart strings thrumming loud
　As you draw near?

RHAPSODE.
　　　　　New life for me.

WHISTLE.
　Again you'll play, and feel, and see!

AFTERWHISTLE.
　Let no profane hand sully her;
　You alone are her master.
　He stole her from you; free her again!

WHISTLE.
　She yearns for you, alone of men...

AFTERWHISTLE.
　She'll play —

RHAPSODE.
　　　　　Whatever I command! —

WHISTLE.
　Shh, hush, shh —

RHAPSODE.
          The dawn breaks —

We see the copse, the Vistula,
Orchards.

AFTERWHISTLE.
    Reach out your hands!

WHISTLE.
          Boldly, now!

RHAPSODE
    Approaches the buttress.

AFTERWHISTLE.
                    Take!

RHAPSODE
    Reaches out his hand
    Grabs the lyre,
    Pulls at it.

LYRE
    Is unmoved,
    Soundless.

WHISTLE.
    Ingrown!

AFTERWHISTLE.
        Ha ha ha! Grown into the stone!

RHAPSODE
    Gazes round in terror.

WHISTLE.
Hoo hoo hoo — — —
Runs off.

AFTERWHISTLE
          Ho ho ho!
Runs off.

RHAPSODE.
Evil that laughter — from below!

He falls
Onto a bench outside the church.

ACT II

(Act I of *Bolesław the Bold*)

THE ACTION TAKES PLACE AT BOLESŁAW'S CASTLE
ON WAWEL HILL, IN THE YEAR 1097

SCENE 1.

A horn sounds.

KING.
A horn. Hear that? A horn is blowing…

KRASAWICA.
The cattle's a-pasture. Lowing.
Or maybe it's a castle ghost
Greeting the sun-god as he soars.

KING.
They're blowing! At the gates, almost —

KRASAWICA.
>   A shepherd. Or some lad of yours
>   At the stables. What other reason?

KING.
>   If a response sounds, then it's treason.

KRASAWICA.
>   Skałka you mean?

KING.
>   Shh! Listen…

A horn sounds again.

KRASAWICA.
>   There —
>   The response.
>
>   *Pause.*
>   Sire, how you stare!
>   Your soul's completely in your ear —
>   You're angry… Pale — and lost in thought.
>   Can it be vengeance that you plot?

KING.
>   You heard that trumpet as it skirled!
>   From Skałka, yes! I know the world —
>   And know my kin. They chose this morn,
>   When all my men are out hunting.
>   I recognised my brother's horn —
>   He and the bishop hunt… the king.

KRASAWICA.
>   Can that be hoofbeats that I hear?
>   Along the castle-road. So near!
>   Yet on the bridge, the thudding's soft…

KING.
> They wrapped the horses' hooves in cloth.

Hoofbeats.

KRASAWICA.
> The sun soon breaks the water's pane.
> Skałka already bathes in flame.

KING.
> The bishop thus dispatches war?
> Soon he will choke on his own gore!

KRASAWICA.
> A war — with Skałka! Tread with care —
> Charmed is that place with ancient spells.
> The sacred grove chants nearby, where
> Stands the temple, the holy well...
> Both simple folk and runic sage
> Honour Skałka with song, holy from age on age —
> This wreath of holy leaves I wear
> First grew upon the branches there,
> The sacred grove, where is jasmine...
> And my home, toppled in ruin.

KING.
> That's where you're from...

KRASAWICA.
>   You didn't know?
> I only spend the night with you...

KING.
> You disappear each day at dawn,
> As does my memory, when you're gone...
> The rubies, gems, the golden shine
> Of crown and sceptre blind these eyes of mine...

KRASAWICA.
>   Your words are jarring, out of tune —

KING.
>   Farewell — it's time that you were gone.
>   Go. Wait not for the light of dawn.

KRASAWICA.
>   The new day sends you misfortune.

KING.
>   You're a rusalka?!

KASAWICA.
>   A Wiślanka, sire.
>   I chose you as my heart's desire.
>   I foresee, for you, undying fame!

KING.
>   So quick the night. I blink, it's gone.
>   Now you must go, as breaks the dawn.
>   Love even spilt blood justifies.
>   You've bound me with love's vow,
>   But now the sun breaks through the skies.
>   You'll be seen here. Go, now.

KRASAWICA.
>   I spent the night in love's embrace;
>   I go — my youth and strength restored.
>   I blossom here... But, open the gates
>   And I'll slip out. Come now, the door.

KING.
>   So quickly comes the parting hour.
>   The eastern sky's now bright with dawn,
>   And still love holds me in its power.

KRASAWICA.
>   I go. One last embrace... And still
>   The blood comes raging through my veins.
>   Again passion oversways my will.
>   I want you — So I still remain.
>   Once more — I can't control my heart...

KING.
>   Come then, once more before we part —
>   My lovely one, my love, my life!
>   For you I spurn my wedded wife;
>   For you I shun her, and my son.

KRASAWICA.
>   You tell me I'm your only one;
>   I'm beautiful — so you declare.
>   And yet, your brow is furrowed, glum.
>   Am I to blame for this... despair?

KING.
>   There is no blame in you — alone! —
>   If now my soul writhes in despair
>   As if tainted with pestilent air,
>   My jealous brother is the reason;
>   My brother, who conspires at treason;
>   My brother, who'd knock me from the throne!

KRASAWICA.
>   Unbounded is your mighty sway;
>   You — human fury scarce can touch.
>   Nightmares and bugbears melt away,
>   But human life — it weighs... so much...

KING.
>   They'll never guess where lies my will.
>   It rages, like a stream in flood!
>   It's nothing — to spill a man's blood.
>   Death herself sits on my council.

> But now, fate weighs down hard on me.
> My heart burns with presentiment;
> My brother — my one impediment;
> My brother — is my enemy!

KRASAWICA.
> A strange necessity now nods
> In your direction. You must kill
> Your brother, though he come with God
> And open arms. For now your life
> Totters on the edge of a knife:
> For you shall die, and die adored,
> Just like a sacrificial bull,
> Butchered by a sacrificial sword.

KING.
> Quiet now, girl. The dawn is nigh.
> You speak now like a simple fool.
> I swore to let my brother live,
> And all his wrongs I shall forgive.
> But love me now. Come, let us press
> Together, tightly — breast to breast.
> Your hair... is like a fleece of blooms!
> Its spring-night scent fills all the room;
> It shines... a golden germination...

KRASAWICA.
> You lord it over the whole nation!
> You are the first among all men.
> The gathered throngs acclaim you lord —
> The whole earth's shadowed by your sword!
> You can accomplish wonders! Yet...
> Come, love me, press me to your chest —

KING.
> First, bind your hair into a tress.
> Your braids are undone, hang like threads,
> Like widely-spreading spiders' webs

That shine like rainbows in the light,
Tousled by loving this long night.

KRASAWICA.
Shh!

KING.
Someone is walking through the yard…

KRASAWICA.
The dawn creeps through the window sash
And stains you with its crimson splash.
Your servants tread toward the barn…

KING.
It's not them — hear the mastiffs growl
Down in the kennels, where they're kept
So they will not impede your steps
Here to my chamber in the night.

KRASAWICA.
No — they're just hungry. They want their bowl.
Kiss me again! — Nobody's there —
I hear nothing. What's there to fear?
Surely you don't mistrust your might —
You're ringed about with loyal swords
To greet the thug that slinks at night,
To crumple at the feet of his lord!

KING.
Is it to Death your tempting leads?
You'd like to see somebody bleed?
That's why you hold me here entranced?
Let go. I'll just go have a glance
About the gates. Cease your caress,
Rusalka! You siren, temptress!

KRASAWICA.
>Your words were not so pitiless
>When your men mocked me "sorceress."

KING.
>Unloose the coral strands with which I'm bound.

KRASAWICA.
>They drag behind you, on the ground,
>Wherever you go.

KING.
>>Again ringed round
>By your white arms, held by your lips,
>I am your captive, and time slips
>From dawn to forenoon. Hear the men?
>You won't slip past unseen again.
>I hear their voices, just outside.

KRASAWICA.
>You hear the mill wheels as they grind.
>We were watched over by the night;
>The dawn betrays us with her light.
>*Suddenly:*
>I hear them coming! I was wrong —
>They come now, armed, a massive throng!
>And your men? Say, when will they come?

KING.
>My love, my sweet, my only one!
>And I — the only man afield…

KRASAWICA.
>At you they point the swords they wield!
>Call out your men, before they harm you.
>And I myself shall arm you.

KING.
>Say rather, "with love's wiles I'll charm you…"

KRASAWICA.
>You must kill your brother.

KING.
>My brother I shall never kill.
>I'd rather bend to God's harsh will.

KRASAWICA.
>And spread wide your gates to foreign lords?!

KING.
>Love here lies chambered with a sword,
>And envy's blade hacks at the door…
>Yet I'll arise, by God above:
>My soul shall envy crush, and love!

KRASAWICA
>*Runs in and out of the inner chamber,*
>*Bringing forth his accoutrements.*

SCENE 2.

KING
>*Dressing.*
>Whoever calls so early a meeting?

KING'S BROTHER.
>Your brother, who brings a brotherly greeting.

KING
>*Taking up his cuirass.*
>Heavy the doors, brother; stubborn the baulk.

KING'S BROTHER.
>Open them, brother. I'm eager to talk.

KING.
> First let me don some accoutrements meet.

KING'S BROTHER.
> I'd greet you just as gladly in a winding sheet.

KING
> *Fixing his swordbelt.*
> Let me just fasten my sword to my side.

KING'S BROTHER.
> How you try me! I'll have the doors hacked open wide!

KING.
> You do me such honour, to bear a sword;
> Brother, you'd flush me with deceitful word?
> And say you're not yourself outfitted so?

KING'S BROTHER.
> I'll smash the baulky doors with one axe blow!

KING.
> How many armed men wait with you below?
> You come with axes raised against your brother?
> While he's alone, with no one save his lover?
> While all his men are hunting far afield?
> Alone, unto my flesh and blood I yield —
> The heavy doors I now unbar myself!

SCENE 3.

Enter: the King's Brother, Sieciech, several knights.

KING.
> I greet you, brother, and you, first in the land,
> With sheathed sword. The knife... is in my brother's hand.
> *Pause.*

So, are we off to the hunt, today?
Over the hills and far away?
Is it elk hooves your greyhounds worry,
Or are you chasing a bolder quarry?

SIECIECH.
You are an eagle, a falcon, sire!
As when you smote the Kiev gates,
Sparks leap from you like living fire.

KING.
But you will have me in your nets?

SIECIECH.
You think we'd run you to ground?

KING.
Only to lift from thence this crown!
You were the guardian of my son,
And now — you nurse another one.
But know: treason's been tried before.
At dawn, you face your king with war!

SIECIECH.
Your chopping block respects no hours.
This father never spares the rod!

KING.
Gripe not at my judicial power —
Who leap into the hands of an angry god!

SIECIECH.
To whom I kneel not, nor am I alone!

KING.
You were not last to kneel before this throne
— When conquered cities kissed my royal sword —
To lick some crumbs then fallen from my board!

SIECIECH.
> Those crumbs were earned by this right hand,
> And can be measured by its span!

KING.
> Great was your progress, great your goods
> From me, in youth —

SIECIECH.
> Won by my blood!
> Blood I regret not; blood that's dried
> There on your shield of wood and hide —
> Blood that weighs heavy on your scale.

KING.
> Be not so bold!

SIECIECH.
> As bold as you,
> Whose boldness faithful knights now rue.

KING.
> Regrets rush in where courage fails.
> They lose their heads, who turn their tails.

SIECIECH.
> So long at war, so far from home…

KING.
> They ran, and left their king alone!
> Deserters find no mercy here!
> While I fought on, they fled, cut loose!
> Who flings his sword shall find a noose!

SIECIECH.
> It was not fear, but faithless wives
> Drew them back home. And now the lives

Of your best knights you'll sacrifice.
Clear now, the sense of your device!

KING.
My nickname?

SIECIECH.
Are you The Bold? The Generous?
Both! The king makes lavish with the truss:
How boldly all his knights are strung!

KING.
How brazenly your wield your tongue!

SIECIECH.
I didn't come to jabber.

KING.
I'm ready for your actions, then.
I'll face alone your brace of men.
You thought to find me here unarmed?
And so you came here in a swarm,
Led by my brother? Yet I greet
You with my sword slipped from its sheathe.
I am your king, and your captive —
So come now,
Brother, take what I have to give.

SCENE 4.

Enter King's Wife, with train of handmaids.

KING'S WIFE.
Well, this is something new, indeed:
Hemmed in by armed men all around,
Before sunrise? Just what I need —
I wished myself to hunt you down!

Won't let him speak.

> She's safe behind a padlocked door,
> Your charming little whore —
> You've shamed your son, you've shamed your wife...
> He's ten years old! Go — take his life,
> Drown him in the Vistula now.
> Three years ago you gave your vow,
> There in the castle church, you swore,
> When first you wore the royal crown,
> To love me, and to have no more
> Than me, your spouse, wedded for life;
> Those promises at your coronation —
> What? Merely bold prevarications!

KING.
> Me, lie? Silence! I've never broken troth!

KING'S WIFE.
> This lie once more proves false your oath.
> I've come not to be sent away
> Or stifled with your bluster.

KING.
> Well then, if you must
> Know what's afoot, by all means, stay.
> My brother's come to pay
> A visit — that I make so bold —
> With muscle — before the dawn's quite old.
> It seems the stake here is my life,
> And you, my queen, my wedded wife,
> Come not to stand in my defence,
> But nag me! On the mere pretence
> Of catching scent of some young bitch
> Padding about the hallways — which
> News — Look at their mouths agape!
> Divert me — pardon, gentlemen —

From matters of import to the state,
To air our dirty linen!

KING'S WIFE.
    I've caught your whore!

KING.
    Keep your nose out of that. No more!

KING'S WIFE.
    One of your servant girls, I'm told
    Has spread the news, you make so bold
    As to pull her into your bed,
    Tired of my charms — it seems you've said —
    What good are your marriage vows?

KING.
    I made a vow, I made a vow!
    And if I broke it? What's the crime?
    A king can't keep a concubine?

KING'S BROTHER.
    The king is bold! Each oath, a breach.

KING.
    I toss that back into your teeth!
    You'd teach the birds to rhapsodise,
    Such honeyed words you gaily sing,
    While underneath lurks a sharp sting!
    Behold the man who never lies:
    My brother! He of spotless word!

KING'S BROTHER.
    It seems I've touched you to the quick.

KING'S WIFE.
    Forgive me, my husband and my lord
    For rushing here. My heart was sick.

KING.
>   You see I stand here with drawn sword!

KING'S WIFE.
>   Was it not of your ordering
>   That there should be such rejoicing
>   Among the captives in the tower?
>   The prisoners released unharmed?
>   And all the peasants stoutly armed —
>   By your authority and power?

KING.
>   What? No! By whose leave? I expect
>   The bishop, hasting to impress
>   The churls with clemency and largess
>   Before my axe-blade meets his neck...
>   Thank you, my sweetling, my one treasure
>   For regaling my guests with such pleasure
>   At your verbose, timely arriving.
>   Now hear what Brother's been conniving!
>   Our good old Sieciech he seduces
>   — That wise old fox, with wise old ruses —
>   And offers me a poisoned cup.
>   I do not fear the Church's curse,
>   My heart is sick with something worse,
>   As if I'd lapped the venom up!
>   *To his wife.*
>   It's jealousy poisons your heart,
>   Because I've dandled with that tart.
>   You say my oaths I thus foreswear.
>   You are my love. My only care
>   Is to find favour in your eye —
>   To bring you glory, or to die.
>   I, by the Church's law, am bound
>   — Like two palms wrapped my throat around! —
>   And this sacred necessity
>   Impels me now to settle sums

With our bishop. It's him or me
Must die. I swear!

KING'S BROTHER.
                And here he comes!

SCENE 5.

Enter the Bishop, in armour, dressed like an Archangel. Behind him, a group of armed peasants.

KING.
Hear this, Bishop. As long as I wear the crown,
Nor you, nor anyone else shall lead
My subjects. As for knocking idols down,
That is my task. Your help I do not need.

BISHOP.
The truth is mine! — It's you that spoils to fight.

KING.
What I decree, I execute with might.

BISHOP.
You've soiled the sword of law, filthy with blood!

KING.
That blade shall clear my ground of rotten wood.

BISHOP.
You are the faggot soon to fuel the pyre.

KING.
Mine is the banquet, and as for the fire,
Dry weeds and sticks will at my pleasure feed
The flames that gorge themselves on hefty logs,

> While round the hearth shall crouch my loyal dogs
> To lick the sap that from the timber bleeds.

BISHOP.
> And so, this matter, King, must end in blood.

KING.
> In blood it ends! And it shall end for good!

CHORUS.
> 1.
> He rages now cruel
> In pitiless ire.
> No mercy can cool
> His eyes, burning like fire.
>
> 2.
> His red face is ablaze;
> Like a vulture's, his eyes.
> Now his sword is upraised,
> Comes the bloody assize!

BISHOP.
> It's slaves for sacrifice you'd have, not men!

KING.
> The scrapied sheep must be cut from the pen!

BISHOP.
> This blessed flock is hale, free from disease —
> Who at another's fortune waxes sore,
> Revels in blood, the wretch, and cruelties.

KING.
> Speak to the winds! I'll hear you prate no more.

BISHOP.
> You vulture!

KING.
>   I'm your King!

BISHOP.
>   I see the drake
> Now coiling fast about you, like a snake.

KING.
> How boldly you spit your treason! But know —
> Such words as these will not unpunished go.

BISHOP.
> As shepherd of this flock, mighty I stand.

KING.
> My power's from Heaven! And you're at my command!

BISHOP.
> No more for that fear I a martyr's fate.

KING.
> Farewell.

BISHOP.
>   My might returning, from your pate
> Will strike that diadem, into the dirt.

KING.
> Is that a threat I hear in your brash words?

BISHOP.
> A threat, and a will — not my will, but the Lord's.

CHORUS.
> 1.
> The venom bubbles at his lips;
> Like smoky torches burn his eyes.

2.
What sort of hidden crime now slips
To action, as he prophesies?

KING.
Amen! God is the judge! His will be done.

BISHOP.
The people form a palisade that runs
Around me.

KING.
      Armed — scythes the weapons they wield.

BISHOP.
They're set to go to harvest in the field.

KING.
Yet first they come here — not with empty hands!

BISHOP.
To set before their King their just demands.

KING.
It's me shall cut you down!

BISHOP.
            As the Lord wills!

KING.
The sun sets early for you. Look your fill;
You'll soon see nothing.

BISHOP.
            Though you hold the sword,
You're raving mad!

KING.
> Groom!

BISHOP.
> Men!
The Bishop now stands at the head of a wall of peasants.
> With us, the Lord!

The Groom enters and stands by the King.

KING.
Behold your death!

BISHOP.
And you, behold your fall!

KING.
I'll drag your corpses through the mud, one and all!

BISHOP.
O, conquering King!

KING.
O, shattered thing!

BISHOP.
Be like your father: our enemies strike!

KING.
You bring your own doom, coming here armed with pikes!

BISHOP.
Vulture!
Be like your ancestors. Spurn carrion!

KING.
Treason!

BISHOP.
    Come kiss the Cross, and be cleansed of all your sin!

KING.
    And you, by that same Cross, kneel at my feet,
    And in the sight of all, call back your threat!

BISHOP
    Kneels.
    And so I kneel before the judgement seat,
    But if you pardon not these humble men,
    May God restrain His hand —

KING.
                        It's you seduced
    These rebels!

BISHOP.
                Whom I gather in His Name,
    If that the King choose not to do the same —

KING.
    You gather them?

BISHOP.
                With might!

KING.
    Deceiving them?

BISHOP.
            By right!
    We come from God.

KING.
                Liar.

BISHOP.
                        We come in peace.

KING.
  Be gone!

BISHOP.
      But first, I beg that you release
  Those prisoners, whom you keep close confined
  In little less than hell, so that this crime
  Not call down punishment upon your head,
  Nor on your son, nor brother. Set by the dread
  Through which you rule your people, from the day
  When I that crown upon your brow did lay,
  There at the altar steps. My flock you slay,
  To you entrusted; their flesh is your food;
  From your chalice you swill your people's blood;
  You punish with the sword and cleave apart
  Your people from you, when you cleave their heart;
  Hearts filled with gall, and then upon their bones
  You raise the dais of your selfish throne.
  Anointed once — God shall mark you again —
  This time your brow shall bear the mark of Cain!

All kneel.

CHORUS.
  They kneel before him, bow their heads,
  And at their feet they lay their scythes.
  Are these petitions, then, or threats?
  To whom, the judgement of the skies?

KING.
  I am your King. And you should seek my grace
  At my footstool. My people, there's your place.
  You, peasant lads, suckled on peasant song,
  Is it for you to fight, in armed throng,
  Against your King? Your very soul rebels

At the idea! And you know it well —
Without the King, you're what? Brutes of the field.
But with your King — what power do you wield!
And for that God has set me on the throne,
So that the King's will, and the Lord's, be done.
Humbly I now reveal these mysteries.
But know this: grovelling wins no clemency!
Whom I condemn to Death, Night shuts his eyes,
With no appeal — however sharp his scythe!
The King decrees, the Lord God shares his crimes!

SCENE 6.

KRASAWICA
in the open chamber doors.
Choose blood, choose blood!
See them lie there supine.
You rule over them, a king, a lion!
And they — slaves, men of mud.

CHOIR.
A rusalka! A sprite!

KING'S WIFE.
Your king's dearest delight.

BISHOP.
A witch, in the king's inner room!

KRASAWICA.
Silence, you man of venom!
You, who orphaned me by slaughter,
Impaling on a spear my father,
Ravaging the sacred trees
With fire, casting the idols down,
From out their hives chasing the bees,

Smashing the temple — Sacred that ground
From age on age; stronger its might
Than any man's — and for that reason
You'll pay sharp for your blaspheming,
Your riding against your king and scheming
With your pet — the king's brother — treason!

BISHOP.
Bind up her hands, and stop her tongue!
Why do you stand there, as if stung?
Spellcast are you, frighted by spooks?
Wake up! Someone go get a noose!

KRASAWICA.
Well then? You're waiting on the king?
That's wise! As long as I have might,
As long as I'm the king's delight,
I have no need of spellcasting!
Yet should the king renounce me, priest,
Then shall my fury be released,
And, by my word — you both — deceased!
To the King:
Choose blood, choose blood,
Choose blood, you bloody king!
Don't waver, don't kick against the goad!
Take up the sword of reckoning
And cut, and cut, your path through them.
Here they all stand, the treacherous men,
The rebels scheming at your life;
They've come here hand in hand, agreed
To put you to the knife!
King, as you've taken love of me
In the dark night — night after night! —
Make use now of my mystery.
Like thunderbolts, my secret might;
Just say the word, unloose my tongue,
And by my spells I'll strike them dumb!

SIECIECH.
>   Your wife, king! Look — how pale the queen!

KING
>   *Rising and moving towards Krasawica.*
>   You pagan asp — you thing unclean —
>   *Looks to his wife.*
>   *She pales — spell-struck —*
>   *Pointing at Krasawica.*
>   Bind her in chains!
>   *To Krasawica:*
>   Begone! And never come again!

KRASAWICA
>   *Frees herself from the Knights.*
>   Spawn of Rycheza — bind me yourself!
>   I gave you power, I gave you love;
>   With lightning's might I burn, the wealth
>   Of the once-charmed, now plundered grove.
>   I'm called by everlasting Fame —
>   A thunderous voice, not like the lame
>   Mewling that fills his treacherous church!
>   Bind me. Let's see what your strength's worth.
>   I'll burst your chains as if they're straw!
>   Upon my brow there shines a star —
>   Ruler of floods, sprite, water-maid,
>   I stand among you, unafraid!

GIRL 1.
>   The queen is dying!

GIRL 2.
>   Quick, some water!

GIRL 3.
>   She cast a spell, that eerie jade —
>   A black charm from the pagan altar!

GIRL 1.
    Cover the wicked serpent's eyes!

KRASAWICA.
    I see your blood-choked throes, as each one dies —
    Nothing can hold back now the murderous hand;
    In jealousy you burn; both, to Death damned —
    But you can't see her, though she's near at hand!
    Instead of me, wrap chains round one another —
    The curse now thickens, by which you shall smother;
    Rather than chase me, fall down on the ground
    Before the living flames that ring me round.
    Your death I prophesy — and he first dies
    Who first shall dare to look me in the eyes!

All look away, save the Bishop, who stares at her unflinching.

ACT III

(Act II of *Skałka*)

The sun is high and very strong
Still, at the zenith,
Shining on Skałka
In a golden shimmer.

RHAPSODE
    Stands
    Beneath the church
    Gazing rapt at buzzing swarms of flies
    Above the waters of the pool.

RUSALKAS
    Emerge from the water
    And stand
    On the steps leading to the church vestibule.

RUSALKA 1.
    Heartsore here, without the lyre,
    Without her strings a-hum.
    No song to smooth this sad desire.
    The font of lore's gone dumb.

RUSALKA 2.
    Gone is your youth, gone is your love,
    Time, father, now to bid farewell
    To bee-swarm and to blooming grove —
    The world's grown old as well.

RUSALKA 3.
    Such was it not, in days long gone,
    When the sacred altar's fire roused
    The sun from bed in the early dawn.
    The sacred flame's been doused.

RUSALKA 4.
    Świetlec today is… just the sun.
    Above the pool scum buzz the flies.
    Your spirit sorrows, guardian —
    Your old heart breaks, and cries.

RUSALKA 1.
    Come, temple fire, once more to burn
    Inside our hearts; come, god of day,
    Świetlec, god golden, O, return!
    Forever past, once sacred May.

RUSALKA 2.
    No more the idols, as of old,
    Shoulder to shoulder, proud and firm.
    They lie deep in the waters cold;
    Their eyes bored through by reckless worms.

RUSALKA 3.
>O Lyre, who once ranged wide and free,
>Today immobile, petrified —
>Once more look on our mysteries,
>This one last afternoon, abide.

RUSALKA 4.
>Expand your heart, fill full your eyes
>One last time, on this final day,
>While Świetlec yet creaks through the skies,
>Before he too passes away.

RUSALKAS
>*Disappear into the pool.*

BOAT
>*Fancily carved and decorated, appears;*
>*A woman stands therein.*

PANDORA.
>From all the stars and worlds that run
>Through the unmeasured vaults of space,
>That swing through the flames of the sun,
>Fed by his strong afternoon rays,
>I snare the brilliance in my tresses
>To fill my treasure chest.
>If you desire, I'll give you wealth:
>Gems and gold,
>All you can hold,
>But you must reach for them yourself.
>*Displays her box.*
>Here they are — all enclosed
>For you to find — or not to find —
>Lily and rose
>Coral and pearl
>All twirled
>Into priceless wreaths, entwined.
>I can roll back your dread

To joy — your fate, from black to red.
As the scent from its chalice expands,
Gaze deep into the lily's eye
There you'll see truth, and lie —
But you must yourself stretch forth your hand.

RHAPSODE.
I know the path of falsehood and sin.
In my young age I gathered flowers,
And wormwood, too, from love's garden.
No wreath of yours has any power
To resurrect my youthful hours,
Nor can the treasures of your chest
Which Cupid flings wide as largess
Return to me my long past years,
Love's dead rejoicings, and dried tears.

PANDORA.
Your youth returns at your command —
You need but to stretch forth your hand.
You know what's true, and what's a lie?
Choose then among the treasures I
Have here to offer from my box.

RHAPSODE.
First lift the lid, undo the locks.
Let's see what you've on offer there,
What liquor brims your chalice rare.
Perhaps its savour I well know.
Or can it a new life bestow?

PANDORA.
Until you roll it on your tongue
Its wonders you shall never guess,
And your complaints — foundationless.
Give it a taste — I'll make you young
Once more, but you, once more must run
The path you've trod before, and hymn

The same old songs, over again,
As you enjoy your youth restored.
But if instead you will refrain
From my help, you've but yourself to blame.
If you reject my magic trove,
Enter no more this charmed grove.

RHAPSODE.
Not me, not me — return me those
Who shared with me the paths I trod.
Only on their account still glows
The ember faint of song, once hot;
One glimpse of them, and I'd be glad —
No matter, were they good, or bad.

PANDORA.
The only shades I can entice
Are such as crowd about the gates
Of the dead regions; those whose eyes
Would gladly feast upon the place
They've left forever, and the days
They've lived through, once again,
And thus — they think — to sooth their pain.
For you alone frame your request —
I'll give you all that I possess.
For he who stands in yearning sore
And spies my craft upon the waves
Shall take from out my secret store
All that his willing heart may crave.
But so it is with mortal life:
Fight on through pain and tears and strife;
The coral, lily, and the rose
Are to be won by endless striving.
Soon you must follow and join those
You long for. Where desire is driving
You, there must you go to burn
In the very flames toward which you yearn.
The soul may balk at meted pain,

But you must hoist the burden up
Upon your shoulders, which you've here
In this life bundled, and drink up
The chalice pearled with our own tears.
All that you love, all you detest
Are stored up for you, in that chest.

BOAT
Moves off and disappears.
From the depths
From the direction of the castle,
Through the grove
Comes running

KRASAWICA.
She runs up to the gate
On the opposite side of the pool
From the side of the grove.
She stands there
Listening to the silence
Then calls toward the gates.

Keeper! Hey! Let me inside!
Fall apart, you barricades!
Back now, barriers! Open wide!
You gods! Arise now from your graves!

The gates open
And the heavy wooden log fastened to them
Sinks into the waters of the pool
Causing a ripple
After which peaceful disturbance
Two wooden idols arise from the water
And in circular fashion approach one another.
These are the

LELE.
They fall into each other's arms, embracing.

KRASAWICA
> *Sits down on the steps*
> *Near the gates by the pool*
> *Gazing into the water.*

KEEPER
> *Arises from the water to her waist*
> *And listens.*

KRASAWICA.
> As he from the castle races,
> May these waters split apart,
> So unhindered may speed the braces
> At the hooves of the doomed hart.

KEEPER.
> Ha, ha! There will be such a din
> When that one acts out his sin!

KRASAWICA.
> A maiden shall come to the knight
> From the secret water's depths.
> Her lips shall give him such delight
> The world will stop its breath...

KEEPER.
> Ha, ha, ha! Now the fun begins,
> When that one acts out his sin!

KRASAWICA.
> ...Till rumour, born on a soft breeze,
> Shall knock the king upon his knees.

KEEPER.
> He'll wish to give the tale the lie,
> And at his own hand, see him die!
> *Disappears beneath the water.*

WHISTLE
> *From the grove, beneath an oak.*
> Listen, hey —

AFTERWHISTLE
> *From the grove, beneath an oak.*
> > Listen, hey —

WHISTLE.
> Take the pitchy torch.

AFTERWHISTLE.
> I'll bring the spark. Get to the church.

WHISTLE.
> Climb up on the very altar, high —

AFTERWHISTLE.
> Which one of us can reach it? Not I.

WHISTLE.
> Sh! Someone's there...

AFTERWHISTLE.
> > Someone snuck in.

WHISTLE.
> The old boy.

AFTERWHISTLE.
> In search of his instrument.
> In vain he punched at the dull stone
> Into which his lyre has grown.
> He hangs his head, he wipes his nose...
> Ho, ho, ho!

WHISTLE.
>   Hee, hee, hee!
>   Now he'll be cursing you and me.

KRASAWICA.
>   Fire it!

WHISTLE.
>   Light the torch.
>   *Grabs a flint.*

AFTERWHISTLE.
>   *Grabs a stone.*
>   *They work to raise a spark.*

WHISTLE.
>   Flint on stone
>   Stone on flint,
>   The spark is born,
>   The fire is lit!

AFTERWHISTLE.
>   The spark is sired,
>   Leaps on the wood,
>   And in a trice, its blood
>   Becomes fire.
>   A raging flame,
>   A gift of God,
>   Power unrestrained.

WHISTLE.
>   Go now, run!

AFTERWHISTLE
>   *Pointing at the treetops.*
>   Now brother, come!
>   Up to our aeries, and fast!
>   Puff and curse, blow and blast,

>   Until the cursed
>   Temple roof bursts
>   Aflame, and all
>   The walls
>   Ringed, are afire, at last!

WHISTLE
>   *Climbs an oak.*

AFTERWHISTLE
>   *Climbs an oak.*

KRASAWICA
>   *Runs with the torch*
>   *To the church vestibule*
>   *Over the steps through the gates at left.*

WHISTLE
>   *Swings in the oak.*

AFTERWHISTLE
>   *Swings in the oak.*

>   *A mighty wind.*

KRASAWICA
>   *Stands before the baptismal font,*
>   *Lifts the torch high above it,*
>   *Sets fire to the ceremonial cake.*

>   *A powerful storm.*
>   *Lightning bolts.*

FIRE
>   *Burns in the font.*

CAKE
>   *Burns.*

TEMPLE
> *The roof of which overhangs the pool*
> *Totters,*
> *The gateposts fall*
> *And on the fallen posts*
> *The temple roof falls to form a bridge*
> *Stretching over the pond to the church vestibule.*
>
> *From the Vistula*
> *Through the grove*
> *At the head of a crowd*
> *Of singing peasants and prisoners*
> *Comes:*

BISHOP.
> *He steps onto the bridge over the pool*
> *Stops at the midpoint of the newly-fallen bridge,*
> *And notices the flames in the font.*

All spirits are in Thy service, Lord,
All elements Thee obey.
Thou didst cleanse them from the power abhorred
When Thou didst put on clay.

Fire and earth, and air and water,
Are Thine alone, by right.
Kill, and revive, almighty Father,
Through Thy unmeasured might.

Ineffable Ghost, to me incline,
And strengthen my soul's will.
Faithful to Thee shall I remain,
Even though my blood be spilt.

Then, Pathmaker, even though this road
Of Thy Law lead through pain,
Thou gavest the breast pierced, and the blood:
Receive them, with thanks, again.

A people freed Thee I restore,
No more the prize of Hell.
Above the flood Thou'st thrown these boards;
Almighty Thy Gospel!

There in the den of kingly pride
If Thou but willst it, Thy Word
Will give the hangmen's crown the lie.
We implore Thine aid, O Lord.

Assist us with Thy storm's great power.
See — fire now pairs with water!
Through murderous hearts speed now Thy plough,
God of this world, great Father!

He crosses to the church
Over the bridge of the fallen temple.
Catching sight of the Rhapsode
Suddenly
He is transformed;
He makes to run to him.
With arms outstretched crosswise,
He forbids those behind him
Entrance.

RHAPSODE
   Draws close
   And kneels.

PEASANTS
   Fill the vestibule, a portion of them having entered
   Through side gates.

BISHOP.
   You — in God's church! What is it you wish?

RHAPSODE.
   All that I had, you have stolen from me!

BISHOP.
    Why do you bow before me like this?

RHAPSODE.
    You took my lyre. She's in captivity!

BISHOP.
    I took your lyre — your device and your might —
    Here at the gates. But it can be restored,
    If God reforms you into His knight,
    And of his gifts, you henceforth serve the Lord.

RHAPSODE.
    You slew me, when by force my lyre you seized.
    In her are kept all of my mysteries.
    Without her, my life isn't worth a pin —
    All that was green in me's withered; herb and bloom,
    No longer nourished by my blood run thin.
    If you now bear a mighty Angel's arms,
    Allow me, in the rags of a vile groom
    To crouch before you, begging of your alms.

BISHOP.
    It's song you want? For that you're shedding tears?

RHAPSODE.
    I want to go where you were! There to stand,
    And look Death in the eye, proud, without fear,
    Without a sword, but with my lyre in hand;
    To sing my runes, to cast my wondrous spells,
    And hear my song, as through the wind she swells!

BISHOP.
    So take it.
    He goes up
    To the church pillar
    Takes the lyre from the wall
    And holds it out.

Take it!

RHAPSODE
Receives the lyre,
Kisses it;
His face is transformed.
He shivers,
He cries out.
Back from the dead!
Silently, he bows over the lyre
In rapture.

ALL
Tensely waiting
Bend over him
And observe him closely.

WHISTLE
From the grove, from the high branches of an oak.
Fly little swallow, fly
Through the thick-spread orchard nets,
Over coops and cotes pass by,
Over the ox-ploughed frets.

AFTERWHISTLE
From the grove, from the high branches of an oak.
Ring out lark, and play.
Soar up into the dawn,
High over plough-land and lea,
Hide yourself in the bright sun.

PEASANTS.
She wakes! She wakes! She wakes!

RHAPSODE.
Quiet! — — — She sobs...
Long captive, her song throbs
Again in her breast, and glows —

A different song than was before,
A different musing.

WHISTLE
From the grove, from the high branches of an oak.
Hither now, eagle, swing.
Blot half-heaven with your wing,
Swooping and circling
From Ledno even past Tyn.

RHAPSODE.
Time was, the springtime grove would sway
With song. Now axed, it rots upon the sod.
A man will be hacked down this foison May,
To arise eternal, a demi-god!

A killer wears the crown. The land
Lies prone beneath the cursing hand;
The nation, flailing in a gory flood,
Flows with the current of the holy blood.
A nation conceived in blood and torment!
He rises.

You who returned my lyre! Your God
Has tinkered with its runic power!
Farewell. I leave, before you're bathed in blood.
She woke — but barely for a quarter hour.

A moment's space yet; where spirits brawl
I shall do battle, as a spirit.
Recall my lyre's song, as I fall,
And with my own gore smear it.
Sings prophetically:
Before my eyes pass hordes of folk
Stretching wide like that circle of oaks.
They fall and moulder, before long
New shoots arise from the black earth:
New generations' birth;

Arising like this my song,
They pass on, followed by my song.

Their fates already set in books;
They flow on past — a cloudy stream
And my thought passes them abeam;
I fish them out, with runic claw
All that along the stream-bed crawl,
Judging and sentencing them all.

An ancient tale — the ever more
Returning wheel, eternal round;
They rise above the steep-cut shore,
Their foreheads wreathed, and proud.

The nation's song, a many-voiced choir,
A thoughtful, emotive flood
Of pain, of mourning, and of ire
Runs living through my blood.

Looks toward Bishop.
Sower of souls, accept my thanks,
Imperial will, whose nod is deed;
Shaman, I stand in the same ranks
As you — whom yet I must precede.

After me, Spirit, you shall fly,
O man in the might of God;
You I bequeath these flaming eyes
Before I wash this path with blood.

BISHOP
Makes the Sign of the Cross over him.

RHAPSODE
Departs
*Over the bridge spanning the pool
Along the path through the grove*

> *Over the bridge spanning the Vistula*
> *Toward the castle.*

ALL
> *Follow him with their eyes.*

KRASAWICA
> *Crawls up*
> *From the posts, at which she fell to the ground*
> *Until she lies at the Bishop's feet*
> *Her head bowed.*

BISHOP
> *Turns*
> *And catches sight of the supplicant.*
> Whoever you be, lift up your face
> And from these hands accept my grace.
> And you — whoever's without sin
> And wish to blame her, come, begin!
> The pure soul who lifts up his hand
> Should first be sure he won't be damned.
> But come, you spotless, heave your stone.
> The sinless only — him alone.

PEOPLE
> *Stand in silence.*

KRASAWICA.
> At your feet, trembling, I bow my head
> As once trembling, I sought his bed.
> It's true, I strove to cause you grief
> By the fire that through the heavens runs;
> Now have I fallen, a trembling leaf —
> For you are of our holy ones.
> In you there glows the lightning's might
> And thus I proffer homage, brash,
> For you illuminate our night,
> Your embers glowing in this ash.

Before the people, father, raise
Your immaculate hand;
Touch me, and free me from all stains
Of the ancient, sinful man,
So that my youth might, for all time
As it in my two eyes plays,
Sing out the spring-hope of my prime
Amidst the Vistula's waves;
So that above the river floods
My virgin song may resound,
As you offer your holy blood
Which to the Spirit redounds;
So ever about this riverside cliff
Should echo this your story;
For this I take of you this gift,
My Lord, for your eternal glory.

BISHOP.
The power that animates each soul
And all the earthly elements
Is given over into my rule
As the Lord's lieutenant.

KRASAWICA
*Rises
And goes off
Toward the Vistula.*

WHISTLE
From the grove, from the high branches of an oak.
Come to us, come
For tears, for laughter,
Unto the cold waves' bedding.

AFTERWHISTLE
From the grove, from the high branches of an oak.
Young, ever young,

Sweet dreams we'll waft her:
Delights, lustings and regrettings.

WHISTLE.
Return now, come on
Sister, to the deep.
The waves won't disown you, girl.

AFTERWHISTLE.
And every dawn
And every eve
We shall sing, we shall dance, we shall whirl.

BISHOP
In the church vestibule
Among the gathered crowd of people.
Now you are free — and free I've led you here —
Only to God you owe obedience.
There is none other over you.
On wings of eagles, fly unto our nest,
O Lord, arise!
I summon Thee to this assize:
Shine in the skies, eternal, clear
Light of all justice; make now present
To our eyes Thy righteous judgement,
That we might come to know immutable
Thy faith, of all our sins and errors shent;
That we might see how the fate of mortals
Is bound within the circuit of Thy will,
That fate, from which we would escape, in vain,
We bear upon our brows, indelible.
May the dark earth part, and uncover plain
Unto our eyes the sin too-long concealed;
From darkest dungeon freed, at last revealed
In all its deathly pallor and mouldy shroud;
Whatever sin or error lies
Within a man, before his eyes
Let it be out today; let it arise

And, where he goes, let it go too —
Always behind him, at his heels
Until with righteousness his debt it seals.
But those whose pure souls Thou blamest not, Lord,
Who shall burn forth a lamp unto this nation,
Reveal them to us, by Thy flaming sword:
A bardic troop unto all generations.

He looks around at the faces of all assembled before him.
Whose spirit bears a guilty trace,
May it now stand before his face,
Self-judged as undeserving grace.

Who'd hide his sin before man's eye
In deepest tomb or tower high
His own tongue will that sin belie.

Self-sentencing, you shall denounce
Yourself, no more to be renounced
The pain that seals the just accounts.

These flowers upon the altar set
Are tokens for the innocent.
If there be here a sinless man
Now, pluck one forth, with your own hand.

CHORUS.
Who'd hide his sin before man's eye
In deepest tomb or tower high
His own tongue will that sin belie.

These flowers are only for his hand
Who sinless before God may stand.
Him alone shalt God give the grace
To look Death boldly in the face.

BISHOP.
    Now set the ringed candles alight
    Until your sins are burned off quite.
    In witness to the cleansed soul
    Myself I set the wreath aglow.

He nods;
They hand him a white sacrificial stole
Which he puts on;
He plucks some lilies
And binds them into a wreath
Which he sets upon his own head.

    With lilies wreathed, I stand here, Lord,
        Before Thy people, as they kneel.
    Now, bring to pass Thy promised word
        And all my acts, dear God, reveal.

CHORUS
    Chants.

    Blessed lily, purest flower,
    Death-in-life from life outscour,
    Although this be death's princely hour.

    The world sinks in night,
    Is swallowed quite,
    But lilies wreathe a sinless knight.

    A leader stands before us now;
    No smudge of sin upon his brow;
    Around which blooms shine, pure and bright;
    The flames glow, the world sinks in night.

BISHOP
    Touches with his hand
    The scorched ceremonial cake upon the font.
    The ashes crumble

    And sink into the fire
    Still burning.

CHORUS
    Move off toward the castle.

BISHOP
    Moves off behind them.

    The earth before the altar opens;
    The sod sinks
    And from below there emerges

DEATH.
    She waves a handkerchief
    After the departing throng.

    The grove crashes down
    Oaks and lime-trees fall;
    Only bare trunks remain standing here and there,
    Grey, dry, dead.
    A broad vista is thus revealed
    Toward the Vistula.

ACT IV

(Act II of *Bolesław the Bold*)

SCENE 1.

KING.
    Bring forth my chest.
    The one that rests
    Beneath the royal bed.

Therein, my crown
Of gold torques wound,
Blue sapphires, rubies red.

Sceptre and apple too, it holds,
As well as shirts of cloth of gold,
Gold buttons, golden clasps.

Sandals, with pearls shining white,
My cloak with pearls embroidered bright,
Locked safe, with iron hasps.

The chamber-men dress the King in his ceremonial robes.

Ha, ha! Your tongue is hanging out!
It would be nice to be tricked out
In rags like these? The hour may come
When we'll change stations...
Patience, patience!
You know I've got an only son —
Sometimes, does it pass through your head,
"What if both King and Prince were dead?"
Slit, poisoned or smothered?

What says old bishop Stanisław?
What says the Czech king Vratislav?
What say you, my dear brother?

PEASANT.
    This crate is a damned heavy thing
    For two poor arms to lug around!
    Why put on all these baubles, king?
    The weight of gold will weigh you down.
    Who cares for jewels anyway?
    You're king. That's bright enough, I'd say.

KING.
>   And what do you say there, who sighs,
>   With labour, rolling round your eyes?
>   Stooped and shuffling, bent and sagged?
>   By gold-envy are you stung?
>   Speak! Or has the cat got your tongue?
>   Take all you'll carry. Fill your bag.

SERVANT 2
>   *Throws himself into the chamber with a bag.*

PEASANT.
>   Look at the fool, rejoicing, weeping!
>   He can't believe his blessed fortune!
>   All he can carry, his for keeping,
>   Measuring his golden portion!
>   Now the bag is bursting full
>   And still he packs it, still he drools,
>   His greedy eyes are shining bright.
>   Now comes the time to bind it tight
>   And lift it up — he strains and strains
>   But can't lift it, for all his pains.
>   He groans, he grunts, he skips around —
>   The golden dream has weighed him down.

SERVANT 2.
>   O the ill fortune, O the weight!
>   I've overreached, sad is my fate!
>   My back is broke; I'm done for, dead!
>   Sire! Tear the eyes out of my head!
>   I cannot look — the gold, bright, burning!
>   I can't look on — I'll die of yearning!

KING
>   *Helps him to lift the bag, only to drop it on him,*
>   *Crushing him beneath its weight.*

SERVANT 2
>   Dies.

KING.
>   Drag out this garbage. Sink them both
>   Deep in the water. You can't say
>   I wasn't generous. He pled
>   A salary, and took his pay.
>   He'll sleep now in the bed he made.
>   Drag it out; dump it in the moat.

SCENE 2.

SIECIECH
>   At the King's side.
>   The Bishop is at prayer.
>   He fills the church with plaintive moans.
>   It seems he's coming here, with men.

KING.
>   So, let him come here with his men.
>   Let him come with cross pectoral,
>   Let him lead his monks in choral
>   Wailing before the black crucifix.
>   Let him light the death-bed tallow:
>   Still he's but a wretched fellow.
>   Let him bless his cup and his bread:
>   Still I'll see him bow his head.

SIECIECH.
>   He's coming here, it seems, in song —
>   Crow-like, croaking doomful words.
>   In your chapel he means to pray.

KING.
>   And you — have you no more your swords?
>   None of you know what role to play

When this priest comes to do us wrong
With curse and interdict? Come, up!
Or are you bold but in your cups?
A priest draws close, you cover your eyes!

SIECIECH.
Your horse is ready, sire. Today's
A good day for a hunt. Why wait
Upon the Bishop? Why remain
To see you excommunicate?
A crowd he wants, to hear his word;
Well, let him come and prate in vain,
Then go back empty, the old wizard!

KING.
I fear nothing.
I'm not afraid.
No terror shakes me!
I shalt falter
Though you all quake with dread,
Though all the court shiver with fear,
I'll reach him at the very altar!
I am the one who all things dares!

SCENE 3.

KING'S WIFE
Enters; her train stops at the door.

KING.
The queen! Of mourning weeds you make a fashion.
Are you commemorating some long-dead passion,
Or do you walk in fear of late-cast spells?
Why do you visit the hall where justice dwells?
Is it from legal curiosity?
Or would you simply catch a glimpse of me?
Today I've placed the crown upon my brow,

The same I wore when I gave you my vow.
Though Emperor Konrad my insignia stole,
In these I live again, and am made whole.
Only an Archangel, like a hurricane
Might tear it from my forehead once again.
And so I fear not your conspiracies —
Your petty treasons, or your urgent pleas.

KING'S WIFE
Falls to her knees before him.
I beg you, prince, prostrate here at your foot,
Restrain your hand, and further scourging spare.
Have mercy on your folk — spill no more blood —
Of vengeance you've already the lion's share.

KING
Raises his wife from the floor and gently strokes her face.
Then he leads her to the doors leading to her chamber.

SCENE 4.

KING.
And now, my brother, the cups are filled with mead.

KING'S BROTHER.
Drink first, my brother. Primogeniture
Will have its rights.

KING.
                  Does this mean you're unsure
Of gifts from my hand? Look around and see,
How lap and slurp the aristocracy!

KING'S BROTHER.
Raise the cup to your lips and taste it first.

KING.
>I've had mead enough. I have no thirst.
>I'll drink no more, but I would see you gay
>And ruddy, who are always sad and pale.

KING'S BROTHER.
>There was a King named Popiel who pressed mead
>Into his uncle's hand, and thus did speed
>Him on his way — deep in Lake Gopło's depths.

KING.
>O, such a poisoned cup I hold reserved
>For those who dare neglect the court today —
>For those who would so gladly do away
>With me — I'll do away with them, and would,
>Were the conspirator my own flesh and blood.
>Such a sweetened cup I once was served
>In Russia, by the princes there, who drank
>My health, as they stood round in humble ranks;
>They sipped — the clever venom, though, was hid
>At bottom; came the cup round, I was bid
>To drink last — but I couldn't be surprised:
>I read the treason in their flapping eyes
>As I read yours. I've learned my lesson: Sup
>From your own trencher, drink from your own cup —
>With which I'll toast your health — or otherwise,
>Pour a libation, where the traitor lies.

SCENE 5.

KING
>*To Strzemion.*
>You, old faithful Strzemion,
>When I sit upon the throne,
>With your sword, stand at my side.

STRZEMION.
> Your friends are all assembled here,
> As is your brother. What have you to fear?

KING.
> Just watch their hands, eyes open wide.

STRZEMION.
> For you, sire, I'll lay down my life.
> But God forfend there should be strife
> Between your brother and you, my king!

KING.
> Ah, my old friend, be watchful still
> As my brother the cups shall fill.
> Watch well the cup from which he'll drink.

STREZEMION.
> These eyes will close before they see that, I trust.
> So I take that chalice — and I drain it thus.
> *Drinks from the cup*
> A toast... your health. I am not good with words.

KING'S BROTHER.
> What have you done!!

KING.
> Strzemion!

STRZEMION.
> It burns! Leave off — your health... your health, my lords.

He dies.
All lean over the dead man.
The King and the King's Brother look at each other.

SCENE 6.

SIECIECH.
   They plot against you at the Tyński court.

KING.
   So, take some men and cut their plotting short!
   Set fire to it, cut down all inside;
   I'll spread my vulture wings above it wide,
   Just like a burial shroud.

SIECIECH.
                    Sire, I don't dare!

KING.
   Attack! And let the charge put paid to fear!
   Soar on the trumpet's roaring!
   Remember storming
   The gold Kievan gates?
   And the rush — like a flooding river — of our mates
   At my cry — "After me, the bold!"
   And, like a flood, over the gates we rolled…

SIECIECH.
   Many knights died that day.

KING.
   You don't say?
   I don't recall. But we were spared —
   You, young; I, king — A king who dared!

   Pause.

SCENE 7.

KING.
    While we're all at pipes and beer,
    While we toast with golden wine,
    Sieciech — with mug drawn and drear —
    Glumly bides his cheerless time.
    Why are you sunk in remorse?
    Have you lost your favourite horse?
    Has your falcon fallen, spent?
    Does his mate tire you with her laments?

SIECIECH.
    Cease guessing, sire. You'll never learn,
    And each word makes my heart to burn.
    Set it down to an addled head,
    And a sick heart that beats with dread,
    That drains my face of colour quite.

KING.
    Some maiden holds you spellbound, right?
    That makes you stoop and glance away?
    You yearn for the Kievan charms
    Who vied to leap into your arms
    When we took Russia, long ago?

SIECIECH.
    It's not those eyes that haunt me, no —
    But those you just now chased away.
    I burn — she holds me in her spell.

KING.
    Now I regret my haste that day.
    I cede her to you. Search her out,
    Even if you have to scour Hell.

SIECIECH.
>   Eternal love to me she vowed,
>   But I may only win her hand
>   If first, for her, I kill a man.

KING.
>   All right, old friend. So, kill away,
>   If you so love the crazy maid.
>   As long as you're up to the trade,
>   With stout, resolved arms, kill you may
>   Whomever she desires, your fair.
>   By God in Heaven, this I swear,
>   Kill whom you will.

SIECIECH.
>   It's the king I'm to kill.

KING.
>   Take this rose wreath into your hands
>   And bid another to the dance.
>   Hey now, fiddlers, strike a tune:
>   My friend calls, at the hour of doom.
>   Look there — Death stands before my face.
>   Set loose the dogs! Begin the chase!

>   *Music.*

KING.
>   It's me that you're to kill for her,
>   My love-besotted courtier?
>   My fate's unchanged — immutable.
>   No sword may touch me. I need fear
>   No one as long as this arm here
>   Is with me — this arm, and this will!

>   *Laughter.*
>   *Music.*

SCENE 8.

RHAPSODE.

    I.
    1.
    At Konrad's court
    The nobles disport
    At the court of the Emperor Konrad.

    2.
    Both page and knight
    In gifts delight
    Yet partakes he of no cup himself.

    3.
    He muses, he schemes
    Gnawed by unease he seems,
    On the table he rests his head aching.

    4.
    Lord, drink up your wine,
    Take a new concubine,
    Let the dogs of war rest till tomorrow.

    5.
    For brave Bolesław's son
    Bears thee down at a run
    With the Polish crown fast on his forehead.

    II.
    1.
    But enjoy life for now,
    And unfurrow your brow,
    Overlong, Caesar, twist not in worry.

2.
For a princess Teutonic
Brings thee much needed tonic —
To thy throne all her fealty vowing.

3.
From her husband she flees,
With her son, to thy knees —
Thou wilt teach him to pray in thy jargon.

4.
Here she falls, at thy throne,
And the crown that she's stolen
She sets on thy imperial brow.

5.
Hide it deep in its chest,
In the dark may it rest,
In the secretest underground chamber.

6.
For they're plotting thy wreck;
Feel their breath on thy neck!
As thy enemies draw near, with vengeance.

7.
Bind the royal orphans down,
Chain their small wrists around,
That these chicks never fledge into eagles,

8.
Their sharp talons to rear,
At thy crowned head to tear,
Till they bear off your empire, exulting.

III.

1.
Hey there, son of Rycheza,
Would it not give you pleasure
To win back your grandfather's lands?

2.
So just bow you down low —
Kiss the Emperor's toe,
Caesar Konrad is kind to his servants.

3.
"I will grant you great trains,
Stallions of warlike strains,
Many swordsmen and knights will stand by you,

4.
"If you but give your word,
And acknowledge me lord,
Over you and yours, all time to come."

5.
"Thus, I give you my word,
And acknowledge you lord —
Merely give me my forefathers' crown!

6.
"Is this not fitting praise
Now that all Poland lays
Here before you a handmaid subjected?"

7.
"It suffices. The crown's
Buried deep underground.
Go and dig for it, take it, it's yours."

8.
"But the underground chamber
We enter in vain, for
The smoking torch now is extinguished.

9.
"And the heavy doors slam!
Konrad has me in hand!
I'm imprisoned in dungeons of gloom!"

10.
So rejoice and be glad
You imperial lads —
See the emperor toast you, rejoicing!

11.
"In the dark dungeon deep
Safe and sound will he keep,
Once my hangman his head has off-stricken.

12.
"But now who rushes up?
The turnkey? Fill his cup —
What's the news that he brings us so breathless?"

13.
"Such misfortune, my lord!
Your guards — put to the sword!
Both the crown and the prisoner, departed!"

14.
"All to horse! All to horse!
Take up halberds and swords!
On their hot trail, before it grows cooler!

15.
"Take the traitors who've fled!
Take them living or dead!
I grant peerages to all the captors!"

16.
But look — What a surprise!
None there present arise,
Nor mayest thou rise from thy drunken bench.

17.
Ah, such excellent wine!
Play with thy concubine.
Only wind will rush after the fleeing!

18.
Jar and goblet he flings.
See him rise, tottering,
Drunk, among his retainers besotted.

19.
Barely shines the new morn,
To the crypts see him borne:
Caesar Konrad is choked on his bile.

Pause.

20.
But sleep well, lord. You should.
He's of Rycheza's blood,
With that blood comes appropriate vengeance.

The King rises to his feet.

21.
King of Kraków, take heed:
You're of Rycheza's seed —
Guilty blood, violent, criminal your rule!

KING.
>A pretty song, a pretty tune.
>How may I now discharge the debt?

RHAPSODE.
>The mould gnaws at my dwelling's ruins.
>Return to me my youth that's sped.

KING.
>I can bestow but what I've got.
>Money, perhaps a laurel crown;
>A necklace of thick gold braids curled.

RHAPSODE.
>The freshest flowers soon turn brown;
>Leaves fall away from stems, and rot.
>I'm called now to another world.

KING.
>Honours you spurn? You disdain wealth?

RHAPSODE.
>I'm richer than you are yourself.
>Rule is a lie; lying is wealth
>When one's heart dies in enmity.
>
>Hatred I bear within my heart;
>Hate eats me through like rust.
>I seek death — killing is your art.
>Give death to me. Be Generous
>
>As you'd be called. The only things
>I seek are past that unknown bourn —
>And all I see, whenever I sing
>Are those very things, for which I mourn.
>
>I go now, never to come back;
>Nothing can save me now but Death.

You're strong, but such power you lack,
Though you be Generous with your wealth.

KING.
What is it you seek — — — ?!

RHAPSODE.
A blush on your cheek.
I'd like to see your visage blush.
Can you even do it? Come now, try:
You, who, unmoved, make thousands cry —
Can your face with shame ever flush?!

KING.
What's your desire — — —?!

RHAPSODE.
You! Light that fire!
I want to see an angry king!
I want to see you put the lie
To your great power. Of that I'd sing!

KING.
What do you want?!

RHAPSODE.
                I want to die —
But first, to kill him, who killed fame.
Rycheza's grand-whelp, I curse thee
And these thy bloody hands.
Thou'st murdered many, now kill me!
And then, eternally be damned!

KING.
You'll die for that!

RHAPSODE.
              Kill me — alone
Of all men you. No one else dares.
In the ruined temple is my home —
God's sentinel, sacrosanct seer.

The people honour me with loaves;
The nation praises me of old.
My curse about thy head now roves;
Kill me — thou only art so Bold!

For he who raises up his hand,
Weaponed, at me, with ill intent,
The lightning shall cut forth his span.
He'll fall, crushed by God's punishment.

You are no ruler, — I am king!
A deep yearning anoints my soul.
Incurable its constant sting,
And viper-like, it twists and rolls.

This churning worry I would still.
The saviour Death alone I trust.
Hey, royal killer! Come now, kill!
For that they'll sing you Generous!

Death stole from me my children dear;
Death stole from me my loving wife.
My eyes have no use, save for tears;
Death only can save me from life.

But Death can't reach me with her hand;
Wretched I squirm in life's embrace.
I see your power, your glory, grand,
Yet read the vacuum in your face.

Yearning, my soul's eternal sting
Eats through my tired heart like rust.

Come, kill me, open-handed king —
For this they'll hymn you Generous!

Kill me! Or you shall have my curse
As I've been cursed, as I've been lugged
Through life. You call yourself God's scourge?
You're nothing but a thug!

KING
Fatally strikes the Rhapsode.

SERVANTS
Carry out the wounded man.

KING
*Summons his Knights into the chamber with his sceptre
Then sits down on the judgment bench before a chest.*

SIECIECH
Bears the royal standard.

KNIGHTS
Take their seats around the chamber.

SCENE 9.

FIRST UNFAITHFUL WIFE
Under guard.
Tyrant! You rabid dog! In my defence
I've nothing but the quick tongue in my head.
I spit on you, shameless and wolfish thing!
Be now a reptile — voiceless, spluttering!
You killed my man: for that you have my curse.
Would he could see me now. So much the worse —
Because I took a lover to my bed,
You crush me in your prison, and you steal
My lands, and judge yourself the scourge of God.

Perish! And may rot eat through your loins.
For daring to judge me, and my passions,
I curse you!

KING.
Take her beyond the palace and set dogs
At her breasts, to suck forth the venom
And bile that sours her. Bind her — take her hence.

FIRST UNFAITHFUL WIFE.
Butcher!

They take her out.

SCENE 10.

SECOND UNFAITHFUL WIFE
Under guard.

KING.
Tell us his name, who soiled your husband's bed.

SECOND UNFAITHFUL WIFE
Is silent.

KING.
I've confiscated your goods, and your servants.
The servants I've put to death.

SECOND UNFAITHFUL WIFE.
Not all of them.
One is beyond your reach. I'd call you Bold
If you could find a way to prick his breast.

KING.
What — — ?

SECOND UNFAITHFUL WIFE.
   My conscience.

KING.
   Ha, ha, ha!

SECOND UNFAITHFUL WIFE.
               Come, bring your punishment.
   Set your pups sucking at my breasts, to purge
   The bile and venom that you judge are there.
   Passion has burnt me dry — as it does you —
   Your burning pride, of stallions or oxen,
   Keeping a tally of your Russian rapes;
   Of girls helpless at your whim. No less mortal
   For all that, we're a pair alike in shame:
   That ring of brass that circles round your skull
   Sets you in judgement over me. Arbitrary
   Arbiter, censor morum!

KING.
   Bind her — take her — break her on the wheel.

The guards take her out.

SCENE 11.

THIRD UNFAITHFUL WIFE
   Under guard.
   Unjust, the charges brought against me
   By your hand, strong — in banditry,
   By your most German hand,
   Since you refuse to hear out my defence.
   To that pale face of yours I'd lend some light,
   That you might know what eaglets feel at sight
   Of prey delightful — If you were so bold,
   Perhaps you'd come to know what passion is,
   Desire, when set aglow. Perhaps you too

Would take fire, with that splendid flame, unlike
　　　All others — Mine, I mean, were I,
　　　Unfaithful wife, to mire me in your sty.

KING.
　　　A noose! And drag her through the palace courts.
　　　Makes a sign with his sceptre
　　　To indicate that the court is adjourned.

KNIGHTS
　　　Rise from their seats.

SCENE 12.

KING.
　　　Hey there, rouse yourself, my page,
　　　And lead to court some pretty maids
　　　Of the queen's service. Let there be
　　　Feasting and dance and jollity.
　　　We'll find a squire for each maid,
　　　And for their beauty, they'll be well paid.

PAGE.
　　　I'll whisper this into their ear
　　　So that their mistress should not hear.
　　　I'll win their favour, they'll be gay.
　　　But should the queen chase me away?

KING.
　　　Pluck some roses from the garden.
　　　Plait some wreaths for knights and maidens.
　　　Toss one on the Vistula's waves
　　　There past the battlements, where my love
　　　Chooses to wander, far from me.
　　　The second bring her with a smile
　　　If you should find her, lost in thought.
　　　I'll wreathe my brow, and all the while

I'll wait here, in some westing plot,
To watch the dying sun expire.

Music.

SCENE 13.

MAIDENS
Enter.

KNIGHTS
Take them up to dance.

FEMALE SINGER.
I.
Race on, race on, Vistula flood,
Past the Niepołomski Wood.
From my love I depart at dawn;
At eve, again to him I'm drawn.

They dance in a circle.

II.
The best loving, my lover gives;
His touch, it makes me thrill and live.
Each night my wreath's despoiled and gone;
Each morn he gives me another one.

They dance in a circle.

III.
Sail on, wreath; on Vistula's waves be tossed.
What reck I, should you be lost?
What reck I, should my love depart?
I'll lodging find in some new heart.

They dance in a circle.

IV.
Race on river, race on fast.
Soon river waves and life are past;
From love though I depart at dawn,
At eve to love again I'm drawn.

They dance in a circle.

SCENE 14.

PAGE
Brings forth wreaths of roses
And sets them on the heads of the dancing Knights.

KING.
Set the wreaths upon your brows;
Step up to the whirling round.
Now begins our dancing swarm.

Come now, maidens, come to play.
Come celebrate love's holy day.
Bedeck with roses your sweet forms.

Though I wade through blood and crime,
Gaily would I spend this time.
Tonight my sadness would I slay.

Fill my cup full to the brim!
My granddad — you remember him,
You, my faithful chamberlain?

Dancers dance, the music swells;
I was told you know some spells.
Say: what's in my future?

CHAMBERLAIN.
                              Pain.

KING.
> What's your meaning? I don't follow.
> Spit it out — Why do you swallow
> What I'd learn, deep in your maw?
>
> Why do you totter afraid,
> Setting atremble cup and plate
> Balanced atilt there in your paw?
>
> You see the wreaths, their rosy blush;
> You see the gay dancers aflush;
> You hear the toasts, course after course?
> Go then, old fool, and fill the cups.
> They're thirsty. Hear? The music stops.

CHAMBERLAIN.
> Sire — banners approach — a hostile force!

SCENE 15.

FOURTH UNFAITHFUL WIFE
> *Runs in from the courtyard.*

FIRST MAIDEN.
> Look there! Look there! Oh, see who comes!
> Her head is turned! See how she runs!

SECOND MAIDEN.
> She's running close — she's running here.
> Her eyes are wild, her shirt is torn;
> She flees like someone's chasing her;
> Someone's behind her — can you see?

THIRD MAIDEN.
> Is there a spectre at her heels?

MAIDENS
    Laugh at the crazed woman.

FOURTH UNFAITHFUL WIFE.
    It's me — it's me — your husband.

    Whomever she approaches, they draw back.
    Pause.

FOURTH UNFAITHFUL WIFE.
    Let me go! I must see the king.

    Whomever she approaches, they draw back.
    Pause.

FOURTH UNFAITHFUL WIFE.
    Beyond the pond — quite near at hand,
    My husband's — and my — castle stands.
    With Bolesław the king, my man
    Invaded the Kievan land.
    Pause.
    Steep is the road of virtue, slick!
    The boys! Around they crowded thick —
    And I betrayed my marriage vow!

FIRST MAIDEN.
    She's out of her head!

MAIDENS
    Laugh.

FOURTH UNFAITHFUL WIFE.
    You'd like to prosecute me? Come —
    Let us draw near the royal throne.
    Here — here, look down on me, my lord,
    And deign impart a merciful word.
    My husband was unfaithful too:
    In Kiev he abandoned you,

And so — for you — with my own hand,
When he returned, I killed my man.
I will not colour what I did;
I will not have my action hid;
As you sit there, dispensing blame,
Say — are our actions not the same?

At the crossroads I killed my love;
There, where the meadow meets the grove.
I dug a grave, I dug it deep ...
And rolled him in. And there he'd sleep
Beneath the flowers and the sod
Had I not this one thing forgot:
To bury him face down! You see:
His ghost, it's risen, and it follows me!

He's burst the grave! You see my plight;
This is perverse! Set it to rights!
He's standing here in your presence:
Pronounce upon him your sentence!
Put him to death, King. Grant me peace!
Judge him, and make this haunting cease.
He will not go — he will not budge;
I beg your justice, lord. Now, judge!

KING
    Laughs.

The lights of the chamber dim.

KING.
    Unfaithful woman! Vain your fears.
    The dead no longer reappear
    Once they've been dispatched to the grave.

    But if you wish, I'll sit me down
    And once more death I shall pronounce.
    He who is dead, dead should remain.

Let him but stand before me here
And charge you with audible breath.
You from that same charge I shall clear
And sentence him to death.

He stands on the dais of the throne.

What's his, I'll make over to you instead.
Keep it, or waste it on a whim;
Take whom you wish unto your bed,
And sin, and sin, and sin!

Just let him stand before my eyes
And make his plea at this assize,
And I'll judge him: once more he dies!

FOURTH UNFAITHFUL WIFE.
He's coming! Ha! He's coming close!

KING.
Here beneath the chamber floor
A vault is hidden. There within
I'll have him thrown. Oh, look — you see?

He points to the floor.

ALL.
They're in the courtyard!

FOURTH UNFAITHFUL WIFE.
Oh — with the bishop he draws close!
Bishop comes, arm in arm, with ghost!
He props the corpse up with his hand.

The worm has eaten through his face,
On his pale cheeks the candle plays;
A dried asp curls about his head!

PROCESSION
Enters through the great chamber doors.

SCENE 16.

A step before the bishop treads
The spectre, wrapped in his grave shroud.
As he has lain in the ground a year
So now the royal hoplite does appear:
Clay and gravel stick to his armour,
A snake entwines his brows
A bloody discharge flows from his snuffed eyes.
His shirt is torn in rags.
But he has been called to judgement
And so he comes.
Only the King
And the criminal wife see him.

SIR PIOTR.
   It is I, your husband.

FOURTH UNFAITHFUL WIFE
   Faints.

ALL
   Kneel.

CHORUS OF MONKS.
   Land him forfend;
   Forbid him fields
   Forbid him strength
   Forbid good will.

   May he be
   Unsought;
   By land and sea
   Forgot.

>   Forbid him salt
>   Forbid him bread
>   Forbid him board
>   Forbid him heaven.
>
>   May he wend his ways
>   Crazed;
>   Unsought,
>   Forgot.

BISHOP
> *Lifts high his arm.*

MONKS
> *Extinguish their candles,*
> *Break them in two,*
> *And toss them to the floor.*

KING
> *Takes a step forward, and the crown*
> *Falls from his head.*

ALL
> *Run off, chaotically.*

PROCESSION
> *Moves off.*

SIR PIOTR
> *Sinks beneath the floor.*

KING
> *Sits, immobile. Alone.*

KING'S MOTHER
> *Enters at a side door,*
> *Moves to the centre, propped on a cane.*

KING'S WIFE and KING'S SON
> Enter and stand near the doors.

KING'S MOTHER
> Pokes with her cane at the candles and the wreaths.
> She notices the crown,
> Stares at the immobile king,
> Crosses herself,
> And gathers the candle-pieces into her apron,
> Continually crossing herself.
> She departs, with the King's Wife and King's Son following.

SCENE 17.

KING
> Starts, as if roused from a deep sleep,
> Runs into the dark depths of the chamber,
> And sounds a horn.

KNIGHTS
> Enter to him,
> And stand around him.

KING
> To Sieciech.
> Betrayed me, you say? That is a curious thought.
> I'd like to see, today, the man who dares
> Betray me! And you, why are you loyal?
> Why are you loyal? I need not your loyalty!
> And so, you do not fear such punishment?
> Ha, ha, ha! I will call the lightning down
> And strike you all — see you all underground!
> You are all traitors! I betray myself
> In telling forth the secret of my soul.
> As long as I'm alive, glory too lives.
> Farewell — depart — your presence makes me ill.
> You may be many, still am I alone.

Farewell, farewell. I'm from another world...
My iron helmet! Now! And my horse!
Saddle my horse! I'm off.
Farewell.
It was us thundered over the Czech king,
Pummelling shields and taking prisoners!
It was us who hunted all through Hungary,
And as there was no castle left to rule from,
We harried off that wretched little Salmon
And gave the throne to Władysław. And Russia?
We were the lords of Russia! Russian princes
And Russian kings lay prostrate at our feet —
It takes a king to do such kingly deeds!
Three castles I shall grind beneath my feet,
Then I'll return, with three crowns on my head!

KNIGHTS
Raise their swords aloft.

KING.
And you — waste no more time — take armed men —
Angry men — And lead them — there!
He points toward Skałka.
See there? The walls are black with people
Who cry out. Cut them down! Drown! But the Bishop —
Bring him to me, alive.
You're not afraid?

SIECIECH.
   Of what?

KING.
    A miracle!

SIECIECH.
With me, lads!
To the king.

> Swear to me just one thing —
> That if I come back, red with guilty shame...

KING.
> I'll go myself!

KNIGHTS
> *Run out.*

KING
> *Watches them depart, from the porch.*

SCENE 18.

KING'S BROTHER
> *Enters from the courtyard and takes his place*
> *On the porch next to the King.*

KING and KING'S BROTHER
> *Enter the chamber, sit down beside one another.*
> *Pause.*

KING'S BROTHER.
> Brother, your opinion — —?

KING.
> The court's still out.

KING'S BROTHER.
> You've got your vengeance, true?

KING.
> Who's the avenger?

KING'S BROTHER.
> Who else but you?

KING.
>You think it torments me,
>You think I'm burdened down
>Because he throws some candles on the ground,
>Because his peasant-monks
>Some litanies have sung?

KING'S BROTHER.
>I think it bad, that such a one
>Lives, who dares to raise his hand
>Against us.

KING.
>>And are you not his man?
>Who knows what's churning in your head?

KING'S BROTHER.
>Hatred.

KING.
>>That I know. Terror. Dread.

KING'S BROTHER.
>Do you not see? His venom's spread
>Throughout our veins! And while he grows,
>You're shrunk to nothing.

KING.
>>>So he's flown
>A black flag, and pronounced a curse;
>Cursed me from water, field and bread
>And salt — Is my destiny the worse?

KING'S BROTHER.
>He ought to be put down.

KING.
>With blood?

KING'S BROTHER.
  With blood.

KING.
  Those are your words.

KING'S BROTHER
  With blood, and quick. Before he flee.

KING.
  Unlike you, he's not cowardly.

KING'S BROTHER.
  It's only you I fear,
  Who smote the golden gates.
  I cede no other the field.

KING.
  Kill whom you wish. His fate
  Is in your hands.

KING'S BROTHER.
            Oh, no. I yield
  To you the first fruits of shame.

KING.
  After which, you'll carry on our name.
  It's too early for tears
  On my part.
  Vainly you strive to shake my heart.

KING'S BROTHER.
  You need to humble him somehow.

KING.
  Ha, ha! My thoughts — can anyone know?
  Do you know who I am? And whence
  It comes, this incarnated strength?

The thought that furrows my brow?
Do you know whom I'm fighting against, now?

KING'S BROTHER.
A man.

KING.
And if he wields a power —

KING'S BROTHER.
What sort?

KING.
The kind that wields the lightning's doom.
The power that crushes with the tomb.
He's not just a man,
With whom I grapple, hand to hand!

KING'S BROTHER.
You are bold.

KING.
These hands have never shivered with cold.
In me I trust, in me alone my faith.

KING'S BROTHER.
I have no such faith, truth be told.
And after all, what does yours rate?
Hack as you will,
The spirit can't be killed.

KING.
So you say. Still,
You are — nothing.
Pale and sickly with thought, overwrought,
And shall be nothing, while so fraught
With fear of death.

KING'S BROTHER.
>It's not in my hand,
Death.

KING.
>Then it's in whose?

KING'S BROTHER.
>I don't know.
Death is a mysterious power.
Whence comes it? From beyond the stars?
A giant, wreathed with withered grace...

KING.
You fear to look her in the face?

KING'S BROTHER.
I see her in your eyes. You bear
Her marks — as if you were her butcher.

KING.
Ha, ha, ha! Such the weight of my robes?
I am a spirit!
You shall witness my deeds!

Pause.

If he's the one
Sent against me by God
To stop me mid-road,
I will kill him.
For I have that of God.

Pause.

If those I sent against him
With swords
Come back empty-handed

After snivelling in his presence
I will kill him.
So let it be,
What hides in me a mystery.

Pause.

I saw
That in his eyes there glow
The lamps of many centuries —
And you dare to judge us?
As if we were your peers?
Ha, ha, ha…
Look — you're treading on roses.
My thorns ought to be back by now…
I must be off.

Pause.

Do you even know what action is?
You saw the singer fall to the floor
Tangled in his harpstrings
Which thrummed
Beneath his falling weight?
He died from a blow to the neck
Given by me — by this arm!
Ha, ha, ha!
I shall renew the world,
I shall redeem the world,
Through blood!

SCENE 19.

KRASAWICA
Runs in, chasing Sieciech before her.
Lover, lover, lover!

SIECIECH
  Raving.
  Where am I?

KRASAWICA.
            Ha, ha! Make way!
  Laughs.

KING'S BROTHER.
            The fool.

KRASAWICA.
  Ha, ha! See how he shakes!

SIECIECH.
  Where am I? I ran to the sacred grove,
  And there... I blacked out...

KING'S BROTHER.
  He totters!

SIECIECH
  Collapses to his knees.

KING
  From the bench.
  Get up!

SIECIECH.
  The king's voice!
  Looks about himself, confused.
  Look! The candles on the altar, all aglow!
  Hollowly.
  And all around it, winged warriors,
  With visors covering their faces —

KRASAWICA.
>   You see? — — Look down, deep down:
>   The water's all rushed into the abyss.
>   The trees choke dry in the sun...

KING
>   *Rises and moves directly in front of Sieciech's face.*

SIECIECH.
>   You slaughtered my soul, you deceiver!
>   *Pause.*
>   You sent me out, a butcher with a knife
>   To cut down those who stand opposed to you.
>   But I saw through you! Holy shamans bathed
>   Me clean in holy water — I forgot
>   The spell, the anger, and the evil rush
>   I had in gift from your royal hand, you,
>   Who leashed me like a dog in your kennel
>   Of butcher-slaves!
>   *He tosses away his sword.*
>   Here! Take the blade! I want no government.
>   I want no king!

KRASAWICA
>   *To the king.*
>   Behold your courtiers!
>   I charmed him with my eye. This eye!
>   A shine reflected from the candles,
>   A cloud of birds,
>   And he fell prone before what terrifies him.
>   He can't hear a word you say.
>   So, you alone remain, knight of the spirit!
>   Through blood! You want to go? Then go yourself!
>   Go and conquer!

SIECIECH
Rises violently from his knees.
Lies!
He chases after Krasawica.

KRASAWICA
Runs into another room.

SCENE 20.

SIECIECH
From the door, watches her dive into the Vistula.
Screams.
Trembling, he totters and falls
Pointing towards the room.

KING.
Boy! Hey, boy! What are you calling for?

SIECIECH
Points to the sword laying on the floor.
It takes a king to do such kingly deeds.
Pause.
I have returned. I can't do it. The others
Soon follow me... I led them there...
And all of them will throw their swords before you,
Never to go to such a battle again.
The people there, were quiet, and quite helpless.
They stood a wall, all gazing at the embankment,
At that knoll on the Vistula
Above the water — on the Skałka bridge...
He can't speak further.
And from the waters — they cry out — RUSALKAS!

One hears the Rusalkas singing.

KING'S BROTHER
To the king.
You're trembling like a willow tree.

KING.
The waters themselves are mocking me?

SIECIECH.
The masses cry: your hand will rot away
If you dare raise it against the bishop!

KING
Stunned.

KNIGHTS
Enter the porch and cast away their swords.

KING.
I'll kill him!
Eagles his flesh will peck and flay!

He pulls his sword.
He rushes out.

ACT V

(Act III of *Skałka*)

Toward Skałka, through the empty fields hastens the

BISHOP.
He enters the church porch.
At the font, wound in a shroud, stands
DEATH.

DEATH.
   I am your truth's guardian.

BISHOP.
   My words in flesh, incarnate.

DEATH.
   You called on God. Foresaw your fate.

BISHOP.
   My words become flesh, in fact.
   I am the judge of human sin.

DEATH.
   Hard upon your words comes the act.

BISHOP.
   Which I accept, my folk to save.
   This corpse I owe unto the grave.

DEATH.
   A death-rattle sounds through the world
   And hastens onward unimpeded
   One thousand years.

BISHOP.
   Where the eagles of Piast
   Perch high upon their royal aerie…

DEATH.
   Ruins, and a chock-full cemetery.

BISHOP.
   The act is done.

DEATH.
             That act, your own.

BISHOP.
>I stand fast to the Truth alone.

DEATH.
>The Truth has one, eternal course:
>The wheel turns, sin gnaws at life's source.
>The fate of all who live's the same:
>To bear the blows of mutual crime.

BISHOP.
>And my Truth?

DEATH.
>   Yes, that Truth of yours
>Only in death endless endures.
>When the living their true life begin
>You will not be among them, then.

BISHOP.
>Along the roads of Hell you've trod
>Here to arrive —

DEATH.
>   There is one God
>Of Hell and Heaven. My might is great
>Over all who live, and all who die.
>I've come to give the truth the lie.

BISHOP.
>How did you pass the forbidden gate?

DEATH.
>The words that called me here, you spoke.
>The thin-fired clay of your dear folk
>You crushed in your creative hands.
>You are subject to the doomful word
>As the only cleansed soul in this land.

BISHOP.
>   What must I do —?

DEATH.
>   Accept the sword.

BISHOP.
>   Whose is the hand this passion brings?

DEATH.
>   The hand is God's. God's, and the king's.
>   Your truth will give the truth the lie.

BISHOP.
>   The judgement —

DEATH.
>   Shall come from on high.

BISHOP.
>   And me, whom God takes in this net,
>   Among the hosts of Heaven has set.
>   What is this power, that God bestows?

DEATH.
>   The spell of words, of words the faith,
>   Above all earthly filth below.

BISHOP.
>   To whom do you give the word's strength?

DEATH.
>   To you alone.

BISHOP.
>   And with it I
>   Shall save my people?

DEATH.
> God on high
> Through you will perform a wonder.

BISHOP.
> What must I do?

DEATH.
> Re-weave what's sundered
> By the fevered hands of lust.

BISHOP.
> Whose hands unwound it?

DEATH.
> Your will must
> Be done, for these, and for these ends.
> Such is the law of violence.

BISHOP.
> Am I to truth thus to give the lie?

DEATH.
> What you've unbound, you must re-tie.

BISHOP
> *Covers his face with his hands.*

DEATH.
> You've paused the wheel in its turning;
> You're elevated above time;
> Above the world, above life clear
> One thousand years.
> What one man's lifetime can embrace
> Passes in one moment, one brief space.
> The aged oak crashes down through the glade
> It towered over, age on age;
> Crumbled in dust, the great trunk lies;

Above the corpse, the freed soul flies —
Strong, liberated, a free shade.
As long as you see me with your eyes
Your sand has not run through the glass.
As you back your folk with your word's strength
A miracle shall come to pass,
As you fall beneath the bloodied blade.

BISHOP.
 What must I do?

DEATH.
  Before God's bench
 Confess your missteps and your sin.

BISHOP.
 And my Truth —?

DEATH.
  Still that truth of yours
 Only in Death endless endures.
 When the living their true life begin,
 You will not be among them, then.
 Living oblation, offer up
 For souls departing holy prayer
 So that they drink not from your cup,
 But of its merits fully share.
 As from a tree the dry leaves fall,
 Before your eyes you'll see them all
 Brawled by the wind's savage attack,
 But you must not take one step back
 Or your death will be all for nought.
 The guilt of gravest sins you've brought
 Upon yourself — God's hand restraining
 From judgement on the flock remaining
 Under your care; a votive flame
 You'll burn throughout all generations
 To words of prayer bestowing grace.

You've conquered Death; you've won the race;
A man may put your corpse to shame
Only to more exalt your station.
The murderous sword
Serving your word.
Pray for him too, whom God has set
You as your judge, that his grave debt
Be washed clean by your sacrifice,
His soul freed, at so great a price.
I kneel down at your feet today;
I serve the Mass you celebrate.
Now offer up the fourfold prayer:
The power of their words is rare.
Above the flame your hand extend.
Pray that you be strong, to the end.

BISHOP
*Raises his hands
Above the votive flame.*

DEATH
*Kneels
Like a deacon.*

BISHOP.
I.
The Book of Genesis in Thy hand
Thou dost reveal the guardians
Of Thy altar, and of my land,
And how Thy Spirit multiplies them.

Above the dreaming head, this night
A spreading tree Thou dost unfold,
That figures those battling for Thy right:
All wearing royal crowns of gold.

Thou set'st them first among all men,
Of thy Blest Spirit inspired and skilled,

From plough to sceptre Thou'st raised them
And through them work'st Thy miracles.

II.
Before thee my angel goeth,
Who shall thy roads prepare.
In the hides of animals clothed,
His realm is the desert bare.

He shall shatter the chains round their wrists;
In the river he shall cleanse them from sin.
With beast's hides he shall cover their breasts;
By his words thou shalt win through to the end.

"He who follows exceeds me in power.
Stronger far is the strength of his merit.
You with man's might alone I endow:
From him you shall have might of the Spirit!"

III.
The two of them are without blame.
Righteous they live before Thine eye,
With none to carry on their name,
No issue to bring them delight.

But him Thou stood within Thy fane
To sacrifice before Thy folk;
An angel in gold armour came
And in prophetic tones thus spoke:

"Thy wife to thee shall bear a son,
And he shall be thy great delight,
Thy clan's joy and benediction:
He'll rule thy nation, by God's right.

"Led by the Spirit, he'll walk in grace,
And father with son shall reconcile;

Walking in faith, he'll build in faith,
A nation that no guilt defiles."

IV.
In the beginning was the Word;
Above the waters mused the Ghost.
The Word inspired was the Lord;
From Him the world took life, and grows.

The matrix of the Word creates
All things; the Word fires star and sun;
Season and times He duly plaits;
Unendingly, the grand chain runs.

A clot of clay, by the Word's will,
Grows into man, like strong grain in the field.
The sower seeds the ploughman's till,
And God's earth bears its awesome yield.

Far off on the Vistula's waters
An immense circling throng arises
From the frothy waves
Hiding from sight the castle and the hill.

THE RING OF THE CLAN OF PIAST.
Over this circle, as if on a rainbow,
Piast after crowned Piast
Appears at the summit,
Before descending to disappear in turn.
The shores of the Vistula fill with song.

RUSALKAS.
A king from river waters born,
Shining in raiments of pure gold,
With sceptre and with mighty sword,
In dream he sees his fate unfold.

You rise in glory, vibrant fame,
And leaves of oak adorn your crown.
Your fortune waxes, and it wanes:
The wheel turns, and spins you down.

The water flows, the wheel flies,
The pulsing river never stops.
He at the zenith faints and dies;
He from the nadir climbs aloft.

Thus Fortune's wheel spins fiercely on,
Like to the ever-fleeting wave.
No sooner do we see the sun
Than we lie blinded in the grave.

A moment's time we call our own.
It passes, no more to return.
We cede to new generations,
And just as brief is their sojourn.

A king from river waters born,
Shining in raiments of pure gold,
With sceptre and with mighty sword,
In dream he sees his fate unfold.

You plough the field your son shall reap;
Your wine shall make other eyes gleam.
Soon you recline in wakeless sleep:
Another's turn it is to dream.

The water flows, the wheel flies,
The pulsing river never stops.
He at the zenith faints and dies;
He from the nadir climbs aloft.

Thus Fortune's wheel spins fiercely on,
Like to the ever-fleeting wave.

No sooner do we see the sun
Than we lie blinded in the grave.

A moment's time we call our own.
It passes, no more to return.
We cede to new generations,
And just as brief is their sojourn —
And just as brief is their sojourn.

ACT VI

(Act III of *Bolesław the Bold*)

SCENE 1.

Night in the castle.

KING
Returns at a run
With naked sword
Halts at the threshold of the room
Sheathes his sword
Enters the room
And notices the crown lying on the floor.
He picks up the crown and sets it on his head with both hands.

RUMOUR 1.
The eagles are guarding the body.
They let no one near it.

KING.
They guard the body, but the spirit?
Do the eagles guard his ghost
So that he shan't pass post
And lintel, and arise
Here, before my very eyes?

I send eagles to fight,
To crush his might,
To sip his blood and lap his gore,
And they — shivering — take fright,
Freezing in terror!

RUMOUR 1.
You wanted them to tear his flesh
And they — ever so gently rest
Upon his violated breast,
As if they were sentinels, lest
The least scrap go astray.
You want them to be chased away?

KING.
Disperse them!

RUMOUR 1.
If that be done,
What if they come here?

KING.
Before me? If they come,
Surrounding me, crowding — ?

RUMOUR 1.
They're not allowing
Anyone near;
They won't be dispersed; they brood
About the temple, on the charred wood,
And contemplate the bloody wounds,
The blood, the body cruelly hewn;
They brood over the blood that sinks
Into the pool; they confer, they think...

KING.
Begone, man.

RUMOUR 1
> *Exits.*

SCENE 2.

RUMOUR 2.
> The lights, the torches! The people raise
> Their voices in the dead man's praise —
> The bishop's corpse yet lies upon
> The turf that saw his martyrdom
> About the pool, dark, green and fair,
> And a scent of roses fills the air.

KING.
> Have someone come and stoke the embers!

RUMOUR 2.
> All of the members
> Of your household are dispersed.
> They left, in fear, when you were cursed.

KING.
> What is that shining on the floor —
> Over there — sparkling blue?
> Dead, rotting flowers? Phosphor?
> Wax from the candles that he threw?
> The tapers spent?
> . . . .
> My brother — did he go with them?

RUMOUR 2.
> Of brothers I know nothing.
> Had you one, ever?
> Today you have none, king.

KING.
>   Call my wife here to me.
>   Let her speak to me: gaily, clever —
>   I am so thirsty
>   Of a kind word — and she
>   Was always so jealous, protective of me...

RUMOUR 2.
>   She now has no kind word to say.
>   She presses her son to her breast
>   Sobbing, in ash-stained sackcloth dressed,
>   At Skałka, where the martyr's splayed,
>   Guarded by birds.
>   No hope for you; no soothing words.

KING.
>   Begone man! Out of my sight with you!

RUMOUR 2
>   *Exits.*

SCENE 3.

RUMOUR 3.
>   At Skałka — your wife, your son,
>   Mourning, sobbing,
>   Hear them crying — — ?

KING.
>   The rain is plashing — winds are sighing —
>   The roof tiles drum
>   The gutters
>   With water
>   Are throbbing.

RUMOUR 3.
>Your four knights,
>True to their king,
>Wash the blood from their blades in the spring.
>Will you send them to fight
>Anew, when their swords are bright,
>Scoured and shining?

KING.
>Mists flicker at the door...
>Who are you? What is your name?
>I've never seen you before...

RUMOUR 3.
>These words of mine, in your heart store:
>You are misled by your fame.

KING.
>Recall those words!

RUMOUR 3.
>   My prophecy.
>Your fame is your calamity.

KING.
>Ill-omened breath —

RUMOUR 3.
>Your fame among your folk: your death.
>*He exits.*

KING.
>He disappeared — the evil sprite —
>How dark in here! How deep the night!
>The wind is howling along the plains,
>And how they plash, the rains...
>Nought else I hear...
>Shh! Something else buzzes in my ear...

SCENE 4.

WHISTLE.

   1.
Whence, whence comes it, sire,
From the wild brakes, from the hunts?
The gore that from your swordblade runs,
The blood that stains your rich attire?

   2.
Whose blood is it, that so burns?
That you so turn
Away in shock, your eyes to hide?

   3.
Whose blood is it, so hot
That you have locked
Yourself away, from all men's sight —?

AFTERWHISTLE.

   1.
To the islet's blooming glen
Led the warlike king his men...
To quarter a man by the water.

   2.
Holy grove, nymph-haunted pond — there
Lies he, who offered daily prayer,
The Bread, the Cup, the Pater Noster.

WHISTLE.

   3.
The eagles watch over that blood;
Eagles, voracious
Eagles — that royal brood!

SCENE 5.

Enter from the side the Lieutenant and the Sexton.

SEXTON.
  All for candles broken!

LIEUTENANT.
  Look — he stands at the altar!
  His eyes, his eyes are on you!

KING.
  "Have you no swords?"

LIEUTENANT.
  They measured with their swords,
  But — see: they've checked their haste.

KING.
  "Cowards!"

LIEUTENANT.
  Support them with your right hand!

KING.
  "Now!"

LIEUTENANT.
  They fall down prone!

KING.
  "Dogs!"

LIEUTENANT.
  Kill, yourself!!

KING
> *Rushes to the wall, stops at the great beam,*
> *When he turns,*
> *He sees the crowd of people approaching.*

SCENE 6.

KING.
> Who are these people
> Who come, blocking my road?
> Whence come these mobs of starvelings?

WHISTLE.
> You hear what they sing?

KING.
> I can't hear a thing.

WHISPER.
> Your deeds and his they cantillate;
> And the dead bishop they claim a saint.

AFTERWHISTLE.
> The years flow by.

WHISTLE.
>   An age is gone.

KING.
> I thirst — ha, water — the sting!

AFTERWHISTLE.
> Bear it — you are a king.

WHISTLE.
> An age is passed.

AFTERWHISTLE.
> The fame of thugs. Shh! Can you hear it?
> No one recalls the butchers' names...

KING.
> Hey — Who are you?

AFTERWHISTLE.
> >A spirit.
>
> I flee, I flee,
> Each hop, a century.
> I halt my tread:
> A hundred
> Years go.
> Like the seeds that blow
> From a dried bloom,
> Men fly to their doom.
> I am man, I am breath,
> And my brother: dumb, deaf.

KING
> *Whispers.*
> Who are you, who?

WHISTLE.
> I fly, I flee,
> Each hop, a century.
> I halt my tread:
> A hundred
> Years fall.

AFTERWHISTLE.
> From the vacant castle walls,
> Over meadow, over lea,
> Over thorns I flee —
> I was there when they hewed,
> And when the birds they shooed.
> Empty hall,

Whisper, call.
I will second your song
All along.
From castle towers
Hour on hour,
From battlements' height
Far and wide,
I shall chase, harry, pursue…

KING.
Who?

AFTERWHISTLE.
Yesterday, and the day before.
And the centuries, score
Upon age in career,
After joys past.

KING.
Nightmare!

SCENE 7.

CHORAGOS and CHORUS OF CRIPPLES.

1.
The king cuts him in four —
But we praise him all the more.
Relics dear and gold-plated
For all time venerated.

2.
Come the feeble poor, reeling
To exult in their healing:
Crippled limbs are unbound;
Once-blind eyes gaze around.

3.
They press close to the tomb,
Silvery-bright in the gloom.
Gathered in one body,
Sundered never to be.

KING.
These crowds, somewhere flowing
In the day sunny-bright,
In the dark of the night...
Tell me: where are you going?

CHORAGOS.
We go to that place
That you fled in such haste.

4.
Lamps glow above the tomb,
An azure womb.
The quartered body grows
Together, a hand uprose
On the altar-dressing
Comforting us, blessing.

KING.
You lie!
That hand curses with damnation
Me, you, and all generations!
Take it away!

CHORAGOS.
That statue of stone
Emerged from the pool.
It brings us cool,
All our sufferings — flown.

KING.
   The water heals! Forget!
   The spring is sacred. In it
   Rusalkas live — age on age
   It is sacred, like the dark grove.
   From its leaves she wove
   Wreaths for her gold braids —
   I know the mysteries, clear, sage —

KRASAWICA
   Appears at the chamber door.

KING.
   I hear the whisper of leaves…
   Do they betoken her arrival?
   Forget! Draw some water,
   Bend your face to the pool.

CHORAGOS.
   The statue forbids it!

KING
   I will crush the damned idol!
   He races to the back.

CHORAGOS and CHORUS OF CRIPPLES
   Block his way.
   He's a saint!

   At the rear of the throng come: King's Mother,
   King's Wife and the Princeling,
   All advancing on their knees.

KRASAWICA
   At the chamber door.
   Choose blood, choose blood,
   You alone are bold —
   Nourish yourself, with cold

    Blood; you've the lion's portion!
    On, on, forward, never back!
    To the bold act!
    To fortune!

KING
    Turns back from the depths.

KRASAWICA
    Held captive in the waves,
    I comb my hair, I wind my plaits;
    In time I cannot wind my braids;
    I can't approach you — it's far too late.
    Before I rush into the grove,
    Before I pick a spray
    Of jasmine fresh...
    I've river mud smeared in my hair.
    My hair is thick with river sand
    Farewell. They'll see me, I fear
    As I rush away
    At the flash
    Of dawn, breaking above —
    Shh... Shh... Your dogs — will they lie still?

SCENE 9.

WHISTLE.
    Water come; all to water turn,
    Repand, expand, enchanted pool,
    From wall to wall
    Bright waters, all
    Encompass, from castle door to castle door;
    Inundate the floor.

AFTERWHISTLE.
    Here they come — the knights of blood
    To wash their rusty blades.

Leaps up on a bench.
See how they're mocked by the waves!
From my perch upon this bench of wood
I'll pipe a tune; I'll pipe the dance.
And you mark time with your two hands.
Here comes the one who struck first blow.
See him bend his knife to the pool below.

RUSALKAS
Emerge from the waters.

AFTERWHISTLE.
Rusalkas in the watery mists
Play, skip about and dance.
I'll pipe whatever tune I wish —
You flub the metre with your hands!

WHISTLE.
It's not my unmelodious ear,
It's just — he is so young,
And already bloody; hence my tears.
Play on, as you've begun.

AFTERWHISTLE
Plays.

SCENE 10.

KNIGHTS
At the side doors, they lean out over the porch
And submerge their swords in the water.

KING
Turns away suddenly from the porch
And stands on the threshold of the great gates.

RUSALKAS
> *Disappear.*

KNIGHT 1.
> Look — his mouth gapes open wide.
> He chews his curse like cows the cud.

KNIGHT 2.
> Look at the wounds! They pulse with blood,
> The pristine spring envenoming.

KNIGHT 3.
> That mouth wound — that was my hacking.

KNIGHT 4.
> He's whispering a prayer, it seems.
> You hear the echo from the stone?

KNIGHT 1.
> You hear neither prayer nor groan.
> A lizard hisses at my feet;
> A reptile, crawled out from the spring.

KNIGHT 2.
> Look how the water's muddying.
> The blood has made the spring unclean.

KNIGHT 3.
> The blood you see is from my blade.
> My sword is stained with it, like rust.
> The whole sword's covered with it, just
> Like a sheath of cloth, fresh-made.

KNIGHT 4.
> Look how the skull is shining through
> The scalp — the flesh is quite off-scored.

KING.
>   I struck at his head with my sword.
>   A weighty blow — my aim was true!

KNIGHT 1.
>   Look — now he turns his eyes on us!

KING.
>   The sword is gripped tight in the fist,
>   But frozen solid is the hand.

ECHO.
>   Cursed to the soul's core. Lost, and damned.

KNIGHT 2.
>   Oh look— he stands, just as he stood
>   Before we hacked, before we crushed —
>   Your armour drips anew with blood —
>   The corpse — he's looking right at us!

KNIGHT 3.
>   Don't look at him — quick, turn away.
>   What horrid mystery is here!

KNIGHT 4.
>   Dip from the spring. Water shall cleanse
>   Us and refresh us, though he may
>   Curse all the issue of our loins.
>   Today all of the people join
>   In worship, after pilgrimage.
>   Whatever sin may chance to rage
>   Within the soul, this water clears.
>   This water sloughs off pain and fear!

KNIGHT 1.
>   O sacred pool, o sacred spring,
>   Thy waters bring us cool healing!

KING.
> O sludge — o blood — o pestilence!

ECHO.
> O soul justly sentenced!

KNIGHT 2.
> Do you see the corpse in the pool?
> The quartered limbs swim together,
> Look — the limbs unite!
> Look — hands joined, conjoined...
> Look— he rises, rises before us!
> Look how he shakes his head at us!

KNIGHT 3.
> What a hideous thing!

KNIGHT 4.
> The dam's sluicing —

KNIGHT 1.
> Look — deep below:
> The church foundations.

KNIGHT 2.
> The candles on the altar glow.

KNIGHT 3.
> He lifts his hand up to his brow.

KNIGHT 4.
> Go to him —

KNIGHT 1.
>   You go first.
> You cut him! —

KNIGHT 2.
>   I am the worse?
>   My sword weeps with a bloody dew…

KING.
>   It's me — — — — !

ECHO.
>   It's you! It's you!
>   The wind soughs through the glade.

Wind is heard.

KNIGHT 3.
>   Brother, there's rust on your blade.
>   Brother, it's time your blade to scour.
>   The moon bears hence the holy hour,
>   You shall not lift your sword today.

KNIGHT 4.
>   I cannot lift my swordblade more!
>   I need to sit beside the spring
>   And with a rock scour off the rust.
>   The rust of blood, the bloody must.
>   When swords are dipped into such sludge
>   It's like they're netted — and can't be budged!

KNIGHT 1.
>   O brother, see now my hard plight:
>   I rinsed my eyes here in the spring —
>   The blood has taken off my sight.
>   I cannot see a thing!

KNIGHT 2.
>   Brother, I scrape and scrape in vain!
>   Eternal, endless, the soul's pain;
>   Endless compulsion!
>   The bloody emulsion —

Is this rust, or blood?
I can't scrape off the glut —
My sword has been shamed!

KNIGHT 3.
See — the charmed swords wade
Through the depths — now they've made
A cross. Now they spin
In the waters — the cross
Begins
To soar — to soar aloft!

KNIGHT 4.
O look — in the depths —

KING.
Someone stretches out his hand to me...

KNIGHT 1.
Someone from the depths calls...

KING.
              Me!

KNIGHT 2.
What do you hear?

KNIGHT 3.
              Look!

KNIGHT 4.
              Look!

KING.
Someone is bending the stone foundations.
The waters slosh in wild rings.
Someone tears a sword from a hand;

It sinks unto the lowest sands...
Someone — like a corpse there stands...

KNIGHTS.
Against us!
The water in great rings is tossed.
Look at the statue!

STATUE
Emerges from the water.

KING.
He raises up an arm of stone!

STATUE
Raises its arm.

KING.
After me! Hack him to the bone!

STATUE
Disappears, as does the water.

KNIGHTS
Disappear through the doors.

WHISTLE and AFTERWHISTLE
Rush through the porch.
Rain.

KING.
After him — where did he go — — ?
They ran away,
And I'm alone!!!
Where are you? — Hey — — — The pouring rain...

KRASAWICA
> *Runs to the porch, stops, gazes toward Skałka.*

KING.
> Whence that brown-eye
> That through the courtyard flees?

KRASAWICA
> *Runs off through the courtyard.*

KING.
> She's gone...
> *He turns to the porch, walks to the back.*

SCENE 11.

KRASAWICA
> *Returns now.*

KING
> *Backs away from her into the room.*

KRASAWICA.
> 1.
> I plait the braid that's come undone
> As I enter your home;
> I hastened to you, beloved one,
> Because you are alone.
>
> 2.
> The spilt blood in the water flees
> As the waters churn;
> I plait my undone braid to please
> You — when I return...
> *She runs into the chamber.*

SCENE 12.

KING.
　Where are they...? They disappear.
　When I fix my eyes, no one is here!
　Madness? Hallucination?
　Am I spellbound?
　There's no one around!
　Hey! It's me! No one's at hand.

ECHO.
　Damned. — — —

KING.
　What is that? On the hinges — rust?
　And on the door-jambs — rot?
　The lintel creaks, the jambs near crushed
　Beneath its weight — There's rust
　On the armour where the blood spattered —

　My eyes are burning. What a clatter
　Sounds through the castle — At the gates,
　A flaming sword... Uff! Stench of plague
　Of graveyards — of decay — —
　I shall be sick with pestilence!

ECHO.
　So is it with him who relents
　Not, in his boldness.

KING.
　What — Is there someone in the gloom?
　What's moving there? — A living tomb!

Lightning.

In the lightning flash,
At times I catch
Something nearing through the blackness.

Who's there at the bridge? A
Grey-stallioned quadriga...
Hey, Porter! The portcullis!

With what effort it nears,
What a burden it bears — —
Is that porter so soundly asleep?

But the drawbridge is down,
And the gates on their own
Open wide — someone's entered these walls.
He moans, and the dogs start to howl.

But as he nears them, they crouch!
Stupid curs! Chase him out!
But they run away from him, instead.

In the yard... now he's there...
Now he's climbing the stairs...
In full armour, that silvery shines.

What a dull, heavy pace!
I can't make out his face —
It's a pillar draws close in the gloom!

Weird the plate-armour groans
As it thuds over the stones
Of the castle. Who are you!?

ECHO.
                                    The tomb.

Lightning.

KING.
> I'm greeted by flashes
> Of lightning — Who are you?
> Who so rules the thunder?
> Who sent you?
> Are you from Heaven, or Hell?

ECHO.
> The Word became flesh, to dwell
> Among us.

> *Lightning strikes.*

TOMB
> *Steps onto the porch.*

KING.
> I can't move my feet, I stand
> Paralysed; my hand —
> Is struck with palsy, and dry.

> *Reaches to his crown with both hands.*
> *Draws backwards.*

KING.
> Leave the crown! Leave it for my son!
> Leave it! I'll be cursed by the whole nation!
> *Backs toward the throne.*

TOMB
> *Enters the room, crosses it.*

> KING.
> Leave it! Not for me!
> I shall be cursed throughout the centuries!
> Leave him the crown! Unhand!

ECHO.
                         Man!

Lightning.

KING
   At the throne.
   Whence do you come? At whose command?
   Begone! Begone! I shall not bow down!
   O fame! Take my life, if you take the crown!
   Fame! God! God — be damned!

   Lightning.
   The Tomb crushes the King.

MUSIC USED IN THE EXCOMMUNICATION SCENE

ACROPOLIS

A Play in Four Acts
(1901)

THE ACTION OF THE PLAY TAKES PLACE ON WAWEL,
ON THE NIGHT OF THE GREAT RESURRECTION.

ACT I

They've gone, the Choir that chanted songs of Rome,
With deep bows toward the silver altar-tomb.
Behind them, puffs of incense wrap around
The columns in the church, twined clouds of gloom,
Fragrant, untwining in the dark anew,
To form cobwebs across the nets of piers.
They come here, on this day of Sacrifice
But once a year.
Once in a twelve-month do they gather here,
To celebrate the holy mysteries
While on each altar shine the candle-trees.
The sentence of the Word is read;
The ancient words once more are said.
Tonight the Spirit's power shall unfold:
He is to come, who vowed to save the world,
Rising anew from death, to life.
They've gone — the rings of smoke still float aloft,
The darkness grows, thick and soft,
And falls upon each pass and notch of stone
Until night reigns upon her ebon throne.
The hammers of the clock high in the tower
Strike; now begins the enchanted hour:
The bell sounds midnight.
Then do those figures clothed in silver bright

Whose backbones serve as columns — strong, if fine —
Bearing the weight of the scarecrow divine
(The silver coffin) lift it from their backs
And set aside their sacred pensum
Directly upon the altar's mensa.
The dull boom echoes through the nave.
Then with their hands they brush away
Grave-worm and dust;
They blink their eyes and gaze about:
Darkness. —
Then one young angel kisses the stole
Wrapped round his forearm,
And gathering up his broad, shining hem,
Descends.

SCENE 1.

ANGEL 1.
    Am I alone? Where are my brothers?
    The stones warp and tremble at my feet.
    Shh! Tears? Is someone sobbing? — Who's that there?
    How my hands ache! — Wherever I tread, a grave.
    Shh! — Sister, is that you? — It's you!

ANGEL 2
    Enters.
    O, how they hurt, my hands, my arms!
    To have to bear in endless pain
    That horrid coffin. The agony!

ANGEL 1.
    My arms, my hands, O how they hurt!
    But now, we're free! And once again
    I feel my youthful strength.
    Strength wells in me anew, and yet,
    Ah, oh, my arms. — —
    The coffin?

ANGEL 2.
>   Tumbled over there.
> It rests upon the altar slab.

ANGEL 1.
> Shh! — Did you hear that? — Murmurs...

ANGEL 2.
>   Sighs.

ANGEL 1.
> The wind races behind the gate
> And whistles at the western porch.

ANGEL 2.
> Oh, brother, how I love you so!
> You read my thoughts; you surely know.
> But how the pain has scarred your face!
> So great a stone, so fierce the weight!

ANGEL 1.
> To stretch my arms! — Ah, once again!
> Ah, oh, such freedom! — Shh! Someone comes.
> Is it him?

ANGEL 2.
>   It's our brother.

ANGEL 3
> *Enters.*
>   Come —
> Shall we have a look around?

ANGEL 1.
> Let's go.

ANGEL 2.
>   But what about
> Our other brother?

ANGEL 3.
> Listen: over there! That rustling comes
> From past the pier — he's kneeling there —
> He's come down.

ANGEL 2.
>   Oh, how weary!

ANGEL 4
> *Enters.*
>   I'm here.

ANGEL 1.
> And thus are gathered we four bards.
> Ah, oh! The freedom!
> And look: our figures are still young!
> My arms, stretch out!
> Stretch out, my wings!
>   That tomb! —
> I'm fed up with that gruesome thing!

CHORUS.
> Ah, oh! The freedom!

ANGEL 4.
> He's not been stingy with our chore,
> Our LORD.

ANGEL 3.
>   Our maker and tormentor.

ANGEL 2.
> How many ages has it been!
> Throughout the day to bear that weight,

Our muscles still, our breathing slight,
So to deceive the mortal eye,
And only for the briefest while
To rest, a short space, in the night.

ANGEL 1.
How many years?

ANGEL 4.
I can't recall.
Such is the predetermined role
That's fallen to us; an eternal
Sentence.

ANGEL 3.
Ah, brother! How you quake!
Atremble like a bird in pain.

ANGEL 4.
And how the pain has scarred your face,
My brother!

ANGEL 1.
Shall we go awake
The sleepers?

ANGEL 2.
Let's go.

ANGEL 1.
Come then, let us join hands!
He leads them to the font.
Let's wash our brows in holy water.

ANGEL 2.
In the name of the Father,
The Son, the Holy Ghost. Now, here,
The hour is ours. We've the world's ear!

ANGEL 3.
    Let's wash our brows in holy water.

ANGEL 1.
    And each with each, let us join hands.

ANGEL 4.
    In the name of the Father,
    The Son, the Holy Ghost.

They pause;
They make the Sign of the Cross;
They fall silent.

ANGEL 1.
    You saw Him, with His thorny crown,
    With tilted head,
    Shaded with dark locks tumbling down,
    There, past the veil.

ANGEL 2.
    I dare not tread
    Near, to behold His dying throes.
    His sighs, how awful! The blood flows
    From hands and feet and face,
    Upon the altar — there
    Where hangs the stirrup in the air.

ANGEL 3.
    When will at last His torments end?
    How sadly heaves His breast; He sighs...
    Can He hear us — so close at hand?
    Or but His own soft, painful cries?

ANGEL 4.
    D'you smell that — — still the fragrant mist
    Of incense rises like a cloud,
    And spins like cobwebs — Candles, ah!

They burn unstifled. In their glow
I sweltered as I strained below
The coffin: in my eyes they glared.

ANGEL 2.
Unblinking must you ever stare
Into their own?

ANGEL 4.
    They have no soul — —
O, listen — — That One in the crown
Moans again — — the mists rise, round
Him...

ANGEL 2.
 Stay. Let's not go near.

ANGEL 4.
       Why not?

ANGEL 3.
No, no, I can't move from this place.
His black chest, bruised, His sooty face,
The blood! Oh, all that blood, the veil
So black, too black! His panting torso,
So cruelly... No! I cannot look
Each day upon His death. O crime
Beyond all crimes, and all the more so
Recalled each day upon this altar!
I won't go! — He's dying up there,
A crown of thorns pierces His hair! —

ANGEL 4.
You're terrified?

ANGEL 3.
    I am appalled.

ANGEL 4.
> You're trembling. — — Come, forget it all!

ANGEL 3.
> Ha.

ANGEL 4.
> We've only got this single hour!

ANGEL 2.
> One hour of life within our power!

> *They pause;*
> *They are silent.*

ANGEL 3.
> What is this gnawing at our soul?

ANGEL 1.
> Once more approach this sacred bowl:
> We've blessed ourselves once, come, again,
> A second, third time, let us try:
> Evil and fear away now fly
> From us in this our living hour.

> *They approach the font.*

> In the name of the Father,
> The Son, the Holy Ghost...

ANGEL 2.
>   Deep night.

ANGEL 3.
> Father, Son, and Holy Ghost.

They make the sign of the Cross;
They pause;
They fall silent.

ANGEL 1.
    Do your arms feel their renewed might — — ?
    Blood, pulsing beneath the silver boss — — ?

ANGEL 2.
    I feel it flowing — —

ANGEL 1.
    My will — a lion's! I swell, I grow.

ANGEL 3.
    My spirit lives in this blest hour.
    My blood is flowing — Strength — and power!

ANGEL 4.
    Night has arrived — and liberty.
    I am like bronze, alive, and light,
    As if I could take wing in flight;
    I'm happy.

ANGEL 1.
    Brothers, we've set our burden by,
    Ah, oh, sweet liberty!
    You know what we must do tonight?

They stretch their wings along their arms,
Their pennons rustle and resound,
Their shadows grow like buzzing scarecrows
As they smooth their feathers with slow strokes.
They turn their eyes each unto each,
Their glowing eyes, that shine like stars,
Then they assume their wonted forms.
With resonant wings they cover all
Their bodies, then again draw close,

Shaking their silver hair; again
Close to each other do they lean,
Murmuring in fragments, frightfully.
They pause — they listen — off they go
Toward the faded memory
Of Ankwicz, whose grave lies behind
Those columns: Cupid rests resigned,
With torch extinguished, against the pole,
Still in a slumber, stony, cold.
The Angels pause, then raise their arms;
They shake the breastplate with their charms;
The statues cold blush, and grow warm.

SCENE 2.

WOMAN FROM THE ANKIEWICZ STATUARY GROUP.
  O the loss!
  The broken column!
  O tomb,
  Engulfing all the joy of life!
  O summer!
  O scythed corn,
  Who was it bound you into sheaves,
  And tossed the sheaves into the fierce gale?
  Whence blow those winds — what do they tear away?
  O tempest — horrid tornado,
  You kill! You toss upon the bed of death
  The fulness of youthful vigour!
  O death — wherever it is you tread
  You leave behind the blasted, empty cottage.
  O my tears — seething, hot,
  O the loss, the loss…

ANGEL 1.
                Quiet now — — …
  Why are you weeping?
  To the Angels:

> Shh!
>
> *To the Woman:*
> Wake up — you're dreaming —

WOMAN.
   Who are you four?

ANGEL 1.
                  The ones who question.
   Why do you weep? For whom do you sob?

WOMAN.
   With ceaseless mourning am I cursed.
   They call me holy in this burst
   Of tears and sorrow.

ANGEL 1.
                  Let it be
   Now. Tear away from this frenzy.
   Bind up your hair, and dry your eyes.

WOMAN.
   Those eyes of yours are all ablaze.

ANGEL 1.
   These eyes of mine: twin thunderbolts.
   I come to you as a herald.
   Arise!

WOMAN.
      Beneath me is the tomb.

ANGEL 1.
   Step down from it! Forget the gloom.

WOMAN.
   What? — Whence that voice? — And whence your speech?

ANGEL 1.
    Stop — Swear not, and cease to weep.

WOMAN.
    I hear something: the sickle's swish —
    The scythe a-mowing down the rye?

ANGEL 1.
    It's not that — it's my locks that sigh:
    In silver plaits they sway and brush
    Against my lily-embroidered robe
    Prismatic in the candle-glow.

WOMAN.
    And I am to forget this tomb?

ANGEL 1.
    Forget it.

WOMAN.
        Forget?! — —

ANGEL 1.
                Nor curse, nor swoon.

WOMAN.
    I'm not to weep? Not to lament?

ANGEL 1.
    Renounce not — but nor sob nor sough.

WOMAN.
    I must remember nothing — ?

ANGEL 1.
                Love!

WOMAN.
    Love? — Love —

ANGEL 1.
                       Yes, love. Expand your heart.
    Prepare you for His coming.

WOMAN.
                       Yes?
    He's coming?

ANGEL 1.
                Yes. The temple's Guest.

WOMAN.
    He's coming?! He — the sweet Desire!!

ANGEL 1.
    The Bridegroom, to the wedding feast.

WOMAN.
    For Him, the deepest love of the heart,
    For Him all youth, for Him the wreath.

ANGEL 1.
    Young maiden, in your beauty's blush,
    You will present him with the wreath.

WOMAN.
    The Bridegroom! He is coming!

    ANGEL 1.
    How beautiful you are, ablush,
    Smiling, in radiant joy awash.

WOMAN.
    I am ecstatic. —

ANGEL 1.
>Ah, how long
For jubilation did you yearn!

WOMAN.
Love! With love I live, I burn!

ANGEL 1.
Love me — Come, kiss my lips.

WOMAN.
Kiss me — Come here, and I will slip
This white shroud round us, none shall see:
You're mine, you're mine, all mine, you, me...
Come, kiss my lips.

ANGEL 1.
>My lover, mine,
Of ivory brow...

WOMAN.
>And how you shine!

ANGEL 1.
Feel you the blood pulse, warm and bright?

WOMAN.
It's night, now?

ANGEL 1.
>Yes, night.

WOMAN.
Night. — — I breathe; my breath, it gives
Forth sounds like music — life, I live!
I love — ... Let's hide in the shroud here.

ANGEL 1.
    Come, with me, into the bright air.

WOMAN.
    There's light — —

ANGEL 1.
            The stars wheeling through space!

WOMAN.
    They shine, fly, fall.

ANGEL 1.
            A stream of grace.

WOMAN.
    On me those streams are beating? Who
    Do I belong to? — Who are you??

ANGEL 1.
    Ask not.

WOMAN.
        I shouldn't?

ANGEL 1.
    Only tonight do I have life,
    And you — only for one moment
    Have waked — yet for the length
    Of its brief course — you own its strength.

WOMAN.
    I live!!

ANGEL 1.
        Come here into my arms!

WOMAN.
 Someone whispers — — can you hear it?

ANGEL 1.
 Other spirits.

WOMAN.
 Spirits? —

ANGEL 1.
 Alive, like you and me.

WOMAN.
 Like you and me... Are they happy?
 Happy... This word seems to remind
 Me of... Someone was with me.

ANGEL 1.
 It was I.

WOMAN.
 No, someone else, before despair,
 When I was just becoming sad,
 A lowered torch, sputtering... there...
 In comfort he raised up his hand.
 Someone is speaking. Who speaks? Who?

ANGEL 1.
 An echo.

WOMAN.
 Forget? — I have forgotten. — Still
 Someone was with me, when I stood
 On that pedestal,
 And now I simply can't recall.
 With Cupid's dart you've drawn my blood.

ANGEL 1
>Smooths her forehead with his hand.
>Don't think about it.

They move beyond the columns.

SCENE 3.

ANGEL 2
>*To the Cupid from the Ankwicz monument:*
>Toss away that smouldering torch.
>Get up — arise.

CUPID FROM THE ANKWICZ MONUMENT.
>A spell?

ANGEL 2.
>Arise.
>A spell! Throw down that torch, my child.
>Jump down from there, boy, make it quick.

CUPID.
>And you — who are you?

ANGEL 2.
>A happy spirit.
>A happy soul, a spirit free.

CUPID.
>Free?

ANGEL 2.
>In liberty. As you may be!

CUPID.
>In liberty! — Apollo cast me in this spell...
>Released now? By Apollo's will?

ANGEL 2.
> This moment's blessed. Arise, and stand!

CUPID.
> I am so called... by whose command?

ANGEL 2.
> You're not commanded.

CUPID.
>   But I'm called!
> I hear the call!

ANGEL 2.
>   Those who hear, shall
> Arise.

CUPID
> *Arises.*

ANGEL 2.
>   Step down.

CUPID
> *Descends.*
>   I touch the earth!
> Ah — what is this?

ANGEL 2.
>   A sort of birth.

CUPID.
> I want to stretch my wings and fly
> And run, like eagles, through the sky.
> What is this shivering?

ANGEL 2.
>   That's life.

CUPID.
    Is it night?

ANGEL 2.
               Yes. — But with the dawn,
    This our brief freedom will be gone.

CUPID.
    I live!

ANGEL 2.
        Now you may run, small friend!

CUPID.
    I live! — I feel the flood of strength!
    Looks back at the monument.
    And where is she, who was with me?

ANGEL 2.
    Forget her, and the past, my sweet.
    Look in my eyes, new-fledged eaglet.
    You see me as a living maid?
    My heart is beating — does yours beat?

CUPID.
    So long immobile, and afraid...
    Yes, — yes — I have a beating heart,
    My heart beats, my lungs breathe and fill —
    I live! — And you, so beautiful!

ANGEL 2.
    Come near, embrace me —

CUPID.
                   What a sound,
    The shining robes that spill around
    Your body.

ANGEL 2.
>   I am richly clad.
> Come, hug me round my waist, dear lad.
> I want to feel your two hands go
> About my breasts, about my face.

CUPID.
> In both your eyes, living flames
> Burn; in both your eyes a fire glows.

ANGEL 2.
> I love. —

CUPID.
>   You lily! Beautiful!
> Your silver robes rustle and sing —
> What's hidden beneath those shining things?

ANGEL 2.
> Your torso is bare;
> Come, pull me close, it's there
> I would repose, my darling boy;
> In your eyes shines a sun of joy!

CUPID.
> Apollo's gift, the ray you see;
> By his grace, he acknowledged me
> His son; this ray is his bestowed boon.
> But you — have wakened me from stone.

ANGEL 2.
> This moment shall be paradise
> Because of you.

CUPID.
>   But who are they?

ANGEL 2.
   Those there? Beyond the column grey?

CUPID.
   Those walking there — and who is she?

ANGEL 2.
   A haunted lover.

CUPID.
              Her I knew.

ANGEL 2.
   You knew her? Ah, but now, let that go!

CUPID.
   They walk just like somnambulists.

ANGEL 2.
   A lover, and her bridegroom fair;
   Like us, another loving pair.

CUPID.
   Like us?! — His mistress?!

ANGEL 2.
   As you are mine, so she is his.
   Oh come now — don't look there — come, with me.

CUPID.
   You love. —

ANGEL 2.
              I love, and secretly
   I'll give you love in the dark night.
   You're mine.

CUPID.
                I'm yours, and you are mine.
Unloose, and lay your robes aside.

ANGEL 2.
It's armour. I'm a virgin maid.

CUPID.
You blush.

ANGEL 2.
                Love me.

CUPID.
                I do.

ANGEL.
I belong to you.

They move behind the columns.

SCENE 4.

LADY DROM THE SKOTNICKI MONUMENT
   To the Angels who are leading her:
   Where are you leading me?

ANGEL 3.
                Into the light.

LADY.
Where are you leading me?

ANGEL 3.
                Into the dawn.

LADY.
> Who are you?

ANGEL 4.
> We're moving on —

ANGEL 3.
> To wake those who sleep this night.

LADY.
> It's not worth the trouble.
> This grave encloses me.
> This slab's imposed on me.

ANGEL 3.
> You were his wife?

LADY.
> I don't recall. No, not his wife.

ANGEL 4.
> You knew him?

LADY.
> I don't know — I prayed,
> And took my lyre,
> And on my lyre I played,
> And had my two arms splayed
> In despair.

ANGEL 3.
> Your hands — unbind.

LADY.
> Unbind...

ANGEL 4.
> Your fingers untwine.

LADY.
And the pain, that I bear in my breast?

ANGEL 3.
Here, wipe your brow. Now put to rest
Your pain. What else do you recall?

ANGEL 4.
Were you ever happy?

LADY.
You ask me was I ever happy?
I don't know. I know that I grew sad.

ANGEL 3.
Why?

LADY.
    I stood on that slab.

ANGEL 4.
And now you've stepped down from that grave.

LADY.
How long do I have?
A moment mere?

ANGEL 3.
Yes, for this hour here,
You are awake.

LADY.
    I feel the stream
Of blood as it flows through my arms.
I was in pain — From that bad dream
You wake me — ?

ANGEL 4.
>I do. Forget your harms,
Your pain.

LADY.
>This is no cruel sleight?

ANGEL 3.
No trick. You live.

LADY.
>I live tonight!

ANGEL 4.
Throw off the veil that hides your face
And you shall see us living, all
About this church, which your stone pall
Hid from your eyes. But lift your palm
To your forehead.

LADY.
>You have the shape
Of Angels.

ANGEL 3.
I am young and strong.
Come with me.

LADY.
>I shall go along
With you!

ANGEL 3.
And all your mourning cease.

LADY.
You lead me where?

ANGEL 3.
>To a wedding feast!

LADY.
Upon your forehead three stars shine.

ANGEL 3.
Stars — The Spirit's light is mine!

LADY.
I hear. —

ANGEL 3.
>He goes with me who heeds;
Who hears, will go along with me!
Into the glow, into the dawn,
Of which we are the harbingers.

LADY.
They do not lie, these words of yours?
Your words are truth?

ANGEL 3.
>My words are might!
My words steadfast, my body, bronze
And blood, alive for this one night.
Like you, I rose and live. Cast away
All sad rememberings, and be gay.
Forget!

LADY.
>Me? I should be gay?
Where is the lute I used to play?

ANGEL 3.
You need no lute now. If you will,
Echoes shall sing back what you trill.
Just listen: there — a bird in flight,

    And tree limbs soughing in the night.
    You hear the wind sigh from the fields?

LADY.
    That light; it shivers as it glows.
    And who are they?

ANGEL 3.
          They're living souls.

LADY.
    They're lovers?

ANGEL 3.
          They are happy beings.

LADY.
    Pointing at the sarcophagus of King Władysław Jagiełło.
    And who is he?

ANGEL 3.
          He was a king.
    He fell asleep, and sleeps like stone.
    To me he is unknown.

LADY.
    He fell asleep a patriarch,
    Buried with pomp, respect and praise.
    I knew him.

ANGEL 3.
          You knew him?

LADY.
                  From tales.
    Before you, beauteous one, my heart
    Transfixed with the shaft of your dart
    Of love and of desire, I did.

ANGEL 3.
> You knew him? — Now, don't think of it.

They pass beyond the columns.

SCENE 5.

ANGEL 1.
> Go wake her, in that chapel over there.
> Her, lost in thought.

ANGEL 4.
> Are you alone?

ANGEL 1.
> I am.

ANGEL 4.
> Your body, then, unstained, as e'er
> It was?

ANGEL 1.
> Look in my eyes. You see? Without blame
> Am I. Look at my robes, and see:
> Lilies unblemished, virgin purity.

ANGEL 4.
> Give me your hand.

ANGEL 1.
> Now go in peace!

SCENE 6.

ANGEL 1.
How to forsake this love? How may I cease?
I tore myself away from her sweet face…
I made a vow. — How may I keep it now?
As lust still pulls me close to the abyss?
I love — I run — I love, I want, in vain
I would extinguish the consuming flame
That burns inside my heart. I can't make out
What this lust is — yet I search for her — in shame.
She comes.—

SCENE 7.

*CUPID and the WOMAN
    Enter.*

WOMAN.
Where is my love?

CUPID.
He's run away?
Why do you seek him, sad, like this?
Why do you remember him, his kiss?

WOMAN.
I don't remember his kiss.
But he kissed me.

CUPID.
And how? Like this?
Kisses her.
Incline your head. Give me your lips.

WOMAN.
That's how he kissed me.

CUPID.
      Kiss again.

WOMAN.
 O yes, O yes — longer this time.
 Come with me now — you be mine.
 This shroud of mine will screen our love.
 Come into this dark alcove.
 Love.

CUPID.
  I love.

ANGEL 1.
 Peering from behind a column.
     False heart!

CUPID.
      Remember?

WOMAN.
 I can remember nothing.

CUPID.
       Where
 Shall we take our repose, my dear?

WOMAN.
 We're like two homeless beings.

CUPID.
       Here,
 Come make your home in my embrace.
 O hug me close! Hug me! Caress.

WOMAN.
 Give me your lips. —

CUPID.
>   Here is our home.

WOMAN.
> But not too boldly — I am pure.

CUPID.
> It's mine you are.

WOMAN.
>   You are my dear
> Young boy — You are my favourite.

CUPID.
> Love me; around you I will plait
> A robe of roses torn from tombs
> And from the altar there on high
> I'll wind a lover's rosary,
> My lady.

WOMAN.
> You my dearest one.

SCENE 8.

ANGEL 4
> Leading *the figure of Time from out the Jagiellonian chapel*.
> Now, old man, throw away your scythe.

ANGEL 1
> *Stepping down.*
> No, let him keep it.

TEMPUS.
>   Who is there?

ANGEL 4.
No one. There is nobody here.
They went on, further down the nave.

TEMPUS.
What would you have me do?

ANGEL 4.
      Cast down
That scythe.

TEMPUS.
How can I? Into this my hand
It was entrusted, by command.
Hold it I must.

ANGEL 4.
    Just a short while.

TEMPUS.
The wheels of time would then stand still.

ANGEL 4.
And so they shall.

TEMPUS.
    What do I hear?

ANGEL 4.
The wheels of time will cease their chase.

TEPMPUS.
And peace will reign for a short space.

ANGEL 4.
There's healing in the shortest respite.
For one night only — just one night.
The first hour strikes. Rise up, alive,

    And cast away from you that scythe.
    Command the wheels of time stand still.
    A short peace soothes the gravest ill.

TEMPUS
    Sets aside his scythe.
    Age upon century is hurled
    Into the yawning abyss.
    A thousand years fly by like this —
    Behold: I've stopped the spinning world.

ANGEL 4.
    Live. —

TEMPUS.
            The pain of labour disappears,
    And with it, faded all my fears.
    My head no longer throbs with pain;
    My arm relaxes from the strain
    Of watchfulness; a peace now reigns
    Within my mind. Ah, I feel delight!
    I'm strong, and light — I might take flight!
    And so I shall! I'm young and bold;
    I'll reclaim my youth, though I be old.
    I feel the blood pulse through my veins;
    I live, — blood feeds my strength again!
    Listen! — Let's take horse, you and I,
    Escape, over those meadows, to fly
    Toward the mountains, — past the river.

ANGEL 4.
    You must return before a sliver
    Of dawn cuts the east.

TEMPUS.
                The new day's light
    Is yet afar. It's night, starlit night.
    Let's go — come — come — let's both take flight.

ANGEL 4.
　　How will you leave?

TEMPUS.
　　　　　　　　Who's got the key?

ANGEL 4.
　　To the cathedral door? Not me.

TEMPUS.
　　Who has it then, if it's not you?

ANGEL 4.
　　The doors are locked from the outside.
　　We have no key. You must abide
　　Here, in the church.

TEMPUS.
　　　　　　　　I don't want to!
　　I'll break the doors down, might and main!

ANGEL 4.
　　With what?

TEMPUS.
　　　　I'll take up my scythe again…

ANGEL 4.
　　Don't touch it!

TEMPUS.
　　　　　　Don't force me to stay.

ANGEL 1.
　　I'll go.

TEMPUS.
>   We will both go away,
> Into the wide world.

ANGEL 1.
>   Yes! To horse!
> I'll go with you!

TEMPUS.
>   Here, you go first!
> Into the bright, the starlit night.
> See? I break the door down with my scythe.

He opens the heavy doors with his scythe.
The clear moonlight enters.

> Into the wide world! In my hand
> Is might! And now the scythe I spurn.
> Goodbye, dark walls! I shall return!!

He tosses aside his scythe
and runs out with Angel 1.

ANGEL 4
> *Retreats beyond the columns.*

SCENE 9.

CLIO FROM THE SOŁTYK MONUMENT.
> This book, my care from age on age.

MAIDEN FROM THE SOŁTYK MONUMENT.
> What profits you its marble page?
> Does it arouse faith in your breast?

CLIO.
>It preserves ancient histories
>And memories
>Of even older acts and gestes.

MAIDEN.
>But faith?

CLIO.
>Is an unstable thing.

MAIDEN.
>Toss it aside.

CLIO.
>The book?

MAIDEN.
>It brings
>You sadness, only. Toss it away,
>And with it, sadness — and be gay!
>Toss it away, embrace me here,
>About my waist, a sister dear —
>Be you the loving soul, with whom
>I'll spend this night alive. Why do
>You care for others' pains and woes;
>Why should you set your tears aflow
>For aches in which you have no part?
>In vain you nurse that breaking heart!
>No, sister. Think no more of that.
>Many long hours have I sat
>In deep thought of myself, and you,
>Wondering: what on earth have we to do
>With brooding, weeping, and with mourning,
>Slaves to a sorrow vain, and scorning
>Freshness, and joy! Come, sister, friend,
>Bring book and mourning to an end.

We'll live our own lives! Come, you'll see —
Joyful, forgetful, happy! Free!

CLIO.
　　I can be joyful?

MAIDEN.
　　　　　　　You shall be,
　　For this one night; heed only me —
　　Put down the book! And feel the might
　　Of this holy, forgetful night.

CLIO.
　　My sister, you are made of stone.

MAIDEN.
　　Ah, in these veins of marble flows
　　Warm blood! I am alive!! With me,
　　Come! Into the sanctuary.
　　Like goddesses, like dryads young,
　　Come, fill with life your marble lungs!
　　Be sad no more, but live! — Be!! Be!!

CLIO.
　　I spurn you, book — get you behind
　　Me, you torturer of my mind,
　　Spoiler of heart-springs,
　　Overtight bindings!

MAIDEN.
　　　　　　　　Forget!

CLIO.
　　The fog lifts from before my eyes,
　　The clouds of thought disperse, bright rays
　　Of sunlight through my pupils pour!
　　Unconscious, I recall no more!

MAIDEN.
    And I shall not remind you.

A silent pause.
They look towards the chapel on the Sołtyk tomb.

CLIO.
                    And she?

MAIDEN.
    She hasn't moved. She is still cold.
    The lid in both her hands she holds;
    Her back to us, fixed is her gaze
    Upon another world, her eyes
    Fixed on that eagle's, which she sounds
    And holds the eagle's soul spellbound.
    The eagle lifts a sword on high —
    We have to wake her.

CLIO.
                    Pass her by —
    She'd drop the lid upon the bird.

MAIDEN.
    You're sad again? Once more you're stirred
    By the old woe. You're mourning still?

CLIO.
    I'll mourn until
    I am no more.

MAIDEN.
    Chase those thoughts away.

CLIO.
    No less than me, you're sunk in thought.
    This carefree smile's a role you play
    To lead me astray.

MAIDEN.
    I'm not pretending anything.
    I wish to be rid of mourning.
    Laugh a bit! Smile! I'm just a girl.
    I'm young. I want to love!

CLIO.
                Absurd!

MAIDEN.
    True love, they say, is pure as gold.
    That's true, no?

CLIO.
                Depends on the soul.
    The truth for each is different.
    And there are those that lie.

MAIDEN.
    Lie? Why?

CLIO.
    Desire holds them pent.

MAIDEN
    Bows her head, deep in thought.

CLIO.
    The door's open. The hasps are burst.

MAIDEN.
    Fresh air. Should it blow through the tombs,
    The dead — will they arise anew?

CLIO.
    No. The dead do not come back to life.
    When one lifespan has been run through,
    New life begins. A grain falls, dies,

And from it, a new bloom arises,
So is it with them. Flesh to dust:
These tombs are filled with bones and must.
And none among them has the strength
To rise anew, and live again.
We are the only immortals,
In spirit. —

MAIDEN.
     What about their souls?
Do they not live?

CLIO.
    They do.

MAIDEN.
      And where?

CLIO.
The stains of sin they must wash fair
Before they enter Paradise.

MAIDEN.
And what to them is Paradise?

CLIO.
It's a return unto a place
Where into spirits of greater might
They are transformed. Others again
Are born among the living, to lead
Their nation, as if to a bride.
In this manner, such souls are healed.

MAIDEN.
And what about those that are freed?

CLIO.
>	Such elevated spirits shine
>	Aloft, on other worlds, far hence.

MAIDEN.
>	Shall they return?

CLIO.
>	 Yes, but not soon.
>	After a long time. Ages hence.
>	When all is changed, and these strong monuments
>	Are crumbled into ruin.

MAIDEN.
>	We, ruins!

CLIO.
>	 Ah, sister: then the Furies
>	Will squat among the splintered stones.

MAIDEN.
>	Speak not of furies. I'm afraid!

CLIO.
>	Whole ages first must pass away
>	Before those spirits will return.
>	Ages upon age.

MAIDEN.
>	 Yes, I know.
>	Speak no more of it.

CLIO.
>	 You know?
>	Here, take my hand then, and let's go
>	Into the light
>	To witness the miracle tonight.

MAIDEN.
> What miracle?

CLIO.
> Why, the Lord
> Comes dressed as King, to be adored.
> His flashing raiment shines of gold,
> A banner in His hand he holds —
> And by His sacred crown of thorns
> He leads men's sinful souls, reborn
> To life, redeemed, into this church!

MAIDEN.
> Redeemed? And resurrected!?!

CLIO.
> Spirits, resurrected!

MAIDEN.
> I know. — He'll send those living souls
> Among the living!—

CLIO.
> Reborn to life!
> He'll send them into war, and strife.
> He has a scale too: on each plate
> He'll place each soul and judge her fate,
> Here at this altar.

MAIDEN.
> Shh! Sister, who made
> That noise?

CLIO.
> Nothing but shades.
> The wind, the clouds it chases
> Through the sky. Nought else. A star.

Come with me, step into these rays;
It's warm here, come and bathe with me.

MAIDEN.
Sister: that beautiful one there. Who is he?

CLIO.
A knight.

MAIDEN.
Oh, wake him, for me! For
I've fallen in love!

CLIO.
Give him a rap
On his breastplate. Farewell, sister, I go.

MAIDEN.
With him I remain, even so.
This air, so fresh, and so intense,
It's sharpened each and every sense:
I feel my heart beat, with the rush
Of blood, and love — I love him thus...
But who are they?

CLIO.
They guard the hoard
Of a great soul.

MAIDEN.
Look, sister, see!
The knight, he heeds your every word!

CLIO.
Give him a rap on his breastplate.
Again — until at last he wakes.

MAIDEN.
I love him so, my heart it breaks!

CLIO
Goes off past the gates.

SCENE 10.

MAIDEN
Knocks at the breastplate resting at the feet of the statue.
Darling.

STATUE OF WŁODZIMIERZ POTOCKI.
Glory?!

MAIDEN.
Nor glory, nor fame.
Delight, desire, sensual game.
And I have come to you tonight,
A girl, to share in love's delight.
Come with me, dear.

WŁODZIMIERZ.
You lead to war?!

MAIDEN.
Unbuckle, and lay aside your sword,
And set it down by your breastplate.
Come down.

WŁODZIMIERZ.
Where are my boys? My mates?!

MAIDEN.
What boys? Only you and I are here.
I've come, because I love you, dear.
And you? —

WŁODZIMIERZ.
I need to save the nation from
A tyrant!

MAIDEN.
What tyrant? There's no such one
Here about. — You're mistaken.
Lean down — and when you've taken
A look around, you'll see:
There's no one else here but me,
Eyes locked on you. Come down.

WŁODZIMIERZ.
You, love me?

MAIDEN.
Come down.

WŁODZIMIERZ
Jumps down.
There now. I'm at your side.

MAIDEN.
Well? You see I haven't lied?
Am I pretty?

WŁODZIMIERZ.
Upon my breast you curl;
You're pliant — like a love-struck girl.

MAIDEN.
And that's because I love you, knight.

WŁODZIMIERZ.
You recall —

MAIDEN.
Set down your sword.

WŁODZIMIERZ.
                              A fight!
   There was to be a battle, sure?

MAIDEN
   With a smile.
   No — the pacts all signed; peace is secured.

WŁODZIMIERZ.
   You smile. You laugh, you grin?

MAIDEN.
   I want you. I am without sin.
   You're beautiful.

WŁODZIMIERZ.
                  And you — gorgeous.

MAIDEN.
   Thus love now takes control of us.
   Come, kiss me — take me in your arms.
   Feel my desire, how my blood warms
   For you; I long for your caress.
   Love me — all else is nothingness.
   Love me.

WŁODZIMIERZ.
                  I must forget.

MAIDEN.
   Forget, then.

WŁODZIMIERZ.
                  So I shall, my pet.
   No — I must regain a clear head... wait...

MAIDEN.
   Your sword. Set it by the breastplate.

WŁODZIMIERZ.
    Cast it aside?

MAIDEN.
                It's useless now
    That we're to exchange lover's vows.
    You want me?

WŁODZIMIERZ.
                I kiss… You're in my arms.

MAIDEN.
    I love you! —

WŁODZIMIERZ.
                I feel your blood. It's warm!
    With me! Come with me, girl.

MAIDEN.
                        One hour
    Is all we have for life and love;
    One hour to feel the coursing blood.

WŁODZIMIERZ.
    I was an ensign in the war.

MAIDEN.
    My darling hero's what you are.

WŁODZIMIERZ.
    What's that? Someone's playing a lyre?
    Whence comes that melody?

MAIDEN.
               Look here,
    At me. — — Shh — Love me, but quiet!
    Come to these shadows — step aside.

I'll take you softly in my arms,
My lover — my true love alone!

WŁODZIMIERZ.
Shh! — you hear the organ's tones?
There in the nave I hear someone hover.

MAIDEN.
With my two hands your eyes I'll cover.
Now, come with me.

WŁODZIMIERZ.
There?

MAIDEN.
There in the dark chapel, my lover…

They go off.

ACT II

DRAMATIS PERSONAE:

PRIAM
HECUBA
PARIS otherwise ALEXANDER
HELEN
HECTOR
ANDROMACHE
CASSANDRA
POLYXENA
PIKEMEN
A PAGE

On the Scaean donjons, battlements, walls
Now report the armoured guards;

On their swords and pikes leaning, they're posted; all
Man this castle, that Kraków wards.

The kings are abed, and their daughters as well,
All the governors fast asleep;
Yet the challenge rings out from their liege sentinels
Who watch over the Cracovian keep.

It's deep night in the town. The Skamander reflects
From the Vistulan waves as they race;
But the sword is gripped fast in the hand that protects,
Though foreboding faint tinges the voice.

Now they look toward the corbel, and now the glacis,
Has the softly sung watch-call been heard?
It's the great hero Hector that they long to see,
It's their leader they long for, their lord.

SCENE 1.

GUARDSMAN 1.
   Be watchful.

GUARDSMAN 1.
         Be watchful.

VOICE.
               God yield
   Good night.

PAGE.
         An echo from the field.
From Skamander's banks the echo flies,
Flags at the city walls, and dies.

GUARDSMAN 1.
> A spy's been caught; have you heard tell?
> He struck the great bell with his wing,
> And thus into our toils he fell.

GUARDSMAN 2.
> Who was this spy?

PAGE.
>   A crow.

GUARDSMAN 2.
>   Flying
> From afar?

PAGE.
>   A bird of grey,
> Who'd snoop out what we have to say;
> He stooped, and, netted —

GUARDSMAN 1.
>   — now lies dead.
> Bloodied, he struggled at the snare,
> And just bled more, till out he bled.

GUARDSMAN 2.
> Now let him our deep secrets share!

PAGE.
> Look there — a spider spins his skein
> From clocktower to campanile,
> And thence unto the temple's spire.

GUARDSMAN 1.
> I see it. Every night, the same.

GUARDSMAN 2.
> And of his toil he'll never tire.

PAGE.
>Look: these two violets are the first
>That bloomed this year on the counterscarp.

GUARDSMAN 1.
>You plucked them?

GUARDSMAN 2.
>>For our two sweethearts.

PAGE.
>You're right. These flowers shall be hers
>When she comes here in search of him
>Fresh from the bed. With them,
>I'll cheer their eyes.

GUARDSMAN 1.
>This morning, the last floes of ice
>Slid down the river, over there.

GUARDSMAN 2.
>Toward the side of Sandomierz.

GUARDSMAN 1.
>Will Rhesus and his horse arrive
>On time? So much depends on them.
>The sight of those fresh horsemen
>Our flagging troops' fire would revive.

PAGE.
>You've heard about the last dictum
>of the Great King?

GUARDSMAN 2.
>>Atreides?

GUARDSMAN 1.
  The lynx with the itch for ladies
  Unscratchable?

PAGE.
            The very one.
  It seems the object of his lust
  Is now Pelides' girl, and he,
  They say, will take her. For he must.

GUARDSMAN 2.
  And how's that make Achilles feel?

PAGE.
  It's made him furious as a beast.
  He said he's laying down his arms.

GUARDSMAN 1.
  And our king's oldest son, then? He's
  Angry?

PAGE.
      Angry, and mocking...

GUARDSMAN 2.
                Hush! no more.
  Here come princeling and paramour.

GUARDSMAN 1.
  Tfu! The two canoodling pets!
  Always wrapped in each other's arms...

PAGE.
  You think he's tiring of her charms?
  Ha! Day by day Helen gets
  More gorgeous, more exciting, her
  Gestures and words enrapture
  Him more; one look: you'll understand;

> One look's enough to fire each man
> With lust; thus she prevails, she captures
> Each living male — just look...

PARIS and HELEN
> *Cross in an embrace.*

PAGE
> *Gives them the violets.*
>
> Fresh blooms...

PARIS and HELEN
> *Smile,*
> *Take the flowers,*
> *Exeunt.*

PAGE.
> They only stir to change bedrooms.

SCENE 2.

GUARDSMAN 1.
> Is that a man? I strive to place
> Him in my bestiary; he won't fit.

GUARDSMAN 2.
> Him? A lover he, our brave kinglet.
> You'd like to have so smooth a face!

GUARDSMAN 1.
> I'd like to be in his smooth place,
> With that smooth girl. Speaking of looks,
> Would you not say our Hector's eyes
> Flash thunderbolts of jealousy
> To see them pet so languidly
> While he's battling the enemy?
> Knowing the while his death is nigh?

GUARDSMAN 2.
   He's coming. It's his watch.

GUARDSMAN 1.
               Password!

HECTOR
   Enters.
   Glory to Ilium!

GUARDSMAN 2.
              Pass, my lord.

A flock of crows start up and fly off from the top of the clock tower;
They fly toward the city, screeching.

HECTOR.
   There's omens in those foul cackles.
   Portending what? When I shall fall?

GUARDSMAN 1.
   Never!

GUARDSMAN 2.
       Never!

HECTOR.
              Who can hold back
   The wheels of fate, of destiny?
   I fight, shall fight, shall die. That's all.
   Where is the girl that prophesies?

GUARDSMAN 1.
   You wish to see her?

HECTOR.
            I desire
   Not, what I know already.

GUARDSMAN 2.
           There:
   She's kept in that tower.

HECTOR.
           And where
   The lovers?

GUARDSMAN 2.
           Seeking a couch.

GUARDSMAN 1.
   They passed from the arcades, and out.

HECTOR.
   Where?

GUARDSMAN 2.
      Back to the castle.

HECTOR.
                Seems like love
   Does not yet bore them. Just like me
   And fighting. I can't get enough.

PAGE
   Enters.
   The king is up, as is the queen.
   They've sent me here to spread divans
   At the Scaean Gate.

HECTOR.
           Go on,
   Then tell them we await them here.

SERVANTS
   Bring forth some rugs and spread them about
   After which they go off.

SCENE 3.

PRIAM.
   My son, I've got some splendid news!
   It seems Achilles now refuses
   The fight!

HECTOR.
              And this should make me glad?
   Why?

PRIAM.
      Rejoice! For now, nothing bad
   Can happen to you. Your life is saved!

HECTOR.
   While I've been hoping for the grave.

PRIAM.
   O son! My only source of pride,
   My sure defence! You'd leave your bride
   Who loves you so? You'd flee your son,
   And from us two, declining, run,
   Abandoning us? Then we are lost!
   We all, and all of Ilium!

HECTOR.
   Such is my will. To fight!

PRIAM.
                     For us?
   Your city?

HECTOR.
        Who are you, that I must
   Weigh my honour and my strength
   On one dish of the balance, against —
   What? That simpering boy who dresses

In flounces, and pomades his tresses,
To please the woman that he filched?
Seek you your pride among that ilk.

PRIAM.
You have a wife.

HECTOR.
I leave you a son.
When my hour strikes, I'm gladly gone.

PRIAM.
What is it that constrains you so?
What damned idea impels you to go?

HECTOR.
My soul!

PRIAM.
He rears up thus against his father,
Seeking to terrify, to make totter
The old man in me. O, my son,
I'll remain here when you are gone,
With my old age. You are abused,
By fame and greatness. You're being used!

HECTOR.
Fame is my father, if I must choose.
And here I stand him to defend.
You gave me life — for that I owe
Respect, but do not hold me in such low
Esteem, that I so boldly impart
To you, the pain that's in my heart.

PRIAM.
I wanted you as king to reign!

HECTOR.
    And I that you should king remain.

PRIAM.
    You say that we are petty folk,
    Too slight to measure up to you.
    You are too proud.

HEKTOR.
              Father, what I do
    I do by my own power, for my own sake.
    I fight, because war is my yoke,
    War is my law, war in defence
    Of all that's holy. Should I endure,
    Then my salvation is secured.

PRIAM.
    What is this holiness of which you speak?

HECTOR.
    Just this, the very remembrance
    Of which shoots fire through all my veins,
    Purging and cleansing my conscience
    To an eternal burnish: Ilium —
    Living, and ageless.

PRIAM.
              My son,
    You're mother is asleep.

HECTOR.
              The sleepy,
    Misty air's overcome her.

PRIAM.
              She's drunk deeply
    Of air, and age.

HECTOR.
                   And I meanwhile
    Will go to see my wife. Farewell.

PRIAM.
    Yes. Go and see your child.
    Where's Paris?

HECTOR.
                You mean Alexander?
    He and his love, as I've heard tell
    Traipsed here not long ago. They'll wander
    Back, before long. And now, goodbye.
    Exits toward the palace.

SCENE 4.

PRIAM.
    Listen: how sweet the carillons
    Sing from the city's towers.
    Hey! Listen — Wake up, woman.
    You love to hear the hours
    Play — Wake up.

HECUBA.
    I was just dreaming of the time
    Our firstborn son first saw the light;
    So small... I held him in these hands of mine,
    And now, he is a knight!

PRIAM.
    A knight in pain. Prey of some might
    That fills him with fire;
    And in his heart, such a desire.
    But that heart of his is locked up tight
    And none can gain admittance there.

HECUBA.
But, he's the best knight?

PRIAM.
              The only one.

HECUBA.
I remember him... small, our firstborn son,
Here at my side, his mother's side;
Long were the hours that he played,
Laughing and babbling... a little child...

PRIAM.
He's grown to be... a fearsome man.
In manliness arrayed;
He towers over all our sons,
In spirit...

HECUBA.
    So many battles won,
Is it not true? He always wins,
He conquers every battlefield;
His very voice makes foemen yield;
Is it not true? You're proud of him?

PRIAM.
By the sword he lives, by the sword he'll die.

HECUBA.
He knows this?

PRIAM.
            Yes. He's quite aware.

HECUBA.
And does he despair?

PRIAM.
>He mentioned something. But I heard not,
>My mind wrapped up in other thought.
>I dreamt, and heard not.

HECUBA.
>   Where did he go?

PRIAM.
>To see his wife.

HECUBA.
>   I knew it, even so!
>A living heart beats in his breast.

PARIS and HELEN
>*Enter.*

PAGE
>*Before them.*
>There they are: talking, taking their rest.

HELEN.
>What do they say? They speak of me?

PAGE.
>They muse on Hector, so it seems.

HELEN.
>Nothing of me?

PAGE.
>   Perhaps, in thought,
>They muse of you; of Hector they talk.

PARIS.
>Have the musicians play something.
>The old folks must share our happiness.

HELEN.
We'll have some music.

PARIS.
                        The lutenists.

HELEN.
The lute that's strung with golden strings —
Have them bring that one, with pearl inlays.

MUSICIANS
   Enter.

PARIS.
Did you see? Today I bear the fleece.

HELEN.
The golden fleece! But the sceptre — when?

PARIS.
Patience.

HELEN.
       Till Hector's dead. And then,
The throne is yours. It is your right?

PARIS.
Not for the taking.

HELEN.
                Just because
You're lazy! In your very own cause!
Too lazy to take what's your own.
Your father would gladly cast off the throne —
Speak with your parents.

PARIS.
                        What would I do
With kingship? When I have all, in you.

HELEN.
    You'll be above all men.

PARIS.
                  So what?
When I behold you, my sole thought
Is lovemaking.

HELEN.
                Am I a stable mare?
I was a queen once, in Sparta, where...

PARIS.
    Speak not of that, just say to me
    "I love you."

HELEN.
                I love you. Maybe.

PARIS.
    Come on, now say, "Let's go to bed."

HELEN.
    Let's go.

PARIS.
       Say one last thing: "I long
For nothing more than lovemaking."

HELEN.
    I want to make love.

PARIS.
                Do you hear the song?

HELEN.
Yes.

PARIS.
The lute our lullaby will sing.

Music.

SONG.

PAGE.
Hey sweet maiden, fairest rose,
Give me of your garland fair.

POLYXENA.
Seated at Hecuba's feet.
Hey there page-boy, here you go:
A feather to stick in your hair.
     Rom tana, rom dyna.

PAGE.
Hey sweet maiden, fairest rose,
Who will raise your bridal veil?

POLYXENA.
Mind your holy water pail;
The priest will tweak you by the nose!
     Rom tana, rom dyna.

PAGE.
Hey sweet maiden, what is this?
You're tied to mummy's apron-bow.

POLYXENA.
And all you want from me's a kiss,
Whether I want it too, or no.
     Rom tana, rom dyna.

PAGE.
> That I would, but if you decline,
> There's plenty other maidens round.

POLYXENA.
> Fondle your lute. I like it fine,
> I'll stay by mummy, safe and sound.
> > Rom tana, rom dyna.

Music.

HELEN.
> The old ones are asleep.

PARIS.
> > They are.

HELEN.
> Above the earth, the stars shine bright.
> Below, we shine like earthly stars.

PARIS.
> Time has stood still.

HELEN.
> > Still is the night.

PARIS.
> Just listen to the old man snore!
> I won't agree to growing old.
> I want to die young.

HELEN.
> I don't want to lose my beauty.

PARIS.
> You're still beautiful. Embrace me.

HELEN.
>   I'm ravenous for your embraces.
>   For them, I forth from Sparta stole,
>   For them, the whole of Sparta mourns.
>   Ungovernable desire tore
>   Me from my home and here to you.
>   These are the actions of a whore —
>   I know — evil, the things I do;
>   And yet I love; yet I desire.

PARIS.
>   My life is sunk in yours, entire.
>   Let's go to bed.

HELEN.
>   I go with you.

PRIAM
>   *Starts from sleep.*

HECUBA
>   *Awakens, too.*

PARIS *and* HELEN
>   *Stand before his parents.*

PARIS.
>   You know what she said? That none of those Akhaian demi-gods have such bright hair as mine.

HECUBA.
>   Oh, my falcon.

PARIS.
>   And she also said that none of those wise Akhaian thinkers have such thought-filled eyes as mine.

PRIAM.
>   And so you think, boy, that she has any thoughts in her head at all?

PARIS
>   *To Helen:*
>   What do you think?

HELEN.
>   Right now I was thinking how you would look, if you combed your hair like the Apollo of Tenea.

PARIS.
>   You see, father? She thinks. Of me.

PRIAM.
>   She thinks of wigs.

PARIS.
>   No, she just compared me to Apollo, and quite rightly so, I think, and I also think that if Apollo looked like me, even I'd find him handsome.

HECUBA.
>   That's what I think, too.

PRIAM
>   *To Paris:*
>   So you think he looks otherwise?

PARIS.
>   I've never really given it a thought.

PRIAM.
>   And yet that's something that deserves some reflection. — Anyway, where have you ever seen yourself?

PARIS.
>   Myself? In the well.

HELEN.
He's always gazing in my little mirror.

PARIS.
The one that Isis is etched upon.

PRIAM.
And so he holds Isis in his little palm.

HELEN.
And in his fist.

PRIAM.
And yet she blushes not.

PARIS
Pointing at Helen.
But she here will blush yet;
Blushing, in her way, more ruddily than the roses
That make up the chaplet she wears round her brow.

PRIAM.
Yes. And yet neither of you know, that this stupidity of yours is our misfortune?

PARIS.
And is this not, in fact, your virtue,
That we can loll in stupidity, while you
Protect us by your majestic grace
And the strength of your majesty?

HECUBA.
That's what I think, too.

PARIS.
There are those who till the soil,
And soldiers, for the battle's broil,
Craftsmen, and journeymen, and all

Who labour at your beck and call;
You can afford us two: divine,
Calm, carefree, loving and sublime.

HECUBA.
That's what I think, too.

PARIS.
If I were to fight, someone might cause me harm,
Despite my nimbleness — oh — just by chance.
Let Hector keep this in mind, who's so warm
To mock me: he's stronger, but I've more... balance.

HELEN.
Let's go, already.

PRIAM.
Go already, babies.

HECUBA.
May the gods protect you, my pets.

PARIS.
To Helen.
Shall we go to our apartments?

HELEN.
Well — straight to our bed.

PARIS.
I think the same.

HELEN.
Bye bye!

PARIS.
Bye bye, Mama!

PRIAM.
    Stay well.

HELEN.
    Your servant.

SCENE 5.

PRIAM.
    You, who live in memories, tell me. Which one do you prefer: me, as I am today, or me as I once was?

HECUBA.
    You're different today than what you were before?

PRIAM.
    The passing years bring changes. Others see them better than we do ourselves, so you must see them in me too.

HECUBA.
    I don't really care about what I see.

PRIAM.
    Because you're always gazing backwards. I on the other hand am looking toward what's to come. The farther off something is, the dearer it is to me, to my soul. Now, how can we draw close to one another, when our thoughts are running in opposite directions?

HECUBA.
    Give me your hand.

PRIAM.
    These hands were once a bridge between us.

HECUBA.
    Are my children pleasing to you?

PRIAM.
   No. That pleasure passed long ago.

HECUBA.
   And the children of my children, then?

PRIAM.
   No. That pleasure's passed, I say again.
   The world has closed behind them,
   Whereas to me, it stands open wide.
   I now see farther — past their lives,
   Which, it seems, will be quickly run —
   Towards the ages yet to come.
   And these, alive, glad in their strength,
   Bursting with vigour and delight,
   Living through this one granted night,
   Before our eyes will meet their death.

HECUBA.
   So have you said. Listen — the hours
   That mark time sound from the city towers.

The bells of different ages sound
From the far-off churches of Kraków:

I. From the direction of the Vistula:
Sing, little bell, O sing
With silver voice the night air lave
Above the sparkling Wisła's wave,
Over the well-washed heather, ring.

Play, little bell, O play
Chase the violet's perfume through the nave
Across the sparkling Wisła's wave
Through the river-washed month of May.

Peal, little bell, O peal
Above the sparkling Wisła's wave

As violet's breath the night air laves,
May laughs at last above the lea.

*II. From the Cathedral clock tower;
Blacksmiths:*
It's time, now it's time
Our hammers strike a fourfold blow
In the metal cast.
Grasp it by the helve;
Hammer, and fire, the embers strike,
Let the name sound! Strike!

From the Zygmunt tower; the lesser bell:
Zbigniew!

*From the Cathedral clock tower;
Blacksmiths:*
The hammer knells
Impel the bell
Aloft: fly, voice of the hurricane!
The roused troops come,
The hoofbeats drum,
Aloft, below, the sound swells!
Let the great name sound! Strike!

From the Zygmunt tower; the greater bell:
Zygmunt!

III. From the higher steeple of St. Mary's Basilica:

CHORUS.
   Shine forth, immaculate gloria,
   Radiant, thy face like a star bright,
   Thy spire basking in heaven's light,

From the lower steeple of St. Mary's Basilica; the bell:
                    Maria!

From the higher steeple of St. Mary's Basilica:

CHORUS.
    Thy brows wrapped in a garland starry,
    Thou standest radiant above the hail
    Of stars winking like a comet's tail,

    From the lower steeple of St. Mary's Basilica; the bell:
              O Mary!

    From the higher steeple of St. Mary's Basilica:

CHORUS.
    Thou, wrapped about in rainbows merry
    Before the daystar lights the east,
    Bearing the sword that pierces thy breast.

    From the lower steeple of St. Mary's Basilica; the bell:
              O Mary!

    From the higher steeple of St. Mary's Basilica:

CHORUS.
    Thou purest one, above the lily fair,
    O Virgin Queen Immaculate,
    The daystar deign illuminate.

    From the lower steeple of St. Mary's Basilica; the bell:
              O Mary!

    IV: From the higher steeple of St. Mary's Basilica: the hourly trumpet call:
    Hey, from on high,
    Stoop falcon, fly
    O'er flower and mead,
    Soar in gyres, skim and speed,
    O'er the town asleep,
    Where dark gates brood and keep
    Their watch...

The Lady, garlanded with stars,
Clad in a robe of azure hue,
Where ringed with gold soars high the spar,
The gold-crowned steeple high in the blue
Night soars, alights, and inclines
Her ear to the music that plays,
Where the golden ensigns
Sparkle in the moon's reflected rays.
She holds a dove against her breast,
While hosts of angels her assist.
Soar forth, O golden bird, arise
To the song of bells and angelic choirs.

Hey, from on high,
Stoop sweet dove, fly
O'er flower and mead,
Soar in gyres, skim and speed,
Reapers and their wives
Bid rise and whet their scythes
For dawn...

The Lady, bright-rayed as the dawn
Now stands upon the crescent moon.

IV. From the direction of the Bernardine cloister:
Arise, monks, to your prayers now hasten,
Don your hairshirts with all speed, to
Chant angelic salutation
And intone the Credo;
Now peals the dawn,
The first bird's begun
Her song, night
Retreats — the candles alight.

Night falls, and night retreats,
Your litanies intone.
The garden, full of chirps and cheeps
Is reborn to the dawn.

The river flows in brawny braids
Beneath the cloister high;
Hey, there on the shingle lies a maid;
On her, knights cast their eye.

The news that Sandomierz has heard,
Soon Warsaw too will know,
Swift are the wings that carry words
When the gusts of morning blow.

Against the flow the galleys strain,
The Wisła's waves roll on and on,
Now set the altar-candles aflame,
Ave intones the dawn.

IV. From the Labyrinth of homes at the castle's foot:

FROM A WINDOW.
    Here am I, left alone,
    By myself in this room,
    And who am I waiting on,
    Can you tell me, fair groom?

LUTENISTS.
    Alone? You're not alone.
    It seems your bed you share!
    Hark! Hooves drum cobblestones;
    Patience — he's almost there!

FROM A WINDOW.
    I have a lover dear;
    I haven't long to wait.
    His charger bears him near;
    He's rapping at the gate.

    He raps at the gate here,
    Clatters at the window pane.

I've known him for a year...
A maiden I remain!

LUTENISTS.
A year, a summer, spring,
And now the month of May.
They come a-matchmaking;
Soon dawns your wedding day.

FROM A WINDOW.
But I won't let them in;
Matchmakers plead in vain.
Rein in that steed, rein in;
With Mama I'll remain.

Alone, here in my room,
I shall remain a maid,
Safe with shuttle and loom,
My Mama I shall aid.

I twitter sweet and low,
Just like the sparrows gay.
With needle and thread of gold
I haft my bodice-stay.

LUTENISTS.
Safe by your Mama's bed,
Tweet like the sparrows gay.
With needle, and golden thread
Broider your bodice-stay.

Sew tight your bodice-straps,
Try it on, and abide;
Hark and hear! Your lover raps,
Come down and open wide.

HECTOR and ANDROMACHE
From the side of the palace
They walk along in an embrace.

ANDROMACHE.
You'll come back to me, with the day?

HECTOR.
I go to fight in the fierce war.

ANDROMACHE.
Husband and lover, bid me goodbye;
Huge, armoured in gold for the harsh fray;
You'll come back to me, with the day?

HECTOR.
I must go where my standard fights
The raging winds of destiny.
It's there, I know, God bids me be,
There I must battle through the night.
Goodbye, my lover, goodbye, my wife;
I know my strength, I know my power.
I know my will. Go in, my life.

ANDROMACHE.
No one knows the day, the hour.

HECTOR.
I'll return, as I have always done,
When, grey and pale, returns the sun.
I throw this body at the feet
Of crow and raven for their meat;
My spirit's with you, my only one.
Stay here, love, and bring up our son.

ANDROMACHE.
And when he's grown, what shall I say?

HECTOR.
>   That he should follow his father's way.
>   I shall not die, no. Don't look glum.
>   Pale, I'll return with the new sun.
>   You know my mysteries. I must away.

ANDROMACHE.
>   I know but this: You "must away."
>   And I remain, a widow bereft.

HECTOR.
>   Such sad parting. You keen in vain.
>   If our foes heard you, how they'd laugh!
>   Nor tears nor plaints can me restrain...
>   What secret words might calm your fear?

ANDROMACHE.
>   Go, and return, my husband dear!

HECTOR.
>   Have my son follow his father's ways,
>   If I should fall...

ANDROMACHE.
>   Glory and praise!

HECTOR
>   *Descends the stairs to the lower circuit of the castle barbican.*

PRIAM
>   *Looking down upon Hector from the battlements.*
>   Sheathe yet your weapon, my dear child,
>   Pause but a moment — look up here.
>   You know, son, how I hold you dear,
>   And wish you well, son, all the while.

HECTOR.
>   Father, my men are standing by the gate,
>   They look up here, to Ilium,
>   And call to war many a son.
>   It's not right that I make them wait.

PRIAM.
>   Lay down your gore-stained shield, my son.
>   Look here — pause but a minute more:
>   Who knows the gnarled paths of fortune?
>   Who knows if I'll survive this war?

HECTOR.
>   Father, you know how dear you are
>   To me, no other person do I hold
>   So dear: wife, child, and you. But war
>   Calls; I can't waver; I must be bold!

PRIAM.
>   Hector, my son, do not depart
>   Just yet: there's time enough for war.
>   Today such sorrow grips my heart,
>   Foreboding… Just a moment more!

HECTOR.
>   My aged father, dear and mild,
>   Go in now, to my family.
>   Go to my wife, nursing my child,
>   I must stand fast to destiny.

PRIAM.
>   It is your steadfastness I fear!
>   For I can see the troops from here,
>   Who'll crush the bones of my bright boy,
>   And pull to dust the throne of Troy!

HECTOR.
> Look then, at this bright battle-axe
> I wield, which shall defend that throne.
> Unhappy man, whom dread so wracks,
> Behold your men: they die alone
> — While I here tarry — in defence
> Of fatherland, palace and wives,
> Their children, and ours. I must be hence
> And join them as they give their lives
> For you, for us. Lost loves, good-bye.
> May my deeds rise before your eyes.
> Be well behind thick castle walls,
> In warm bedrooms; I go to fall.
> In Troy's defence this life I spurn,
> Soon — as your god — I shall return.

PRIAM.
> Good bye, dear child, if go you must;
> In you, dear son, all our hopes rest.
> Our fate entire thus I entrust
> To the great heart that enflames your breast.

HECTOR.
> The words you spill down from on high,
> Dear father, sap me of my might.
> Look, father, how deep is the night;
> Look, father, thus I go to die.

CASSANDRA
> *Descends and stands before her parents.*

HECUBA.
> Beauteous mourner,
> Apollo's forced mate,
> Misfortunate scorner,
> Prophetess fortunate,
> Fall here at my knee,
> Cuddle close to my breast,

And foretell me my death.
What says my destiny?

CASSANDRA.
Ask not, dear mother, of Lord
Apollo, what's hidden by fate.
But look, my aged mother, no sword
Has split the warp of Scaean Gate;
See: Ilium yet stands;
Look there: the fearsome bands
Of her warriors defend her walls.
And listen: the rhythmic footfalls
Beating time: so dance your daughters
Through the many peaceful rooms
Of the palace, to harp, and to lute;
And the many Trojan altars,
With purest sacrifice still fume.

HECUBA.
My daughter, I would know the truth,
Though cruel, of my destiny.
Am I to endure slavery?
Then you'll have time to weep for me.

CASSANDRA:
Mother, you prod the daemon now.
I was enslaved, in that high tower,
In ragged robes, such as I wear,
Since kings deigned hold me captive there.
But now I break my prison walls,
I burst my chains, a fire falls,
— O Mother — here upon my brow;
Apollo's mastering me now!
Apollo, Oh, it burns, your spear,
The spear you've sunk into my breast, how deep!
Crows and ravens will caw and cheer
Above the ruined castle keep!
She rises.

Day will rise to you no more!
No sun, no dawn,
No rosy-fingered dawning light
Of gold.
To Andromache:
Await not your husband's return tonight!
In a trance.
Hey, ravens! bend your gliding, sweep
With cloudy widespread wings to perch
Upon the crenellations steep,
Above the fosse; these curious urge
Me to reveal the destiny
Of Ilion, which now I see
Balanced aloft, against the sheen
Of fire that tincts the angry sky,
While warriors pummel helm and screen
Of flimsy shields, behind which they die!
Chasing Andromache:
Pull her down from the ramparts there,
The madwoman — You are whose wife?
You clamber so that you might glare
Upon the battle? You'd watch his life
Ebb from his throat? Protect her,
Guards, drag her to the palace.
That hag is the wife of Hector!
Alas!

GUARDS
Enter from the rear.

CASSANDRA
Chases Andromache.

ANDROMACHE
Flees.

CASSANDRA.
> Ravens and crows! Come here to me!
> Ravens and crows! Come here!

RAVENS and CROWS
> *Come to Cassandra.*

CASSANDRA.
> Old Black-wing, old Coat-of-jet,
> Favourite gossip of the night,
> Settle down here, and watch the fight.
> Weep, and when you catch sight of one
> Of the doomed knights, then caw!
> Swords tattoo armour like a drum...

RAVEN.
> Kra-a, kra-a, kra-a.

CASSANDRA.
> Your beak is black, sharp is your beak,
> Come, sisters, cuddle close, and clothe
> Me round in black from toe to peak.
> My brothers battle down below,
> Your brothers in a solemn choir
> Waggle like maggots thick, up higher,
> On buttress and on counterfort.
> See how the moon's light they defile,
> Anticipating sport!
> Settle down here, and watch the fight.
> Weep, and when you catch sight of one
> Of the doomed knights, then caw!
> Swords tattoo armour like a drum...

RAVEN.
> Kra-a, kra-a, kra-a.

HECTOR and AJAX
  Appear in the lower circuit of the walls,
  All silver and golden in the moonlight.
  Their swords and bucklers sparkling,
  They trade heavy blows.

CASSANDRA.
  Ice flows on the Vistula.
  Lover, observe, and caw.

RAVEN.
  Kra-a, kra-a, kra-a.

CASSSANDRA.
  The ice-floes on the river rush,
  But who will live till Spring?
  Young leaves adorn both tree and bush,
  Her advent proclaiming...

RAVEN.
  Kra-a, kra-a, kra-a.

ACT III

DRAMATIS PERSONAE:

ISAAC
REBECCA
ESAU
JACOB
LABAN
RACHEL
LIA
SHEPHERDS

HISTORIA JACOBI thus is called
That tapestry — you know it — from the walls
Of the cathedral, in far Flanders weft.
First is that scene where the father (bereft
Of sight) calls forth and bids his elder son
To sate his hunger with some venison,
Meanwhile, before he might prepare that lunch,
His younger brother beats him to the punch.
And thus fulfilled shall be God's servant's dream
When, sleeping in Bethel, he saw, it seemed,
Legions of angels the ladder ascend.
And then he meets Rachel, as his cousin tends
Her flock by the well. In tears they embrace,
But Laban shifts him Leah in her place.

Before you now will be played out this tale
Told on the tapestries, rich, plush... and pale,
That hang between the chapels near the stairs
And double gates. — Isaac hobbles near
On two long staves for crutches. Just behind,
Esau. And thus speaks Isaac to his scion:

SCENE 1.

ISAAC.
  My son.

ESAU.
  Here I am.

ISAAC.
  You see that I am grown old, nor do I know the date of my death. Take up your weapons, your quiver and your bow, and go into the fields. When you hunt something down, make me a meal of it. Thus you know my will. Bring it for me to eat, that I may give you my soul's blessing, before I die.

ESAU
 Goes off.

ISAAC
 Draws away.

REBECCA
 Enters.

JACOB
 Enters, following his mother.

SCENE 2.

REBECCA.
 I heard your father talking with your brother Esau, telling him: "Bring me back something from the hunt, and make me a meal of it, so that I should eat of it and bless you before the Lord, before I die."
 So now, my son, heed my advice. Go to the flock and bring back two kid goats of the better sort, so that I might make a meal for your father of them, which he will gladly eat.
 And when you bring them to him, and he eats his full, he will bless you before he dies.

JACOB.
 You well know, mother, that my brother Esau is shaggy, while I am smooth. Should my father touch me and feel my skin, I'm afraid that he will think I wished to mock him, and I will call down a curse upon my head, rather than a blessing.

REBECCA.
 Let the curse fall on my head, my son. Heed but my advice, and go and bring what I've commanded you.

JACOB
 Goes off.

ESAU
  Enters
  With his quiver and bow
  And halts Jacob.

REBECCA
  Draws away.

SCENE 3.

ESAU.
  Where are you off to, brother?

JACOB.
  I'm about Mother's
  Business. And you?
  In such a hurry?

ESAU.
  I'm off to do
  Father's will. But you look worried…

JACOB.
  I burn with shame.
  Perhaps, brother, you can guess why?

ESAU.
  You are more loved and praised than I,
  By Mother, but I do not blame
  You for that. We're friends, we two.
  My love for you is strong, and true.

JACOB.
  And strong, too, is your memory
  Of selling your birthright to me
  For a gulp of pottage, a heel of bread?

ESAU.
>Is it for that you're flushing red?
>I sold my right — faint unto death —
>An oath that weighs as much as... breath.

JACOB.
>Yes, hunger forced you to give your word.
>But you swore the oath, and Heaven heard.

ESAU.
>Well, another's hunger presses me
>Into the fields to hunt today.
>I'm off into the wilds to slay
>Meat for our father's table.

JACOB.
>   And he,
>In gratitude, does he intend
>To bless you?

ESAU.
>   By laying on of hands,
>To pass on his inheritance.

JACOB.
>Go, hunt, fulfil your destiny.

SCENE 4.

ESAU.
>Off to the hunting fields we go —
>Chase on, you clouds, you fair winds, blow!
>My quiver's full, strong is my bow,
>And strong and fresh am I;
>A fat roebuck shall die
>My father for to feed.
>Blow winds, lead on, clouds, lead!

Shine on, lucky star, shine!
A blessed heritage is mine!
Come, servants, off we go
With quiver and with bow,
The winding horn, now! Blow!

He sounds his horn
Horns echo from all sides.
He moves off.
Behind him come servants and other members of his household
Leading hunting dogs as well.
Armed with bows and spears
They pass on.

SCENE 5.

JACOB
> *Enters*
> *Gazes after his brother and his train.*

REBECCA
> *Comes near, bearing clothes.*
> Here now, Jacob. Put these clothes on.
> The finest sort for you I've chosen.
> Get dressed.

JACOB.
>   Mother, you'd have me stain
> My honour? See, I burn with shame!

REBECCA.
> Long since your brother did the same,
> Selling you his inheritance.

JACOB.
> Father will see through this pretence.
> Will he not see right through our scheme?

REBECCA.
>   Wrap your forearm in this. You'll seem
>   To be your brother.

JACOB.
>   So, I'll lie?

REBECCA.
>   You fear to smear yourself in sin?
>   Do as I say. Then you shall win
>   What otherwise would pass you by.

JACOB.
>   What shall I win? A brother's hate.
>   I grow, by making his loss worse.

REBECCA.
>   Grip tight what's offered you by fate.

JACOB.
>   The price of which: a deathless curse.

REBECCA.
>   To such a curse God blocks His ears.
>   Win His pardon through pious fear.

JACOB.
>   I'll do your will.

REBECCA.
>   My will fulfil!
>   Here — take your gifts. Be off now, son,
>   Before your brother chance to come
>   Back from the hunt. Go! Your father comes.

ISAAC
>   *Enters,*
>   *Sits.*

SCENE 6.

REBECCA
To her son.
Kneel down.

JACOB
Draws near his father and kneels.
Father!

ISAAC.
That's Jacob's voice.
Is it you, Esau? My firstborn son?

JACOB.
It is— I... the unworthy one.

ISAAC.
These hands, which now on you I poise
Raise you in worth above all men.

JACOB.
O, Father!

REBECCA.
Hush!

ISAAC.
Be blessed, then.
He lays his hands upon Jacob's head.
And now, come. Let us share our meal.
Embracing his son
He rises
And leads him to the rear
Leaning his weight upon him all the while.
Your hunt fared well today. And fast.

REBECCA.
   The Lord was with him.

JACOB.
                      The Lord cast
   A bruising hand upon my brother's head.

ISAAC.
   You shall grow great and multiply.
   You shall be lifted up on high
   Above all as their lord.

JACOB.
                      Abhorred!

ISAAC.
   Aged in years, I bless you. May
   You live long.

JACOB.
                In infamy and shame.

REBECCA
   To her son.
   Go now.

JACOB.
          Mother, look! Esau comes!

ESAU
   Enters.

REBECCA
   Retires.

JACOB
   Follows his mother.

SCENE 7.

ESAU.

Arise, father, and have joy of your son's hunt, so that you may bless him from your soul.

ISAAC.

And who are you?

ESAU.

I am your firstborn son, Esau.

ISAAC.

Then who was he, who fed me from the hunt before; who sated me before your coming? Whom I blessed, and who, therefore, shall be blessed?

ESAU.

My swindling brother has beguiled you?

ISAAC.

He came, your brother, knelt in fraud,
And made me faithless to my troth
To you; now he is blessed of God.

ESAU.

If that's so, father, bless us both.

ISAAC.

There was one blessing; your brother came in treachery and stole it from you.

ESAU.

For the second time now he has upended me. First, he took my primogeniture, and now he's swiped my blessing. Have you no blessing for me?

ISAAC.
I have set him above you as your lord. All of his brothers I have indentured to him. You shall live henceforth by the sword, and serve your brother. But the day will come when you shall undo bow and keeper pins, and cast his yoke from your neck.
He goes off
Led by servants.

ESAU.
And the day of sadness will come to you, father, when I kill my brother Jacob!
He goes off.

SCENE 8.

REBECCA
Enters.

JACOB
Enters behind his mother.

REBECCA.
Your brother Esau threatens you with murder.

JACOB
Hangs his head.

REBECCA.
And so, son, heed my voice. Arise and flee to Haran, to Laban my brother.
You shall live with him a little while until the violent anger of your brother cools, until his anger ceases, and he forgets what you have done to him. Then I shall send for you and lead you back here. Why should I lose both my sons on one and the same day?

ISAAC
Enters — led by servants.

JACOB
Shuffles aside.

REBECCA.
The daughters of the Hittites sour my life. Unless Jacob take a woman of our own nation to wife, I will no longer wish to live.

ISAAC
Sends for Jacob.

JACOB
Comes near and stands before his parents.

SCENE 9.

ISAAC
To his son.
Take not to wife a woman of Chanaan, but get you to Syrian Mesopotamia, to the house of Bethuel, the father of your mother, and take as your wife one of the daughters of Laban, your uncle. And may God Almighty bless you; may He grant you a potency unto many generations, so that you may be father to multitudes.
And may He bless you and your seed with the blessing of Abraham, that you may possess the land of your pilgrimage, which he promised unto your grandsire.
He draws away
Led by servants.

REBECCA
Embraces her son,
then retires with her household.

JACOB
Remains alone, descends the stairs
Sits down upon the first step
And rests his head against the jamb of the first gate
And sleeps.

Aloft, the clock the hour sounds,
On the bell the hour strikes,
The time of blest visions rolls round
When Earth is joined with Paradise.

Open the gates of Zion! Broad
The pathway, wide the gate-wings yawn.

Envoys stream from the Throne of God,
A troop of prophets, on and on!

Along the steps they take their post,
Dalmatic-garbed, a shimmering host,

Nearby the gate in tunics long
They stand, the blest, resplendent throng.

They gather close, solemn they stand,
About the sleeper, with raised hand.

SCENE 10.

THE ANGELS FROM JACOB'S DREAM

1.
Spring of new life! To thee all hail.
2.
Farewell, daystar. Thy face grows pale.
1.
Rise, morning star. Shine forth, thou dawn.
2.
Thy beauty is now come, and gone.

3.
Now dost thou rise, thou font of life;
4.
Dying, the day once splendid, sets.

3.
Thou wadest through a sea of light.
4.
Upon a trunk thy head now rests.
Condemned, thou art by death harassed.
3.
Enter this new life. Though distressed,
A thousand powers protect thee fast.

5.
Before thee: wealth, fame, veneration;
Before thee: life, by Jahwe blest.
6.
Behind thee: countless generations
Supine lie, in condemnation pressed.
5.
Before thee: anger, and delight —
With these thy hunger shalt thou sate.
6.
Behind thee yawns the open gate,
Before thee stretches empty night.
5.
Upon thee grace pours down in showers;
By grace, this moment live and breathe.
6.
Thy joy dies with the passing hour,
And dust are all those, who believed.
5.
Ask: granted be thy heart's desire.
In fame and power rest thou content.
6.
Yet Paradise, with this sword of fire
I thee deny. Fear the serpents.

7.
Thou shalt overcome thy foemen's strength.
Thine arms heroic their might shall break.

8.
Thy power feeble, thy might is spent.
Thy glory is all bluster, fake.
7.
To thee my countenance I incline,
And Paradise to thee display.
8.
Thy feet in brambles I entwine;
With thorns and nails thy soles I flay,
Till thou shalt recognise in pain
Thou never shalt the summit gain.

2.
Great are Thy mercies, Lord, Who grants
Me safe repose upon Thy breast,
Who trusts Thy sceptre into my hands
Though my flesh below in terror frets
1.
And when at last Thou shalt me thrust
From out Thy tabernacle on high,
Grant me a moment in the dust
And rubble next Thy gate to lie.

4.
Thou who canst all things, merely nod,
Creator of all life, great Lord,
And I shall rise from the wretched sod
By Thee my vigour new restored.
3.
But should Thy power me dismiss
I must follow my destiny,
My soul cast into the abyss.
Lord, grant my soul Thy clemency!

6.
Thus dost Thou each day freshly make.
5.
Thus dost each back with labour break.

6.
Thus leadest Thou all out from the night.
5.
Thus temptest Thou all with false delight.

8.
Thus temperest me into a power
That once was merely wretched dust.
7.
Thus hour by eroding hour
Thou turnest mine iron bright to rust,
Till crumbled into dust again
I lie, who toward the summit strained.
8.
My glory yet shalt Thou renew
And summon me before Thy throne,
With Thee to reign, never more to rue
My lot, never more to weep and groan.

The gates close with a shuffling rasp
And fixed once more the iron hasps.
See Jacob stir from slumber, rise,
And gaily wipe sleep from his eyes.
He takes a jug of oil in hand,
Pours a full cup, and on the stone
Where he had slept, and dreamt (the land
Called Bethel) pours a libation.
Shepherds approach, and before him stand.

SHEPHERDS
In a group
Rest their chins upon their crooks
In anticipation.

JACOB.
What lies beneath this stone?

SHEPHERDS.
   A pure wellspring.

JACOB.
   And whence do you come, brothers?

SHEPHERDS.
   From Haran.

JACOB.
   Is Laban known among you, Nachor's son?

SHEPHERDS.
   He is.

JCACOB.
   And is he well?

SHEPHERDS.
   He is. Look — Here comes Rachel, his daughter, with her flock.

JACOB.
   It is not yet time to drive the flock back into the sheepfold. First let them drink, and then lead them back to feed.

SHEPHERDS.
   We cannot, until all the flocks have been gathered together. Then do we take away the stone from the well mouth, that all the flocks may drink.

RACHEL
   Enters.

JACOB
   Takes away the stone
   Points to the pure spring.

RACHEL
   Blushes.

JACOB.
> *Kisses her.*

SCENE 11.

JACOB.
> Maiden, your lips.

RACHEL.
> > And yours.

JACOB.
> You lean towards me, in full bloom.

RACHEL.
> Drink of my nectar, lovely groom.
> You travel to us from afar?

JACOB.
> This well my flagging strength restores.
> You've come to the spring, where I stand.

RACHEL.
> I find a haven beneath your arm.

JACOB.
> My journeys end now, in this land.

RACHEL.
> With love's longing my heart now pines.
> My ears thrill sweetly to your words.

JACOB.
> Sing on, sweet bird of paradise.
> I come, commanded of the Lord.

RACHEL.
>   I understand. It's destiny.
>   Come with me, to my father's side.

JACOB.
>   As you will have it, so shall it be.
>   Long did I the Lord's will abide.
>   Your words now make His counsel plain.

RACHEL.
>   I love you. This I wish to say.

JACOB.
>   My Rachel.

RACHEL.
>   My loving lord, my dear.
>   I dreamt of someone drawing near,
>   Carried here, by the winds, to me,
>   Led close by common destiny.

JACOB.
>   My Rachel!

RACHEL.
>   Leading here my sheep,
>   I'd gaze into the glassy pane
>   Of water, and look past my face,
>   Searching yet deeper, for a trace
>   Of someone's features, who should be
>   The husband God would send to me.

JACOB.
>   From my father's house I have been driven
>   Here to the house of Bathuel,
>   Our motherland, our origin.

RACHEL.
>This morning, when I came, the well
>Was covered with the stone. There too
>My reflection awaited you.
>Uncovering the spring's the same
>As if you summoned me by name.
>Look — see? My image disappears
>Beneath the sparkling ripples — clear
>And chaste as glass now is the well.

JACOB.
>Rachel — Rachel — Rachel.

RACHEL.
>This morning through the fields I came,
>Where sunlight sifts through poplar tree
>And bird on bough trills merrily,
>In chorus with the shepherds' flute
>As they pursue their errant route
>Behind their flocks. I strove to hear
>Among the notes, a call — my name,
>From these parts, whence your feet were led —
>To lead me to my bridal bed.

JACOB.
>Rachel!

RACHEL.
>　　My chosen lord.

JACOB.
>　　　　　　Rachel!

LABAN
>*Surrounded by women and men, he emerges*
>*Through the cathedral doors*
>*And halts at the porch.*

JACOB
Approaches, kneels, and embraces him at the hip.

LABAN
Embraces him.

JACOB
Rises.

SCENE 12.

LABAN.
Flesh of my flesh, bone of my bone. Serve me.

JACOB.
As you say. I shall enter into your service.

LABAN.
You are my kindred. Shall you serve me without reward? What will you take in return for your service?

JACOB.
I shall serve you in return for the hand of Rachel, your younger daughter.

LABAN.
It is better that I give her to you, than to another man. Come live with me.

The servants crowd around them then,
And lead the pair before the priest.
The marriage solemnised, again
They lead them out, unto the feast.

The joyous revellers dance in pairs
While happy wedding songs are sung,
And incense wafts up through the air
And the cathedral organ thrums.

The dancing couples disappear
Down the dark sanctuary's nave.
The distant music one can hear
Dying along the architrave.

The youthful groom is then espied
After the guests have bid farewell,
Leading along his chosen bride,
Her face hid by her wedding veil.

SCENE 13.

JACOB.
   Who was it rested in my arms this night?

LEAH
   Unveils her face.
   It was me you cossetted, the gift of my father's hand.

JACOB.
   Not yours the wedding that your father prepared for me,
   nor is your love welcome to me.

LEAH.
   You push me from you, having first sated your lust upon me,
   as if I were no longer worthy of your love. You do me wrong.

JACOB.
   For your sister's hand have I been serving Laban, and it is her love alone
   that I crave. You have deceived me, knowing that it was by your father's
   will that you should come to me, not by my own wish or longing.

LEAH.
   You do me wrong, and my sister too, for thus you sow hatred between us.

LABAN
  Enters.

SCENE 14.

JACOB.
  What is this that you have done?
  Has it not been for Rachel that I have served you?
  Why have you tricked me?

LABAN.
  It is not our custom to give the younger maiden into wedlock before the elder. Serve out your term indentured, and I shall give you the second as well, in return for your labours on my behalf.

RACHEL
  Enters.

JACOB
  Draws away.

LABAN
  Draws away.

SCENE 15.

RACHEL.
  You've taken from me what is mine.
  You are his wife, and I, a concubine.
  Your husband, but — my lover.
  For I'm the one he chose;
  These lips he kissed, not those
  That day at the spring
  Promising
  To love no other.

LEAH.
>   I bore him heirs,
>   Though my share
>   In his love was uneven.
>   Still he held me in veneration
>   As the mother of his nation.

RACHEL.
>   I had him too,
>   Nor shall I be bereaved
>   Of his love and respect, for you
>   And the fruit of your womb.
>   The coral bloom
>   Of my lips, and the starry fire
>   That shines from my eye
>   Will draw him nigh
>   To slake his passionate desire.
>   And I will satisfy
>   His hunger and thirst, for I
>   Am his, and he belongs to me.
>   My house will fill with gaiety
>   Long begged of the Lord,
>   And heirs will I bear him in love,
>   Trusting in God's will, God's word;
>   The nation of my womb will soar above
>   The flowers' pride in Spring,
>   Or that of the sun, summering.
>   I am first mother of his nation.

LEAH.
>   The Lord's word upon you rests,
>   Since you are so loved, so blest.
>   Sister,
>   Let us join hands in reconciliation.

JACOB
>   *Enters,*
>   *Gives a sign to the women to be gone.*

LABAN
> *Enters,*
> *Following Jacob.*

SCENE 16.

JACOB.
> Give me your leave to return to my fatherland, my country.
> Give me my wives and my children, for whom I have served you, and I shall go. You know the merit of my service.

LABAN.
> May I find favour in your eyes.
> I know by experience that God has blessed me on your account.
> Consider the wages I am to give you.

JACOB.
> You know how I have served you; you know how great your wealth has become in my hands. You had but little before I came to you, and now you have become rich, and the Lord has blessed you through my coming. It would only be justice that I might also furnish my own home.

LABAN.
> What shall I give you?

JACOB.
> I want nothing! But if you do what I ask of you, I will yet care for your flocks. But whatever shall be brown, spotted, and of divers colours, among the sheep as well as the goats, that shall be my wages.
> And my justice shall answer for me tomorrow before you, when the time of accounting shall come. For all that will not be of divers colours, brown or spotted among the sheep as well as the goats, will testify to my thievery.

LABAN.
> I accept what you propose with glad heart.
> *He draws away.*

LEAH and RACHEL
  Enter.

SCENE 17.

JACOB
  To both women.
  I see that your father's face is not inclined towards me as it was yesterday, and the day before. But the God of my fathers has been with me.
  You know yourselves that I have served your father with all my strength. Yet your father has deceived me, and changed my wages ten times, though God has not permitted him to harm me.
  And God has taken all your father's wealth from him, and given it to me.
  And an Angel of God spoke to me in a dream, saying:
  Jacob!
  Here I am, I replied.
  And he said:
  I am the God of Bethel, where you anointed the stone and made a vow unto me.
  So now arise, leave this land, and return to the land of your birth.

RACHEL.
  Have we a share in the wealth and inheritance of our father's house?

LEAH.
  Has he not looked upon us as strangers, selling us, and consuming the price given for us?
  But God took away the riches of our father and has given them to us and our children.
  Go then and do what God has commanded you.

  The servants of Jacob's household enter, carrying crates and sacks. They move from the direction of Queen Zofia's chapel towards that of the Jagiellons. Jacob and his children follow them.
  Behind these comes Laban.
  From the opposite side a Servant rushes to him.

SCENE 18.

SERVANT.
The man to whom you entrusted your wealth and your possessions, to whom you gave your daughters as wives, has slipped out of your house in secret, taking your riches with him, escaping from you like a thief, a criminal.

LABAN.
What is this you are saying? Is it Jacob of whom you speak, whom I trusted above all others, accepting him as my own son and giving him my daughters?

SERVANT.
It is the same. He has crossed the river, and makes for the hills.

LABAN.
After him!
He turns toward the depths of the nave
And knocks at the gate.

SCENE 19.

JACOB
Comes out and stands before the gates, closing them behind him.

LABAN.
Why have you done this, taking off my daughters without my knowledge, as if by force, by the sword?
For without my knowledge you have sought to escape, without a word; otherwise I might have seen you on your way gladly, with songs, and tabors, and zithers.
You did not even allow me to kiss my sons and daughters farewell.
You have acted foolishly.
Now, my right hand might well repay you evil for evil, but yesterday the God of your fathers said unto me: Beware that you say nothing foul against Jacob.

So let it be. You wished to return to your own, longing for your father's house. But why did you steal my gods?

JACOB.

I left without giving you notice, for I feared lest you take back your daughters from me by force. But as to the thieving of which you speak, come search! See if you can find your gods among anyone here. Whatever of your own you may find here, take it back.

LABAN
Stands before the cathedral gates,
Which open.

SCENE 20.

RACHEL
Beyond the gates.
She has covered some of the crates of treasure with animal pelts;
On these she is sitting.
Let my lord not be angry with me, that I do not rise in his presence. But according to the custom of women, so it is with me at this time.

JACOB
Standing behind her.
What is my fault, what my sin that you so hotly pursue me and search through all my belongings?
And what have you found there that belongs to you?
Set it here before my brothers, and yours, and let them judge between us.
Why did I remain with you for twenty years?
Your sheep and goats were not barren; nor did I consume a single ram of your flocks.
I did not show you any mauled of a beast, but made good all your losses. Yet whatever you lost by theft, that you blamed on me.
Day and night I suffered the heat and the cold, and sleep did not visit my eyes. Thus did I serve you for twenty years: fourteen to win your daughters, and six for your flocks. And you changed my wages ten times. Had not the God of my father Abraham and the fear of Isaac stood

by me, you would have dismissed me naked. But God looked upon my
suffering and the work of my hands, and rebuked you yesterday.

LABAN.
My daughters and sons, and those flocks of yours, and all you see here
are mine. Yet what can I do to my sons and grandsons?
Come then and let us make a pact to witness between us.

JACOB
To his servants.
Bring up some stones.

SERVANTS
Bring up stones.

LABAN.
May the Lord behold, and judge between us, when we depart from one
another.
If you mistreat my daughters and set other wives over them, you have no
other witness of our words than God, who now beholds us.
May this stone be witness against me, should I pass it to come against
you; may it witness against you, should you pass it, coming against me
with evil design.
May the God of Abraham and the God of Nachor judge between us.

He goes in to where Jacob's sons and daughters are sleeping.

I shall not behold your joy, but may it grow
Like a great tree. Your fortune: may it spread,
May it develop fully, like a bloom
That takes delight in peaceful skies and sun.
And you, be to that man woman, and wife;
A faithful guard, a yet more faithful servant
Than you had ever been to me, your father.
Live by his side, a dedicate of love,
But think on me as well, who in old age
Pursued you, thirsting for your faithfulness.
Between us may the God of Abram judge —

Is it the child, or father, here who errs?
My heart is empty of you.
Accept this last kiss from my lips today.
O Lord my God, you alone behold my tears!

Kisses his sons and daughters,
Blesses them,
And exits.

SCENE 21.

JACOB
>*Goes out to his servants.*
>Say this to my lord Esau:
>Thus says your brother Jacob —
>I have been the guest of Laban, where I dwelt until this day.
>I have oxen and asses, sheep, servants both male and female, and thus do I send an envoy unto you, lord, that I might find favour in your eyes.

SERVANT.
>We went to Esau your brother, and, look: he hastens to prevent you with four hundred men.

JACOB.
>Divide the people who are with me into two companies.
>If Esau comes and destroys one of them, the other that remains shall be saved.

SERVANTS
>*Go off.*

SCENE 22.

JACOB
Kneels.
O God of my father Abraham, and God of my father Isaac, Thou who said unto me: Return to your country, the place of your birth, and I shall do well by thee!
I am less than all Thy mercies and Thy truth, with which Thou hast filled Thy servant.
I crossed that River Jordan with nothing but a stick, and now I return with two companies.
Deliver me from the hands of my brother Esau, for I fear him greatly, lest he come and slaughter the mothers along with the sons.
It is Thou who promised to be gracious unto me, and multiply my seed like the sands of the sea; so many, that no tally would be possible.

SCENE 23.

SERVANTS
Enter from all sides and stand around Jacob.

JACOB.
Take from all that is mine gifts for my brother Esau. Twenty goats, with sire and dam, twenty ewes and rams, twenty calving camels and twenty calves, forty cows and forty bulls, and ten foals of donkeys.
Go before me.
And may a place be made between herd and herd.
To one of the servants:
If you should meet my brother Esau and he ask you: Who might you be? or Where are you going? Whose cattle are these, that you are driving? Say to him — They belong to Jacob your servant; these gifts he sends unto my lord Esau. And after them he comes himself.
To another servant:
Speak these words to Esau, when you shall meet him.
To another servant:
And add unto them:
Your servant Jacob himself comes behind, for he has said:

I shall beg his favour with gifts, which shall go before me; and thus before we meet shall he have mercy on me.

SERVANTS
Go off.

ANGEL
Stands at the cathedral doors.

The flagstones bend beneath his tread;
His buskins mark each step he takes.
The slates crash, the foundation quakes;
With gloomy furrows his forehead
Is lined.

He lifts his hand, and makes a mark
In the dark air — that of the Cross —
A cross of stars behind him toss
Upon the roads he's travelled a spark
Malign.

He spreads his ebon pennons wide,
Gathers his dark cloak round him — on
He strides,
Relentlessly towards the agon
At the crossing, where the man abides.

With flashing eyes, he meets his gaze —
The mortal's eyes are startled blind,
Yet his strong grip the other's finds,
As hand to hand, they fast engage.

Strength matches strength, blow parries blow;
Balanced, now tossed upon the ground
They wrestle, while the hammer's blow
The hour sounds.

SCENE 24.

ANGEL.
   Unlatch me now — unbar my way.

JACOB.
   Submit — your pleading is in vain.

ANGEL.
   Leave off — invoke me not in vain.
   Let me pass to the destined ford.

JACOB.
   I've spoken — here you shall remain
   Until you grant your blessing, lord.

ANGEL.
   No words salvific shall you hear,
   You lying man, you soul accurst!

JACOB.
   Then shall I hold you captive here
   In chains no slave like you shall burst.

ANGEL.
   You cannot match your strength with mine;
   Almighty God has blessed my hand.

JACOB.
   I will stand even to such divine
   Force, though I be forever damned!

ANGEL.
   Kneeling under the pressure of Jacob's hand.
   Eternal torment shall be mine
   Should I bend beneath a human hand.
   To death such creatures are consigned —
   They fall before me — grains of sand!

JACOB.
>	The kingly might of humankind —
>	Man, lord of all created things —
>	Fast through your frightful limbs entwines
>	And your fierce power to ruin brings.
>	You, who no compassion know
>	And strut about in angelic pride,
>	Colossal wings spread open wide...

ANGEL.
>	These wings, when we shall come to blows
>	Will snap the bone joined to your hip.
>	Then shall you to the hard stone slip,
>	Then shall you know angelic might —
>	Late-coming wisdom, through hardship!
>	Blind man! Then, you'll regain your sight
>	And know who's lord of all creation!

JACOB.
>	Winged messenger, you have confessed
>	That, as you go, God's gifts you bear.
>	You shall not move, though the sun west
>	A hundred times, and the dawn rear
>	Her head a hundred more, until
>	You fold your hands in peaceful prayer
>	And the blessing of the Lord distill
>	Upon all future generations
>	Of Jacob's loins.

ANGEL.
>	 Man, let me go —
>	The purple sun begins to glow
>	Upon my wings. It's time!

JACOB.
>	 Even so
>	My strength returns. We still shall fight.

ANGEL.
>   Man, let me go! Lest my curse smite
>   Your hand, which withers, dead and dried!

JACOB.
>   My faith cannot be overcome;
>   It lives in struggle, and in pain.
>   You toss me down, but have not won —
>   Though pressed to earth, I rise.
>   When from my shoot new blooms push forth
>   Then shall you know, who of the earth
>   Is master; with Whom my covenant.

ANGEL.
>   Take then, your blest inheritance.
>   *He touches Jacob's hip.*

JACOB
>   *Kneels.*
>   Who are you, more than man, who shakes
>   Me half from half?

ANGEL.
>   The one who breaks.

JACOB.
>   Whence come you, who arrest me here,
>   Phantom divine?

ANGEL.
>   The one to fear.

JACOB.
>   Cruel is your strength, mighty your hold.
>   I can't squirm free, twist as I will.
>   Your words strike like the thunderbolt —

ANGEL.
   The one who kills.

JACOB.
               Call back that writ!
   For what crimes do you punish me?

ANGEL.
   You but postpone your fateful hour
   For yet more crimes and acts more dour.
   For ages shall you struggle and fight
   As you have battled me tonight,
   Pining for immortal life;
   In constant labour, endless strife
   You'll stumble through an age of pain
   To learn, at last, 'twas all in vain.

JACOB.
   You bless me with such words?

ANGEL.
   As I am lord.

JACOB.
   My soul bleeds at your butchery.
   And you pass on…?

ANGEL.
                  To eternity.

JACOB.
   Your tread has fissured the pavement;
   Your footsteps are like patterns, runes
   Traced as in blood upon the stones.
   What is their meaning?

ANGEL.
                  A lament.

JACOB.
>The blood gathers, and like a river flows.
>Have mercy! As I serve the Lord!
>You drag your wings — Where? One last word:
>You pass on — to eternity?
>What are you called?

ANGEL.
>   Necessity.

From the right, the household and servants of Jacob enter the proscenium. From the left, the household and servants of Esau enter the proscenium. Esau is at the head of his knights:

SCENE 25.

ESAU
>*To Jacob.*
>And what is this? Do these belong to you?

JACOB.
>This is the little flock that the Lord has given me, your servant.

The servants and sons of Jacob bow to Esau.

LEAH
>*Comes forward with her children; they bow before Esau.*

RACHEL
>*Comes forward with her children; they bow before Esau.*

ESAU.
>And the companies I've come across on my way?

JACOB.
>I sent them out, to find favour in your eyes, my lord.

ESAU.
   I have enough of my own; keep what is yours.

JACOB.
   Speak not like that. But if I have found favour in your eyes, accept a small gift from my hand.
   For as I looked upon your face, it seemed I gazed upon the face of God. Take then the blessing, which I've brought you, which was first given me by God, who gives everything.

ESAU.
   Let us eat together, and I will accompany you on your way.

JACOB.
   I know, my lord, that my flock is of tender years; I have ewes with me and calving cows which, were I to drive with violence, the entire herd would expire.
   Let my lord therefore precede me his servant, and I shall follow lightly in his footsteps, taking care of the needs of my flock, until I come to my lord at Seir.

ESAU.
   I beg you, allow at least some of the people who are with me to remain as comrades of your journey.

JACOB.
   There is no need of that; I only need find favour in your eyes, my lord.

ESAU.
   I saw, my brother, that the gifts
   You sent had a deceptive shift —
   As armed you come, and thus I sent
   My knights to fend off ill intent,
   As I myself came to forgive,
   And not to punish; as I live
   In longing for you, thus did I
   Desire to see, before I die
   The harvest grand that you have reaped

By your own labour; wide and deep
Your riches — these I longed to know,
And my forgiveness to bestow.

JACOB
Kneels.

ESAU.
Brother, I thirst to embrace your soul.

JACOB.
Brother, how wretched is the soul that you would embrace!

ESAU.
I recognise the hand of blessing upon you, which rules you.
Confession cleanses the soul.

JACOB.
Accept this soul, then, brother, and comfort her,

ESAU.
I accept you, and comfort you.
He embraces Jacob, and kisses him, weeping.

JACOB.
How many evils did I plan
As in my heart there festered hate!
Fear drove me to wickedness, and
Terror made me unfortunate.

You were my terror, you the scourge
That from my pillow banished sleep.
I kneel before you now, to purge
My sin, as I in penance weep.

Have mercy on my trembling soul;
Have mercy on my wasted years;

For one blest moment, make me whole
For these my infants, by these tears.

Lift not at me, or them, your sword,
Though I deserve your harshest course;
May your heart beat in pity, lord:
I am your brother, though perverse.

Return not ill for ill, though I
From you the blessing basely took;
Restrain your force, pray, do not bind
My children to a slavish yoke.

May we together, with our sire
Live out — Blessed be you! — our lives;
Lead to your town my folk entire,
With me, and these my faithful wives.

Together, then, in divine accord,
If you allow it, may we live;
Speak, brother, but the cleansing word,
Say unto me that —

ESAU.
    I forgive.

JACOB.
  O brother! Such the sin of Cain
  With which the sire infects the son! —
  His guiltless progeny to stain,
  A blight to all generations!

ESAU.
  That crime sinks in oblivion.
  This kiss wipes clean your sin, your debt.
  My name shall be the clarion
  That rings aloud Forgive, Forget.
  He embraces and kisses his brother.

ACT IV

From the organ's tuneful summit
The king leaps, in his golden robe
And, harp in hand, he stately plummets
Into the living world below.
On the cathedral flags he alights
And does a deep obeisance.
Harmonious spells thrice he recites,
Loosens his golden peplum's bands,
Rests harp upon the podium,
Commences the psalmodium.

High in the storied castle tower
The hammer strikes now the third hour.
The royal house is entombed in sleep
As watch the ages over them keep.
Above them flow the centuries
Though here the bell calls forth the dawn.
Beyond the choir's stone filigrees
The fainting stars blink, cold and wan.
The clock still trembles in the tower,
Once more the hammer strikes the hour;
It sounds — the king his instrument
Tunes, his steps ring on the pavement;
Harp resting on the podium,
He cantillates his psalmodium.

SCENE 1.

HARPIST.
   I. I am king and monarch of my peoples, who once was but a simple shepherd.
   I clothe myself in scarlet, and wear the dearest robes of my nation, I who once was a simple servant boy, clad in humble hides, leaping along the streams, when first I learned to hymn Thee my praises.

II. 1. O holy water, rivers blest,
'Twas from your springs I drank the fire
Sacred, that glows within my breast.

2. O holy water, river blest,
It was thy living springs inspired
My knowledge of the times that pass.

3. O font pristine, o waters clear,
Your living floods my soul refresh
Forever young, maugre the years,
And labours which upon me press.

III. 1. Complaint and tears, lament and keen,
The blustering storms and winds intone.
I brood on them — what can they mean,
Such words encumbered with such moans?

2. Along the vaults Jeremiads flow,
Uneasy winds bear them along.
To whom belong the lips that throw
Them high aloft? And whose the tongue?

3. Who is it voices these laments,
Prayers, and earnest petitions?
They creak like yokes on sore backs, bent;
Echoes of spent munitions.

4. From ancient battlefields the sounds
Reverberate, of ancient wars,
And now, like pilgrims, crowd around
Sacred springs, and healing spas.

IV. 1. Behold — a city is afire.
Look — knights in angry companies

Proud pillars pull down to the mire.
Victors exult cruel victories.

2. High towers now infernos grow,
Like mournful tapers tombs presaging;
Stormclouds their lightnings thickly strow
Their thunderbolts, widely ranging.

3. The leaders caper in the gloom,
And bathe themselves in youthful gore.
Old men, like lions, expire on tombs;
Both faith, and wise men, are no more.

V. 1. A brother steals what is his brother's,
Entwining him in sly deceits —
Unworthy son of evil mother!
Dog-like he snaps, as on she bates.

2. Declining age besets their sire.
The younger son wheedles a pact
To win the elder's portion entire,
And seals the theft with treacherous act,
Stripping him clean, the liar,

3. When he was hungry, weak and faint,
Unmindful of the stakes he lays. —
See how your brother lies in wait,
Snatching from your brow, destined bays,
Rejoicing in his successful sleight!

VI. 1. Along the Jordan's banks I cried —
My nation, is it worth the pain?
Do I seek service, or is pride
My goad, riches and glory my true aim?

2. And will the weight of glory prove
Too much for this frail back to bear?
Can my soul rest, at peace, unmoved,
My acts worthy a conscience clear?

3. And thus my nation I bewept,
Striving for honest thoughts, unstained;
As from the Jordan pure I sipped
I raised my prayers to Thee again:
Heavenly Judge, Thy angels send
To me, revealing Thy judgement.

4. Since Thou appointest me as Thine,
Strengthen my arm, Lord, and my soul.
As to a groom, to me entwine
My people. And on the Jordan rolled.

VII. 1. When the brute Goliath mocked
The armed battalions of Saul,
'Twas me Thou called forth from the flock
And planted me before them all.

2. He sneered while I, before the eyes
Of all Thy folk readied my sling;
To me befell the victor's prize
Thou granted — a miraculous thing.

3. The gory, bleeding giant's head
Before the monarch's feet I rolled.
My tunic with his blood splashed red,
Saul covered with a cloth of gold.

4. Then at the very head of those
Who ply the harp, and those that sing,
I took my place, and like swallows',
Our hymns of praise enmassed did ring.

VIII. Already then I recognised
Thee as my Lord, and only God;
When Saul's regal crown met my eyes,
I knew 'twas what I'd ever sought.

2. And when he shunned me with his eyes,
Turning his countenance from me,
Then did King Saul start to despise
Me; and then did grow my enmity.

3. Why didst Thou plant within my heart
This proud disdain, royal desire,
So that, spurning the shepherd's part,
To do Thy will I blazed like fire?

4. Yet gaily in Thy grace I dwelt,
Glorying in psalmodic hymns;
The hosts of angels I beheld
On desert cliffs and canyon rims.

5. I saw the winged angels cleave
The air, their brows with roses wreathed,
Legions of angels, warriors all;
To be the king my heart then seethed,
To grasp, and wear the crown of Saul!

IX. 1. Upon my heart that golden crown
Thou deigned to place, in Israel
Bidding me like the birds intone
Thy music, at feasting and wassail.

2. Thou bade me on the eagle's wing
To fly wherever the psalm should call —
A worthy people's mighty king,
Signed by the angels, ruling all.

3. "Before my people, David, stand
And lead them, as my armed right hand;
In ringing mail, stout in command,
Broadly thy raptor's wings expand.

4. "Sing but be watchful, on thy guard,
Lest no man's plough a furrow carve
Into the land entrusted thee;

5. "Love God, and in blest gaiety
Live in thy nation, as a choir,
With harp and voices in accord.
Sing, live, and love and fear the Lord!"

X. 1. And Thou didst save me from his angry glare,
Guiding my youthful steps afar from death;
Thou knocked aside the vengeance-thirsty spear
From me Thy servant, loving Thee in faith.

2. And well I know 'twas Thou that fostered me,
So that a Prophet grow from the rude youth;
Thou set me over Saul in majesty;
Thou didst declare — Thy word unchanging truth.

3. Thy Word I've heeded since my very birth,
And Samuel revealed this my vocation,
That I should serve Thy chosen people on earth,
Singing Thy praises through all generations.

4. And so I lift to Thee my songs of praise,
As here in the church vestibule I sing;
Harping aloft my psalmodies and lays,
The poet-king hymning the King of Kings.

XI. 1. Many defeats I've known, and many sorrows;
Much joy I've had to abdicate.

Care for my star's lined my brow with furrows,
And Thou hast bid me wait.

2. I've been lashed to a mocking pillory;
Numbered among the shameful crowd.
Shall I be saved? The thought has oppressed me
Since flames of my sins wall me round...

3. Thou'st bid me wait, and not flag in the fight
Though burdened with iniquities.
I must endure the battle this long night,
Before the morning star arise.

4. I've waited long upon the holy fire
Of the new Daystar's rosy glow;
Thy Sun's bright countenance my one desire,
Whose advent Thy sure words did vow.

5. For Thou didst promise, by Thy sacred Word
To bring salvation when Thou come,
And free us here enslaved; Thy mercy, Lord,
Removing all opprobrium.

6. And come Thou shalt, the joyful hour is nigh,
O Sun, resplendent Joy —
Thy beams shoot through the glooms on high,
Thy everlasting voice.

7. Thy voice I hear, I hear Thy mighty Word
Echo along the high ribbed vaults;
Thy flashing cart among the starry sward
Approaches, and all Heaven exults!

XII. 1. As I do, for the memory hasn't dimmed
Of mercy shown me as a boy,
When I so mired myself in mortal sin,
My soul I nearly did destroy.

2. Before me, kings as supplicants did fold
Their palms, bowed low before my throne;
Their crowns Thou gave to me, and cloth of gold,
That I might rule supreme, alone.

3. And yet I lusted for my servant's wife,
The hetman of my armed hosts.
Him I despatched alone into the strife —
Death guaranteed: his appointed post!

4. When (as I knew he must) at last he fell,
Slaughtered through my own knavery,
I cast upon his wife seduction's spell,
And bound her in love's slavery.

XIII. 1. For this Thou raised against me my own son,
Placing the weapon in his hand.
Ashamed and cowardly, then did I run —
But Thou his death of me didst command.

2. A frightful message was then brought to me,
Of Joab, who my axe-battalions led,
When my son Absalom was hanging on the tree —
His was the blow that struck him dead.

3. My son! Who took pride in each flowing lock
Of royal hair upon your head,
Who swore to heaven my death; the heavens mock
You with a horrid death, instead!

4. When in deep mourning I stretched out beside
Him, weeping the death of my son,
Thou willed through sorrow I be purified,
And set me back upon my throne.

XIV. 1. Thou didst command me, "Rise; Arise in Act,
Arise in all your splendour.
Above the city, a Temple erect
Wherein my Spirit may enter."

2. And so did I erect to Thee a fane
Of every ore and stone of worth,
For Thou didst vow my seed, though I should wane,
To multiply upon the earth.

3. O crescent be all future generations
Who shall praise Thee, by thy Name,
God of all gods, hymned by a mighty nation
One, everywhere, ever the Same.

4. And may their faithful praises ever ring
In Thy service, Thy stalwart sons.
Look mercifully upon them, King of Kings,
O Omnipotent, Trisagion!

He kneels.
In the depths, under the arcades of the side nave,
Night appears with her train.

SCENE 2.

NIGHT.
The water-birds alight on the river waves,
In the dark gardens softly rustle the leaves;
Throughout the gardens the trees murmur low,
The birds startle aloft, then stop, then go,
Fluttering their wings against the window sash,
The panes themselves tremble, and now — a flash
Of dawn sets them aflame.
But then again the rising sun's pushed back —
The choirs of ravens blot it out, with black
Wings as they fly about the roofs, and caw —

Charnel-house birds, screeching with raucous maw.
Like vermin seething on the castle walls
The ravens gather, thickly covering all:
Treetop and battlement, plot and architrave,
Thickly they bob upon the Vistula's waves.

She moves along the arcade,
Beneath the columns which prop up the choir loft,
And enters the proscenium.

HER TRAIN
Follows her.

NIGHT.
Shh! My sons — let us escape!
Shh, daughters — gather close your drapes,
Put out the stars that prick the gloom
Of your dark robes — come now, the tomb
Awaits us... Hush! Come on —
It's nearly dawn.
You hear? The hounds — we're soon at bay —
The stars pale at the dawning day —
Come, look not toward the heavy doors;
Someone has split them with bright sword.

Silence.

Shh! Here, the soul's dark keep:
Endless, dark and deep.
Daylight won't rouse us hence:
The tomb our sure defence.
Enter the dark, slide closed the lid,
Here in the depths we're safely hid.
The noisome dawn now taints the flood:
Her light splashes the Vistula.

CHORUS OF EUMENIDES.
  1. Mother, dear mother, the perfume
  Of roses! Ah, close not the tomb!

  2. The scent of living roses pours
  Upon us! Ah, one moment more!

NIGHT.
  No, daughters, turn away the face;
  Treacherous beams — that hateful stench!
  The votive lamp shows you our place:
  Below, with bones, on the grave bench.

CHORUS OF EUMENIDES.
  That kneeling man's harp — how it rings!
  Permit us but to hear him sing!

NIGHT.
  Daughters, the sun nips at our feet.
  Soon you will feel his searing heat!

CHORUS OF EUMENIDES.
  Mother! A bird rests on my palm!
  He throbs, just like the heart of man!

NIGHT.
  Cover your eyes, before the dawn
  That wakes the roses, dews the land!
  Quick! Into the depths with me to hide:
  The heavy doors creak open wide!

CHORUS OF EUMENIDES.
  1. Above the Vistula, the grey dawn breaks.
  2. But in the town it's night yet — no one wakes.
  3. Oh Mother, look at him — hold on a bit —
  4. The harpist stirs anew, flutters his lids,

1. Flutters his eyelids, gazes round about...
2. Mother, a golden crown adorns his brow.
4. The harp he bears is poured of purest gold.

1. Again he blinks, and looks about the grey Gloom...
2.   ... and into the shadows makes his way.

NIGHT.
Harpist! Thou singer of the Lord...

They sink beneath the floor.

SCENE 3.

AURORA
*Runs in from the side of the Church,
Her Train following her.*
Phoebus, my golden lover!
Arise! Toss back the covers
Of the skies, pursue the night
With thy rays — arrows in flight!
Servants! Fill to the very brim
The cups with nectar — to the rim!
And follow, follow, follow
My flight over hill and hollow.
Come my train, follow me, run —
Hot on my heels, O rising Sun,
Spin your golden wheels through
The furrows of the fields, pursue
My steps with rays from your shining quiver
As I precede you, over field and river,
My temples with rose-garlands bound.
Leaning over the Harpist.
Old man! O king! A growing crowd
Awaits your song, awaits your harp —

I wind you with a rosy scarf
That banishes the thinning dark.

HARPIST.
A large crowd's gathered at the gates?

AURORA.
A large crowd at the Jordan waits;
Since dawn, down at the river's bord
For you to sing them of the Lord
A banquet song.

HARPIST.
Me, stained with sin.
On Jordan's banks the people wait?
In large numbers? The crowd is great?

AURORA.
On Jordan's banks they await you, sire,
To hear you harp their one desire,
Exhausted with their journey long,
From far away they come, to hear your song.

HARPIST.
How shall I sing, O dawning light?
The temple still is wrapped in night.

AURORA.
I wind you with a rosy scarf —
The dawning light overcomes the dark.

*She draws away toward the Sołtyk chapel,
Her Train following.*

SCENE 4.

HARPIST.
   XV.
   1. Whole legions of people are massed —
A nation gathers at the gate.
They murmur, the legions, they ask —
Will I, with my song, their thirst slake?

   2. Whole legions of people are massed,
Great, the crowds grow greater still.
Will my song slake their thirst, they ask;
Will I, with my song, feed them their fill?

   3. Exhausted, their limbs they recline
Along the cold stones and the ruins.
Will Thy resurrected sun shine?
Does the harpist his instrument tune?

   4. My nation! I'll sing, and your thirst
Will slake with song. Come then, arise,
O dayspring of the dawn, now, burst!
Wing flashing rays across the skies!

   5. Hear the crowds murmuring, dear Lord:
Hear them grumble about the gates.
Help me sing out Thy comforting Word
To Thy people, who, broken, wait.

   6. They press close: now they're at the door.
The gates bend before the massy throng.
Enliven my powers, dear Lord;
Lend Thy strength to my feeble song!

CHORUS.
   Harpist!

HARPIST.
>Hear them, Blessed one!

CHORUS.
Harpist!

HARPIST.
>Lord, Thy Resurrection
>Hasten, Redeemer of mankind!

CHORUS.
Harpist!

HARPIST.
>With hunger they pine
>Here on Thy temple's stones, O Lord!
>O at Thy all-powerful Word
>The dead shall arise, if but Thou
>So nod Thy omnipotent brow —
>O Thou, who all spaces dost fill,
>Grant mercy, by Thy holy will
>Upon Thy suffering people all…

CHORUS.
Harpist!

HARPIST.
>O Lord, hear them call!
>Step forth upon the altar's height!

CHORUS.
Harpist!

HARPIST.
>All-powerful God, lend my songs might!

CHORUS.
Harpist! Harpist! Harpist!

SCENE 5.

HARPIST.
    XVI.
    1. All pain and tears will fade away
    At thy advent, Lion of God.
    Defeat, deceit were crushed that day
    On which Thou spilt Thy holy blood.

    2. Lion of Judah, come Thou nigher,
    Borne on Thy flaming chariot.
    From Thy brow spills a rain of fire,
    O Mighty, Everlasting God!

    3. Immortal God, beyond all change,
    Who rulest the whole universe,
    Thou put'st an end to slavery's reign,
    Our servile fetters now are burst.

    4. Such is the might of Thy blest wings:
    Chains crushed, forever are we saved.
    Swing, hammers! Let the church bells sing
    His glorious Rising from the grave!

    XVII.
    1. For through Thy Rising from the tomb
    Thou dost renew all of creation,
    Giving new life, dispersing gloom
    For all — Regeneration!

    2. Blessed be Thou, Almighty, Great
    Lord God, in song, mighty in storm.
    Come, Spirit, to us, Incarnate;
    Immortal now our life reform.

    3. Be with us on this glorious day,
    Thou Divine Conqueror of death.

All creatures sing *Laudamus Te!*
With one exultant breath.

4. The trumpets blare, the bells all ring,
The winds blow, and the thunder roars.
Thy praise today all Nature sings,
Thou Lion, our Resurrected Lord!

XVIII.
1. Upon the wilted flowers now falls
Thy dew; refreshed, they fragrant stand —
The beggar and the wealthy, all
Raise up in thanks their prayerful hands.

2. The wretched from their misery
Thou dost raise up, merciful Lord;
Their wing'd battalions rise to Thee,
Strengthened by Thy all-conquering Word.

3. They soar above hovel and combe,
Above the castle and its bells;
With morning dew are slaked the blooms,
Dew plashing down from heavenly wells.

4. Above the waters do they race,
Hymning Thy praise in happy song.
To Thee they rise as one, in haste,
And Thou dost bless the jubilant throng.

XIX.
1. 'Twas not for this that I processed
Before Thy tapers' glow:
Not for this, that I might confess
The secrets of my soul.

2. 'Tis not to fault my enemies,
Their baseness to indict;
Vengeance is Thine — and clemency —
I praise Thy dawning light.

3. With other prayers, that would relate
Here, in the breaking dawn,
Thy grace, in raising to this state,
To this great vocation,

4. Thy wretched servant, whom Thou call'st
To stand, with harp, watchful, to abide
As Thy refulgence golden falls
From the great altar's height;

5. To praise Thee for the holy might
Of Thy will, free and full,
That makes for me all fardels light
Through Thy Word infallible.

6. Come Lord, before my people, bright;
They call to Thee, my nation.
Rise to us, as Thou rose Easter night,
Make tremble this fane's foundations.

7. Before Thee, this grand church shall fall
Upon my people's necks;
Yet after three days, at Thy call
It shall stand new, erect,

8. Of ancient crimes and sins made clean,
Its slavery forgot;
Renewed shall stand, eternal, serene
At Thy Word, Holy God.

9. Tear through the vault, push down the walls,
Tumble down altar, throne;

Come, sweet Redeemer! Thus we call
In the rosy-fingered dawn.

10. I hear a rumble from afar —
Hoofbeats — Here comes the Sun!
Thus rush the hosts of Thy centaurs,
Smashing pillar and column!

11. The mortar cracks, the blocks down slide,
Walls pavements now bestrew.
Thy golden cart majestic rides
Triumphant over the tomb.

12. Thy golden face shines brilliantly,
Thy robes, like golden fleece.
Thine eyes sparkle with victory;
Night's mysteries now cease.

13. Thy wheels roll over the silver tomb.
O Saviour, crush our chains!
Speak, Dawning Lord "I am with you"
Great One, Lord of this fane.

14. Say, Lord: "I come, as God I come"
And on these cold stones write:
"God am I, there is no other one,
None equal to my might.

15. "By the fires which about me play,
By this my Holy Word,
A new cathedral shall stand today,
Where I shall be your Lord."

Thunder in the choir loft.

SCENE 6.

HARPIST
　Lifts himself up from the floor
　Where he had been lying prone.
　His head and harp are shining in the dawn's light.
　A thunderclap;
　From the summit of the main altar we hear:

THE VOICE OF THE SAVIOUR:
　I am!

HARPIST.
　　　　Come, Saviour!

SAVIOUR.
　　　　　　　　Strength, and might!

HARPIST.
　O come, for Thou hast vanquished night.

　Thunderclaps
　About the choir loft.

SAVIOUR:
　I am!

HARPIST.
　　　　Come, Saviour!

SAVIOUR.
　　　　　　　　Strength, and might!

HARPIST
　Is lifted to the summit of the choir loft
　Above the organ.
　Thunderclaps.
　Orchestra and harp resound from the vaults.

One hears
The whining screech of the demolished panels
Of the silver tomb
From the direction of the altar of St. Stanisław.
From that direction:

APOLLO
Rides in upon a golden chariot
Pulled by four white stallions.
Thunderclap.
Brightness.

1. Musicians, pluck your golden strings
In floods of melodious fire —
Flame-like, orchestral chords now ring,
For the Sun is mounting higher.

2. He's risen! Sing His Resurrection!
He, once of thorn-pierced brow
Ascends the altar, His golden throne.
The Sun's full risen now.

3. Play, harpist! Fiddlers, ply your bows.
As Dayspring's floods now crest,
Above the city stretch rainbows.
Hey! Coral adorns His breast!

4. The organs boom, the thunders shock —
Tornados of sound are whirled.
In flame now stands the House of God,
Rejoicing in her Herald.

5. Harpist, reverb your singing lyre!
See how the children run:
From field to nave, from nave to choir,
To vault, where plays the Sun.

6. The fiddlers all accompany
Your psalm, your song of songs!
It's heard in town, and on the lea
Where woodland spirits throng.

7. He's racing, hey! He speeds, he bounds,
Apollo, god of light.
He flies, and from high Tatra mounts,
Nymphs following, flashing bright.

8. The swift wind over the meadow flies;
Smile for the Sun, Harpist, play!
Apollo, come! Apollo, arise
For the Lord's Resurrection Day!

9. With sonorous voice sings Zygmunt's bell —
Its hammer strikes with might.
Trumpets resound over hill and dell,
Joining his regal flight.

10. Trumpets like cannon-fire resound
As once, on these same leas;
As if Poland had risen now
From off her bended knees.

11. As if she'd now good fortune won
After so many years,
And faded in oblivion
Were all her toils and tears.

12. High over the peoples, through the air,
The sacred song takes flight;
Over bloodied Poland, Acropolis, where
Her kings sleep, as does their right.

13. I'll wake the centuries one day;
I've stood before God's face,

Whose Living Word conquered the fray —
His victory I praise.

14. The song is finished, Wawel's rune,
Her deathless fame re-told.
God's finger hovers above these stones,
Once, and again, His scroll.

ACROPOLIS

A Proposal for the Renovation and Expansion of Wawel
Conceived by Stanisław Wyspiański and Władysław Ekielski, 1904–1907[46]

In the Autumn of 1904 — and thus a few weeks after the Royal Castle at Wawel was returned to the nation, Stanisław Wyspiański summoned me to his home. He proposed that we work together on a plan for the renovation and expansion of the entire Hill, with an eye to its future exploitation. At that time, it was a well known fact that the army was not only to abandon the Royal Castle, but the other buildings on Wawel Hill as well, which for the most part had been used as hospitals.

At this moment, so significant for Polish society, when, after 100 years, we could once more call the ancient Royal Castle, and indeed the entire Hill, *ours,* Wyspiański began to ponder just how — over the course of years — the Hill might be developed; what sort of buildings it might contain, what their appearance might be and where they could be located.

Wyspiański's deep respect for our past, and in particular for Wawel, is universally known. Wawel is the setting for his poem *Acropolis*; on Wawel the action of *Bolesław Śmiały, Legenda* and *Liberation* are played out. Among his sketches one finds myriad details from the Castle and the Hill. Just like the Athenian Acropolis, which contains within it the sum of the faith and glory of the Greeks, so does Wawel contain all of our splendour and our faith...

He stated that *In connection with the evacuation of Wawel it is incumbent upon all contemporary artists to give a clear, visual expression of how the future structures of Wawel might be imagined.*

---

46   Please see the Illustrations section of the book to reference the Wyspiański/Ekielski plan. There, the reader will also find several of Wyspiański's individual architectural drawings for buildings referenced in this text, as well as a photograph of the architectural model envisioned by the two men. Once more, I express my sincere gratitude to the National Museum in Kraków for permitting us to reproduce these invaluable visual aids.

I myself had pondered this question more than once. However, I never proceeded to endow my ideas with any visual form. Now, when such a great man, of such immense genius, so fanatically and lovingly devoted to our history and the monuments of our past, proposed a collaboration on "Wawel — the Polish Acropolis," I felt a vital obligation to accept.

I therefore undertook — as much as this was possible — an exact inventory of the existing state of things on Wawel Hill. I was able to examine more than one detail in person, and the visual working up of this inventory constituted a background, against which one might begin to consider planning renovation and expansion among the existing military buildings. Although my inventory was certainly incomplete in some details, I came to see it as sufficient for our purposes: to create an idea of future constructions on Wawel.

Our plan shows all of the buildings currently in existence on Wawel. These are signified in black: the Cathedral (F) with the Treasury (E); Zygmunt's Tower (G), the Tower of the Silver Bells (I) and the Clock Tower (H); the Royal Castle (C) with the Arcaded Courtyard (D), Terraces (A) and Bastions (B1, B2, B3, B4). Further, the Archdiocesan Museum (M) recently restored by Zygmunt Hendel,[47] the House of the Cathedral Vicars (N) and — partially — Buildings O, Y, and W, and finally the Bastions P2 and P4. All of these buildings will remain as they are. The existing Hospital Buildings, Outbuildings, etc., appear only in their general external outlines, while the new buildings which we propose are designated by hatching. Two roads lead to Wawel: one, from the north, leads from the city via Ulica Kanonicza, and the second, as an exit road, leads from the south, beginning at the Church of St. Bernard.

With this inventory in hand, we began our work. Each of us sketched on our own. Later, we defined the purpose and placement of the proposed buildings together during discussions. During these meetings, we came to accept the following key points:

1. Our work is not primarily concerned with the restoration of existing buildings. However, some of the buildings in need of restoration have been included in our plan, within their existing footprints. We started from the conviction that Wawel ought to be the focus of the *life* of the nation, as the most ideal efflorescence of its national and intellectual culture. Thus, we felt that it must constitute a visible symbol of that nation and its culture in the

---

47   See *Architekt*, 1905 (*Author's note*).

form of a series of buildings growing out of its *living* organism. Yet all the same, although our aim was to restore some no longer existing buildings, out of a veneration for the past, we agreed to do this only to the extent that such reconstructions would serve our artistic goals (I am speaking here of the churches of St. Michael and St. George).

2. The Royal Castle was not a subject of our discussions, nor did we ever consider violating its present form. We were aware of the fact that it was to be restored, and we understood that matter as something existing in and of itself, apart from all else. The restoration of the Castle is a separate project. For that reason, in this plan we touch upon the Castle only in so far as the buildings that we projected in its environs demand it; we consider the Castle only in relation to the context of the new buildings in its immediate neighbourhood. The same is true for the Cathedral and the Archdiocesan Museum.[48] I do not wish to expound upon the extent of the projected restoration of the Royal Castle, and its artistic furnishings. That said, I will state that we were convinced that the Royal Castle should remain *the ancient royal castle it is* and should serve no other ends. We were also convinced that there will come a time when its youth will be restored... Any new allocation of the building calculated for the short term should not efface the memory of the past events, the glorious and the sad, which it has witnessed, for it is not right to change the character and purpose of any ancient building — all the more so in the case of so important a national monument as Wawel Castle.

Consequently, its structure and its extensive halls would make it useless for the purposes of a National Museum.

Let us dwell for a moment on the sort of conditions that ought to be found in a modern museum, in consideration of the sort of mission we envision for our National Museum.[49] The plans already made in this regard

---

48 Here are a few of the details taken up in our plans: the development of the garden terraces (A), the completion of the quadrangle of the Great Courtyard (D), the creation of a Cathedral portal (K). These and other minor matters occurred to us almost incidentally, and were not necessarily considered binding (*Author's note*).

49 The National Museum in Kraków was established by the City Council in 1879, on the upper storey of the Sukiennice (Cloth Hall) in the centre of the Main Market Square. Although that space still houses many important Polish paintings and sculptures, the museum collections soon outgrew the space, and at the time that Ekielski was composing his essay, plans were being discussed for the creation

can be summarised in a few points, none of which fit the Royal Castle, because… it is a Royal Castle. And so:

A well-organised museum ought to have rather low ceilings. Paintings and other expositions displayed at a height greater than 2.5 metres cannot be examined properly — to say nothing of sculpture, which in most cases cannot abide even such an elevation.

The halls of a museum should be shallow. At a depth greater than four metres the proper lighting of exhibits becomes impossible.

The great value of museum deposits makes fire-resistant ceilings a *sine qua non*.

Such a museum construction affords the exhibits exactly what they need, and provides visitors with the greatest possible transparency and tranquility, heightening their experience, and allowing for peaceful reflection.

Even if we were to pass over these conditions, essential to a museum, which would be irresponsible, there yet remains the matter of those so immense halls of the Castle. In the very nature of things, our National Museum possesses exhibits neither so valuable, nor materially speaking so large, as some would wish to properly decorate these huge interior spaces. The beautiful Empire or Biedermayer furniture of our old manor houses looks wonderful in the context for which it was designed. In the halls of the Castle, on the other hand, they would make a rather ridiculous impression. How the halls of the Royal Castle might look, properly speaking, might be intimated from the fantasies of the architect Stanisław Noakowski of Moscow. At this time, we possess only one object that would suit these halls: Matejko's *Prussian Homage*…[50]

For these reasons, therefore, we would *prefer an empty Royal Castle* to a failed museum…

---

of a new museum. The construction of the main building of the National Museum in Kraków, on 3rd of May Avenue, was begun in 1934.

50   Stanisław Wyspiański drew up a proposal for a team of painters for the decoration of the individual chambers (*Author's note*). The *Prussian Homage* (*Hołd pruski*, 1879-1882) is a massive historical canvas by Jan Matejko. It depicts Albrecht Hohenzollern's oath of allegiance to King Zygmunt I, which took place on the Main Market Square in Kraków on 10 April 1525. It can be viewed in the National Museum collections in the Sukiennice — just metres from where the historical event transpired. A portion of the Sukiennice building is seen in the background.

3. The gigantic piazza, which would come about after the pulling down of existing army buildings, is divided into three parts, each as it were an individual courtyard: Cathedral Square, Victory Square, and House of Representatives Square. In this way, one might obtain for both buildings favourable distance and proportionate space.[51]

4. The concept of rebuilding two churches: those of St. Michael and St. George, the location and general shapes of which we found — we assume — perfectly sketched on the plan of the Castle from 1796, arose from our piety toward the past.[52] It suggested to us a quaint — in our opinion — architectonic motif of arrangement: St. Michael's stands almost perfectly in the centre and constitutes an important framing focus of the square before the Cathedral. The asymmetrical setting of St. George's tempers the rigidity of the layout of Victory Square.

5. Starting from the Royal Castle (from the St. Bernard side) and continuing to Bastion P1, we propose an arcaded gallery, in especial consideration of the beautiful landscape vistas spreading about these places.

6. We preserve the general silhouette of Wawel as it exists today. We do not diminish the dominance of the Royal Castle, which rests, in any event, on the very promontory of the hill. The new buildings are to be constructed almost exactly on the sites of the existing military buildings, and their elevation — more or less — is in agreement with the height of the former. Only there, where the motif of the plan demands it, would we build taller.[53]

7. For the enlivening of the silhouette, the preservation of the character of a *castle,* and as an expiation for the mistakes of 1820, we would restore in their original shapes two defensive municipal bastions, on the model of those then torn down,[54] Bastion P1 "Desolate" [*Spustoszała*] and Bastion P3

---

[51] It is unclear what "both" is referring to here, since Ekielski is describing the division of space into threes. Most likely, he is referring to the main buildings that dominate these spaces: the Cathedral, or the House of the Cathedral Vicars, on the one hand, and the proposed House of Representatives on the other.

[52] S. Odrzywolski: *Zamek królewski na Wawelu* [*The Royal Castle on Wawel Hill*] and the survey of the cathedral by the same author, printed in *Architekt* (1901) were our important sources. We had no access to any others (*Author's note*).

[53] The roof over the House of Representatives, the dome above the Senate House, the powerful mass of which we take to be a desirable counterpoise to the Royal Castle group (*Author's note*).

[54] King Zygmunt III Waza built the so-called Waza Gate in 1591. Between the years 1820-1827 the "mistaken" restoration of the gate was carried out, in

"Sword-bearers" [*Miecznicy*],[55] preserving the existing Bastion P2 "Thieves" [*Złodziejska*] and P4 "Sandomierska."

8. The Renaissance style, with its thick use of attic motifs, will endow the future group of buildings with a distinct character. The existing castles in Baranów and Krasiczyn[56] seem to argue for the adoption of just such a motif for the future buildings in the Wawel complex.

We must confess that we did not have the courage to introduce Modernism to Wawel. This does not mean, however, that in the future, when that movement ceases to be a field of experimentation and trial, it will not obtain a right of place.

CONTENTS OF THE PROJECT

The ancient *Thieves' Bastion P2*, which stands on that legendary spot near the

DRAGON'S CAVE μ,

constitutes as it were an entry point for the whole complex: directly across from it, on the shore of the Vistula, lies the fantastically conceived

CASTLE OF THE BOLESŁAWS λ,

containing the sarcophagus of

BOLESŁAW THE BOLD κ;

beneath the DESOLATE BASTION P1,

---

testament to which the tablet reading *Senatus Populusque Cracoviensis Restituit MDCCCXXVII* can still be seen carved thereon. Subsequent restorations did not reconstruct the bastions removed in the XIXth century.

55   A. Brabowski: *Skarbniczka naszej archeologii* [The Treasury of our Archeology] (*Author's note*).

56   The castle in Baranów Sandomierski, sometimes called the "Mały Wawel" (Little Wawel), was built between 1591 and 1606 for the Lubomirski family. One of its architects was the Florentine Santi Gucci, who is also associated with Wawel Cathedral. The castle in Krasiczyn was begun 1580 and completed in 1631. Projected by Galleazzo Appiani, it is named for the Krasicki family.

THE FIRST ENTRANCE TO THE INTERIOR;

beneath the THIEVES' BASTION

THE SECOND ENTRANCE;

beneath the SWORD-BEARERS' BASTION P3

THE THIRD ENTRANCE.

These three entrances are aligned on axes with the

COLUMN δ

that stands in the centre of the courtyard of

VICTORY SQUARE,

on the summit of which stands the winged

NIKE, GODDESS OF VICTORY.

The socle of the Column is raised on a broad brick base: on one corner of which is

A SPEAKER'S ROSTRUM ε.

~~~~~~

Along the Thieves' Bastion / Nike axis is found

THE CHURCH OF ST. MICHAEL α

conceived along the model of Sainte-Chapelle in Paris, as a stone construction of one level, and before it:

a FIELD ALTAR γ.

To the side,

THE CHURCH OF ST. GEORGE θ,

planned as a church with two naves.⁵⁷

Let us take up our position in front of the Field Altar. To the right of the House of the Cathedral Vicars N, separated from it by a narrow alleyway, spreads the corpus of

THE NATIONAL MUSEUM O,

constructed within the existing walls of the military barracks as a building of two levels, with a ground-floor annex on Victory Square in which, besides the main entrance, the Offices of the Museum are to be housed. The corpus of this part is connected with the existing corpus by means of a corridor, from which one obtains a view of the Cathedral. The contents of the structure: a number of long, but not wide (5m) corridor-like exposition halls; larger halls and small offices; on the second floor,⁵⁸ halls lit entirely from above (It was this decision that gave rise to the attic motif). Two staircases provide communication between the floors and facilitate circulation in such a way that one need not retrace one's steps overmuch in order to visit the entire building.

The existing building is in a bad state. It must be fundamentally rebuilt anyway, and thus it will be easy to apply the restoration to the needs of a Museum as described above.

---

57   The model for this was the Church of the Holy Cross (Św. Krzyża). The rectangular shape of the plan of the nave argues for the division of the nave into two halves, which, as is well known, is often found in Poland. One of Wyspiański's dreams was to reproduce the Church of the Holy Cross. More than once, in speaking of architectural works, he stated that it was better to copy well a good structure from the past, than to construct a bad, new one — a statement that certainly sounded original in the mouth of a Modernist (*Author's note*).

58   Thus Ekielski, departing from the traditional European numeration of storeys. Where he writes First Floor, read *parterre*; where he writes Second Floor, as here, read *first (European) floor*.

~~~~~~

Around *Victory Square* are set structures which together constitute the buildings

of the POLISH PARLIAMENT:

Q, the SENATE

and S the HOUSE OF REPRESENTATIVES.

Between these lies the apartment of the King, R, for those occasions when there is an Address from the Throne, or when the Senate is in session. The *House of Representatives* is symmetrically divided into *Right* and *Left* sections; with chancelleries chiefly in the *Senate* building and on the upper floors.

The semicircular arcades, with the triumphal arch h immediately in the vicinity of St. George's, closes the

HOUSE OF REPRESENTATIVES SQUARE.

~~~~~~

The Bastion shaped according to the foundations preserved on the plan of 1796 (the Tenczyń Bastion) separates the House of Representatives from the

ACADEMY OF SCIENCES, U:

which is the building that Wyspiański referred to as the *Capitol, Valhalla*. It is thus dedicated to the *glory* of that most respected Institution[59] that we possess, and is intended for the gala *Annual Conferences* and Committee Sessions, which have a connection with the past. In the immediate neighbourhood of the arcades facing the courtyard is a type of ancient

---

59   The Polish Academy of Sciences (Polska Akademia Umiejętności). It was founded in 1872; its headquarters are on Ul. Sławkowska in Kraków.

GYMNASIUM, T

for the use of our votaries of learning. One of Stanisław Wyspiański's sketches presents a view of this part of the project. Another depicts the monumental courtyard and façade of the Academy of Sciences; above the entranceway there is a bas relief: a reproduction of Matejko's *Grunwald*.[60]

~~~~~~

Across from the Cathedral, and attached to the Royal Castle, stands a structure which has been transformed quite a bit: after removing from it the superfluous portion that juts into the courtyard, we shall remodel it as

the BISHOP'S PALACE, Y,

the official *Curia Episcopi*. It will include the bishop's hall, and next to it, the cells of the Canons ρ (on the first floor).

Further, we shall preserve the old, though today much built-over

ROYAL STABLES, W

with coach-houses and a courtyard, X. Because we are only generally familiar with the interior, we preserve their form here only in a general fashion.

One of Wyspiański's sketches presents

the CATHEDRAL SQUARE.

~~~~~~

We have projected the construction of a

GREEK THEATRE, ν

---

60   Matejko's *Battle of Grunwald* (1878) is a large historical canvas depicting the 1410 victory of Polish-led troops under the command of Władysław Jagiełło, over the forces of the German Knights of the Cross.

with a capacity of 700 seats, carved into the cliff, with enchanting views of the nearby surroundings, as well as the Tatras and Babia Góra. Personally speaking, I believe that our late lamented friend Wyspiański possessed all the gifts necessary to bring to life the tragic figures of our history and legends, addressing the soul with concise words and stirring it with tragic speech and dramatic complications.

The idea of a Greek theatre has traditions among us in the Łazienki Park in Warsaw. Above and beyond that, there exists a contemporary movement towards the reanimation of theatrical presentations in the open air. It is sufficient to point to a series of articles on this topic printed in Volume VI of *Architect*. The passion plays at Oberammergau are well known and popular. Periodically, similar spectacles are held in the ancient theatres in Nîmes, Béziers and Orange. The complex of buildings funded by Miss Pheoebe Hearst at the University of California in Berkeley includes a reproduction of the ancient theatre of Epidaurus, where classical dramas are performed in the open air. The creation of so constructed a theatre would suit well the culture of our society which, as is well known, follows our youths' inscenations of Greek tragedies with great interest.

Here we provide only the general plan of such a theatre. As far as the outfitting and equipping of the stage is concerned, I was expecting Wyspiański to direct me, who in his discussion of *Hamlet*[61] sheds such a singular light on the scenic arrangements of that play. Unfortunately, his illness and subsequent passing did not permit him to work up a detailed elaboration of the structure in question.

~~~~~~

At the foot of the hill near the Bernardine church there rises

the FALCON SOCIETY STADIUM, π

---

[61]   Stanisław Wyspiański, *The Tragicall Historie of Hamlet, Prince of Denmarke, by William Shakespeare. Według tekstu polskiego Józefa Paszkowskiego, świeżo przeczytana i przemyślana przez St. Wyspiańskiego* [According to the Polish Tekst of Józef Paszkowski, Freshly Read Through and Meditated on by Stanisław Wyspiański] (Kraków: Drukarnie Uniwersytetu Jagiellońskiego, 1905)

where young men will compete for the laurels of athletic victories, since our nation is to be strong in both mind and body...

~~~~~~

It is our opinion that the military gate in the fortifications that leads to the Cathedral ought to be replaced with

ANOTHER, K

modelled on the gateway to the church of St. Andrew.[62]

We preserve the fortifications of Wawel in their entirety. Certainly, only the battlements (*crenellage*) will be superfluous, especially in those places whence beautiful vistas of the city and the environs will be found. There, it would be proper to construct balconies of the type we propose to set before the entrance near the Cathedral. The barbicans which exist at the fortifications will be easily transformed into

LAPIDARIA, L

one of which we have projected in the shape of the barbican on Floriańska St.[63]

Here ends our work. The question of the slopes of Wawel remains open. I think, however, that we would have opted for their preservation in their present, semi-wild, state.

~~~~~~

---

62   A Romanesque church on Grodzka St., not far from Wawel, built between 1079 and 1098. Its founder was the historical Sieciech, advisor to King Władysław Herman, who appears in Wyspiański's plays centring on the conflict between Bolesław the Bold and St. Stanisław.

63   The Barbakan, or Rondel as it is familiarly known, is a circular defensive structure of brick. With a diameter of 24.4 metres, it is the largest such structure in Europe. Connected to the defensive walls of the Old Town by a "neck" stretching over the city moat (hence the nickname "rondel," i.e. "saucepan"), it was constructed in the final years of the XVth century. Diametrically opposite Wawel, it stands at the beginning of Ulica Floriańska, the first leg of the "Royal Road" proceeding via the Main Market Square (Rynek Główny) and Ulica Grodzka to Wawel.

If it were not for Wyspiański's protracted illness, and subsequent demise, our project might have become more mature and polished. More than one aspect of the plan might benefit from reconsideration! At the moment of his passing I pondered this matter deeply. Certainly, the drawings as already prepared needed nothing more than consolidation. The entire project is brought to completion with his sketches.

I must add that we also planned to work up an architectural model in either plaster or wood,[64] and moreover, I add here Wyspiański's idea of how the effect of the projected monuments, squares and areas set apart for statuary, ponds, etc., might be tested out. He mulled over the creation of theatrical perspectives showing the entire Wawel complex rebuilt according to our ideas, which would have allowed us to finally fix the proper volume of certain objects, such as the bastions, domes, etc. Likewise, such perspectives might also have been constructed envisioning our Cathedral Square, Victory Square, or House of Representatives Square, as decorations for suitably chosen plays, with everything drawn according to a proportionate scale.

~~~~~~

Our project is an idealistic one, yet even at first glance, it is obvious that it has a firm basis in reality. All of the projected structures possess a real purpose and aim, which seem "ideal" only because they are... distant in time.

I am reminded today of that splendid public manifestation on May Third[65] of the present year, and am struck by how differently the structures that we project might have framed it. How differently would the ardent words of Rector Morawski[66] have sounded were they delivered from our rostrum, rather than from the window of the Vicarage!

Is all of this to remain just a dream!!?...

If the realisation of our project were already in the offing, the strength

---

64   See the Illustrations for a photo of the model on display in the National Museum.

65   The Polish national holiday, celebrating the Constitution of 1791.

66   Kazimierz Morawski (1852-1925), classical philologist, rector of the Jagiellonian University, president of the Academy of Arts and Sciences, member of the Upper House of the Austrian Parliament during the Habsburg years.

and life of one architect would not suffice to bring it to a successful conclusion. Nor would that be a desirable thing: such a complex of buildings demands variety in the conception of its details.

However, in the future, when the thoughts of men turn to Wawel, to what should be erected there, and how those structures ought to be conceived, I think that what we have projected should be taken into consideration.

We devoted much time and effort to the goal valued by each and every artist: *the projection of great works.* Perhaps some day there will stand similar structures, in forms recalling ours, there on Wawel Hill, that

DEAREST OF ALL PLACES,

our

POLISH ACROPOLIS,

which remembers our beginnings, our Kings, our Victories, our Catastrophes and Hopes, and which — may it so please God — shall witness our

BETTER FUTURE.

Władysław Ekielski

APPENDICES

INTRODUCTORY DIDASCALIA to *Bolesław the Bold*.

Take wing with me unto those ancient times
To which but dream or memory can lead;
Where from the visions that precede us there
The visions of a yearning soul are born.
There we shall find a palace, sacred with treasure;
There we are led by rhapsode-guardians.
There do they point, arms stretching through the mists:
Look closely: the past now lies clear before you.

I had a dream, and in my dream I saw
Such things to which my heart leapt yearning:
There ghostly figures trod, all bearing swords,
Shields of leather, and some heavy items
Of leathern armour. Dressed in glowing robes,
The train, wrapped in the colours of the moon,
Stood before Wawel castle, and my eyes.

There was a wooden palace there, of linden-planks
Fastened together with rafters of oak.
There purlins, split of centuries-old branches,
Made shelter overhead for the royal court.

And in this court I saw a chamber, immense,
Dim and deserted — behind it, thrums the Vistula,
Its waves beating so, the wind's very roar is dulled;
All this is still present to my ears and eyes.

Amidst the floor a crimson runner led
Toward the spot, whereon the royal throne
Stood, shining, all covered in golden plates.

When I entered that empty room abandoned,
The moon shone in through empty panes.

But then it seemed, someone before me
Had walked into the room, closing the doors behind:
His face was covered with a silver visor.

Who are you? You, who guard the nation's mysteries,
Who led me to this ancient seat of kings?
In answer, he laid his hand upon his lips,
And then, himself, set ear against the door.
And then I heard... behind that barrier,
A horn sound, as horns were wont to sound
When kings were kings, and courts abandoned not —
As if men had returned to that deaf palace.

Here to me, here to me, O souls of my people,
Who populate my dreams!
Here, to me! I shall lend you colour,
Such as you wore yourselves in ancient times.
Let the king gird himself with armour, before me!
Let the king stand before me, dripping blood!

Then did a little gate in a side wall
Turn ... am I in the castle, or on stage?
A light shone then upon an empty notch;
Two shadows flickered: one was maidenly,
The other was a man — as tough as oak!

The man heeds something — hand cupping his ear —
His other hand (the right hand) shakes with ire.

Again the horn sounds, closer now it strikes,
And with its voice immense sounds through the courts,
Carried aloft by the eagle-bearing wind...

Then did the pair begin to speak — I hear them;
Loving their voices, tender, the spellbound pair.
It is the King that coos, and Krasawica.

II. ARGUMENTUM to the drama of King Bolesław and Bishop Stanisław.

From history we know next to nothing. All that has come down to us from the entire rich legend and the long process are their general, very surface contours. But this is quite a lot as it is. One might say that, since the surface contours and outlines are really external, then the silhouette of the events (of the drama) is true. And so within this silhouette *everything* must fit.

What is the appearance of that silhouette?

There was (some sort of) a quarrel between the king and the bishop, or the nation, at the head of which stood the bishop — to the extent that the events took place on the territory of Kraków.

The result of these events — definitive for us — is that we have no kingdom of our own any more, but the tomb (of the saint) remains on Wawel hill. The holy tomb.

The fact that the king retreated from Kraków is proof of nothing. Because at the time, both king and throne were movable — not set in any particular place.

Through how many lands did that king travel; over how many lands did he extend his sway, with force!

When he withdrew from them, so did his "sway" ebb (only to be reimposed after a short while).

The fact that Bolesław did not return to Kraków was a coincidence. And this is the warp of "another" drama, arising from quite different causes (new figures, and hence the new characters in the dramas).

The knightly bishop was a strange person. Especially as his death could become so meaningful — from the very first moment, death made of the "person killed" a person of the first rank!

A national figure!

If there was any animus against him, it was found at the court of the reigning Bolesławs and Władysławs.

What then was the role of the bishop?

He was a knightly bishop; his role was knightly.

An armed archangel. Lucifer advancing upon the burning torch of Bolesław.

Bolesław the king, crowned by many (15?) Polish bishops (in Kraków or Gniezno) takes up his residence in Kraków, marries (with a Rusinka,[67] for his mother was a Rusinka) and sets off on a campaign against Kievan Ruś.

There, his knightly geste ends in shame. His knights abandon him and return to their landed estates. Left alone with his own courtiers, he is forced to escape.

He returns, and wreaks his revenge.

On whom — ?

On the nation —

On those who abandoned him. And since those who abandoned him betrayed the majesty of the state, he wreaks his revenge on traitors.

On those who — according to the Bishop-Knight Stanisław — were against predatory wars of partition and banditry.

The king returns, and engages in a slaughter of his knights. These, perhaps, are already doing battle with their own retainers and peasants (?) who had remained behind, and whom their adulterous wives took to their bed, in the absence of their husbands.

The king moves on to judge the unfaithful wives and execute them as well. He confiscates their goods, enriches his own treasury with the wealth pilfered from them, and takes to himself the produce of their fields.

He destroys the nation, slaughtering the husbands and the wives — according to the Bishop-Knight Stanisław, who makes war on the king.

Who raises his sword against the king!

But the king defeats him with the sword.

The king kills him.

Yet the Bishop-Knight Stanisław is victorious — after his death.

Still, he dies as the defender of traitorous men and unfaithful wives — he dies as a traitor!

---

67   Today we would say "a Ukrainian," although that term did not exist at the time in the same manner as it does today. In our translation, we use "Russian" as a general translation for "Kievan Ruś." Kiev, in modern-day Ukraine, was the matrix of the Eastern Slavic nations. What we know as Russia today — Eastern Slavs further east and north of the Kievan centre of power — was not as influential or powerful as was Kievan Ruś.

"We will not absolve the traitorous bishop, nor will we defend the cruel king."

That king himself must have had quite a few lovers.

Of what sort — ?

Certainly not the wives of others — since he treated adulteresses so severely — (pressing suckling dogs to their breasts).

So, of what sort?

Girls of all sorts — Russians in Kievan Ruś, Cracovian maidens in Kraków, etc. The story of Krystyna, wife of Mściwój, is certainly slander, lies and invention. But it is true that there did occur some sort of misunderstanding between the king and the queen — something dealing with jealousy, since from that grain of truth there grew such a legend (though false in its details).

The legend of Piotrowin[68] is untenable. It does not hold up under criticism. The whole story is an invention, a myth.

But what is the grain of truth it contains?

The image.

The wordless image, without a text.

The bishop, accompanied by the corpse, by a man long dead. (Death).

Where do we find such a man, who comes back from the grave to give witness to his truth?

In Mickiewicz's ballad *Lilies*.

Historians have no faith in the story of Piotrowin. They know that it is a myth. But everyone must believe in *Lilies* — for it is truth — eternal truth.

The person who denies the truth and summons the dead to witness to his lie — must be struck by the lightning bolt of truth.

No one is able to lie with impunity!!

He who dares to lie — must be confronted with the truth — the living truth will stand before his eyes — and kill him.

He who stands at the head of the nation and defends its misery — will not take issue with the king about — money.

It cannot be true, that the Bishop-Knight Stanisław did not wish to

---

68   The ghostly Sir Piotr/Peter.

pay the king an illegal, wrongly exacted payment, for goods long obtained with payments long made. —

Certainly, he would have paid three and four times over, to his own detriment — to the advantage of the greedy man. —

Neither did the Bishop-Knight Stanisław need to accumulate goods, for he probably had quite enough of them, nor was the king such a "greedy" fellow — for his first soubriquet was *Szczodry* ("the Generous.")

So the king was slandered, and the bishop was portrayed as a poor man, miserly jealous of each cent in his inviolable pocketbook.

These were not petty people —
They did not do battle over petty things —
Two great spirits engaged in battle, over great matters.
They met in great crimes; they attempted great deeds.
By blood and by the sword! —
Both of them, by the sword!
Blood stained the hands and robes of the royal killer —
The king was more powerful by the sword —
Stanisław's death — elevated him higher than the king —
He grew through Death.
So, who from this quarrel — from this battle — remained — ?

The king withdrew from Kraków along with his court, which does not mean at all that he ceded to the bishop or to the bishop's allies. But, perhaps he did not want to remain long at the scene — of the crime.

He abandoned Wawel Castle on the Vistula —

His brother remained; Władysław. — And since he remained, this proves that he did so, perhaps only by the will and at the *command* of his brother.

The fact that his brother did not return from Hungary? This is something conditioned by quite different, later causes, which have *nothing at all* in common with the matter of Władysław's succeeding his brother, nor, all the more so, with the quickly forgotten case of Bishop Stanisław.

But his brother — remained,
And his brother was "the father of Kraków."

What then was the relationship of these two brothers? Against the background of events so violently initiated by the hand of Bolesław?

Perhaps Władysław was like those patient and anticipatory people — who extend their strong hand only for certain prey — who set their hand to someone's intended act, but only to such an act that, bringing one person to his finish line, opens a clear road for themselves — — ... ...

"Glamis and Cawdor" — and one more still: The Crown!

Did Bishop Stanisław excommunicate the king? — History is silent on this matter. Or, rather, it says "no."

I think that even the Bishop-Knight Stanisław was unable to "arrange" such a thing. He wouldn't know how such a thing was done — (as they did in Rome and Byzantium, etc.). But to deprive someone of his honour — to take away a person's power — to enchant a person — the idea of breaking candles, snuffing lit candles — (dousing a sacred fire — dousing the hearth in someone's house) — these things are not that difficult at all, nor do they require any sort of special ceremonial. — This act does not require — ritual —

In and of itself, such an act is death-dealing —

It is a spell.

And paganism — is also thus explained.

It is the horrible death of the flame of someone's soul.

It is the horrible killing of the flame of someone's desires —

It is regicide, if the person so dealt with wear a crown.

The Bishop-Knight Stanisław could have wanted to immobilise the King — with a spell!

In sacrifice on the nation's behalf! —

To separate the fiery King — from the nation.

So that he would be alone —

Alone to stand in his place. —

Should he fight further, with the sword?

Fight on... but now only with charms!

The Bold King does not fear charms.

He kills!

The knight — Stanisław falls —

The King remains at the head of the nation — the criminal king — of a terrorised nation.

But that dead man is "Alone" again — Solitary in his greatness, which grows through the centuries.

With a greatness that is useless, unprofitable to the nation.

Its advocate, who listens to their complaints and reminds them of his own great fault —

The fault of misusing charms!

Today he is a saint. Let him remain so.
But that the King was Bold, let it not be held against him.
At the dawn of the nation, these two spirits
Overcame one another, and each was a pontifex.
The Bold King was, and will be again.
As the Bishop entered the walls of Wawel in his tomb,
Let the King, who is to come, smash that tomb,
And let the spirit of the Saint rise above the clouds.
This drama has not been played out by eternity —
So let it be resolved from the earth by God — Necessity.

Are we to look upon them with indifference,
As one's holiness grows, greater with each passing day,
Although we cannot even hope to walk in his footsteps,
And the blood of the Bolesławs begins to weaken
In our pulses... The royal torch once extinguished —
Are we to let it sink into the marsh, and disappear?
Let "Boldness" and "Sanctity" wallop the nation —
When the King confronts the Saint, and the Saint the King.
Arise unto battle, eternal swordsmen,
Your acts will be judged by God — Necessity!

—11 April 1903

GLOSSARY
to the plays.

ANGELS 1-4. Silver-plated sculptures supporting the four corners of the tomb-reliquary of St. Stanisław in Wawel Cathedral. The reliquary was designed in 1669 by Peter van der Rennen; it is the central point of the baldachined "Confessional" designed some four decades earlier by Giovanni Trevino. This is the tomb that falls upon Bolesław in *Bishop, King. Bishop*; it is also the tomb that is broken apart under the wheels of Christ/Apollo's chariot at the conclusion of *Acropolis*.

ANKWICZ monument. Sculpted in Florence by Francesco Pozzi, to commemorate Stanisław Ankwicz (1790-1840). Ankwicz was a Polish legionnaire during the period of the Partitions.

ARRASES. The large arrases hanging from the walls of the Cathedral date from the mid-XVII century. They were produced in the Brussels atelier of Jacob van Zeunen, and were donated to the Cathedral by Jan Małachowski (1623-1699), Bishop of Kraków and Vice-Chancellor to the King of Poland.

BOLESŁAW I Chrobry (c. 967—1025). Second king of Poland, the son of Mieszko I and his wife, the Czech princess Dubrava, under whom the baptism of Poland took place. He is most well known for his friendly alliance with Emperor Otto III, with whom he negotiated the continuing independence of the Polish Kingdom. He is the architect of the Church in Poland; under him, the diocese of Kraków was established. The surname "Chrobry" means "the Brave." He is the great-grandfather of Bolesław II. Legend has it that the coronation sword of Polish Kings, nicknamed Szczerbiec ("notch-tooth") for a notch in the blade that occurred when it was hammered against the gates of Kiev, belonged to him. The sword is on display at Wawel; experts date it to the second half of the twelfth century.

BOLESŁAW II Śmiały (c. 1040—1081). King of Poland from 1076 — he obtained the privilege of his coronation from Pope Gregory VII for his support of the papacy during the Pope's quarrel with Emperor Henry IV. His reign was marked by many wars, often of a dynastic character, in Hungary and Kievan Rus. He also battled with the Czechs. His domestic policies, aimed at curbing the power of the nobles, as well as his frequent wars, unsettled the country during his reign. He is most well known for the murder of Bishop St. Stanisław in 1079, for which he was exiled to Hungary along with his son. The surname "Śmiały" means "the Bold," although he was sometimes also known as Bolesław Szczodry (Bolesław the Generous). Wyspiański deftly juggles these two characteristics — boldness and generosity — in the scenes of his drama.

CRUCIFIX of St. Jadwiga. The Crucifix referred to in Act I of *Acropolis* is the Miraculous Crucifix, also known as the Crucifix of St. Jadwiga. It is located in Wawel Cathedral, near the apse, at the eastern end of the ambit. Made of dark wood, it is dated to the XIV century. St. Jadwiga was known to pray before this Crucifix, and her relics are located beneath it. It is called the Miraculous Crucifix because, according to legend, the Crucified Christ spoke to her once during her prayers. The Stirrup referred to is that of Kara Mustafa, the leader of the Ottoman forces who besieged Vienna in 1683. It was taken by King Jan III Sobieski of Poland when he lifted the siege, and presented to the Cathedral as a votive offering.

DAVID. The choir loft of Wawel Cathedral is dated to 1758. It is decorated with figures of angels and saints, crowned with a sculpture of David, holding a harp. Thus, he is designated as the Harpist in *Acropolis*.

HORNED BEAST (Turoń). A horned figure generally representing a bull; one of the character types popular in Polish folk celebrations during the period stretching from Christmas to Easter. He is a trickster type, whose jokes and dances are often aimed at women present.

JAROWIT. God of war of the western Slavs. The anthropologist Aleksander Brückner holds that, although their neighbours may have worshipped such a god, Jarowit was unknown to the pagan Polish tribes.

KONRAD II (c.990—1039). Emperor from 1027. In 1033, he invaded Poland in alliance with Kievan Rus, on behalf of Bezprym, Mieszko II's brother, which led to Mieszko's flight to Bohemia and Rycheza's flight to Germany. After Bezprym's death in 1034, Mieszko returned to rule Poland, but with the title of Prince, rather than King. He also acquiesced to Poland's loss of autonomy, and dependence on the Holy Roman Empire.

KRYSTYNA, Wife of Mściwój (Mścisław). Wyspiański is probably referring to a story developed by the historical novelist Józef Ignacy Kraszewski (1812-1887) in his novel *Boleszczyce* (Bolesław's Men, 1877), according to which the amoral king Bolesław seduces the wife of Mścisław and keeps her as a concubine. According to family tradition researched and recorded by his brother Kajetan, Kraszewski believed that the murderers of St. Stanisław ("Bolesław's men") had been recruited from the Jastrzębiec clan, to which the Kraszewskis belonged.

KURHAN. In Polish, *kopiec*; an artificial mound raised over the tomb of a leader, or in honour of a respected person. The Kurhan of Wanda (Kopiec Wandy) may still be visited in Kraków today. It has been located near the village of Mogiła (the name of which also signifies "mound"), today called Nowa Huta, since the VII or VIII century. Thus, it is a pre-Christian object, which tradition holds to be the final resting-place of Wanda. Nearby is another pagan mound, dated to the VII century, known as Kopiec Kraka (The Kurhan of Krak). On the territory of Kraków, there are two other artificial mounds commemorating national heroes: the Kopiec Kościuszki, raised between 1820-1823 in honour of Gen. Tadeusz Kościuszko (1746-1817), and the Kopiec Piłsudskiego (1936), raised in honour of Marshal Józef Piłsudski (1867-1935), whose tomb is found in the crypts of Wawel Cathedral. At 35 metres, Piłsudski's Mound is the highest, followed by Kościuszko's at 34. The ancient mounds are much smaller: Krak's is 16 metres, and Wanda's is 14.

LEL (pl. Leli). Pagan idols. According to Brückner, they were honoured by the pagan Slavs on the first of May. Henryk Łowmiański asserts that legends of a pagan cult on Łysa Góra (Bald Mountain, in south-central

Poland), where "Lada, Boda and Leli" were worshipped is "pure literary invention."

LESTEK (or Leszek). A legendary character; leader of the Polanie tribe. Various dates for his era have been given by mediaeval chronicles; these stretch from 400 BC to the IX century AD. In *Bishop, King. Bishop* he is referred to in the context of Polish legends, which claim that the Polish monarchy arose from the simple people, the peasantry.

LESZY. According to Slavic folklore, a mythical wild man, inhabiting the woods.

ST. MARY'S BASILICA. Kościół Marjacki (begun in 1226). Brick Gothic church on the Main Market Square. Every hour, on the hour, the *hejnał mariacki* is played on a solo trumpet, from the higher tower, toward each of the cardinal points of the compass. It is one of the most familiar melodic lines in Polish music. The stanza beginning "Hey, from on high..." during the chorus of the bells in Act II of *Acropolis* approximates the metrical line of this musical phrase.

NIEPOŁOMSKI WOOD. A wooded wilderness near Kraków, approximately 120 square kilometres (46.33 square miles) in area.

PIOTR, Sir (also known as Piotrowin). A legendary figure. In hagiographies of St. Stanisław, the saintly bishop resurrected Piotrowin from his grave in order to testify on his behalf in a lawsuit concerning the transfer of lands to the Church. Wyspiański uses the ghost of Piotrowin in a novel manner, the reasons for which he explains in his "Argumentum" (see Appendix).

POPIEL. Legendary ruler of the territory surrounding the first Polish capital of Gniezno, predating the Piast dynasty (from which Bolesław arose). According to a story mentioned in the chronicle of the Anonymous Gaul, he was consumed by mice in a tower on Lake Gopło.

POTOCKI, Włodzimierz (1789—1812). Scion of one of the greatest magnate families in Poland, a colonel in the horse artillery of the

Napoleonic Grand Duchy of Warsaw. He died in Kraków of typhus. His memorial statue was funded by his wife, whom he married in 1808 — and therefore the scene in which the enlivened Maiden seeks to make him forget warring, and enjoy her love, is all the more poignant. It was sculpted around 1820 by one of the greatest sculptors of the age, Bertel Thorvaldsen (1770-1844). Its position in the Cathedral is near the Chapel of the Holy Trinity and the Chapel of the Czartoryski Family.

RUDAWA. A river in Kraków, which flows into the Wisła (Vistula) in the area of Zwierzyniec / Salvator. The name means "reddish," or "ruddy."

RUSALKA. *Rusałka* in Polish, plural, *Rusałki* (Wyspiański also makes use of an unusual male form of the word: *rusał*). In Slavic folklore, rusalkas are beautiful water nymphs, or sirens, who tempt unwary men to their deaths. According to Aleksander Brückner (citing A.E. Bogdanowicz), rusalkas inhabit the waters from Autumn until "Rusalna Sunday" (the Sunday after Pentecost), during which time it is dangerous to swim. After that date, they emerge from the waters and inhabit trees — birches are their favourite. Wyspiański references this in the story told by the Drowned Herdboy. According to folklore, the souls of children who die before being baptised become rusalkas.

RYCHEZA (c. 993—1063). Queen of Poland, wife of Mieszko II, a Blessed of the Roman Catholic Church. She is remembered in the Church calendar on May 21. Granddaughter of Emperor Otto II, grandmother of Bolesław Śmiały and Władysław Herman. In 1025, she escaped to Germany during a period of political instability in Poland (her husband also escaped, to Bohemia). Her taking the royal insignia with her (they were returned to Poland by her son Kazimierz Odnowiciel — the Restorer) is painted in a nefarious (and probably undeserving) light by Wyspiański.

SALMON (Salomon, c. 1052—1087). Crowned King of Hungary in 1057, in defiance of an earlier pact between his father, Andrew I, and his uncle, Bela, who was to inherit the throne after Andrew. A war ensued, and Bolesław the Bold entered it as Bela's ally, when the latter sought his support. Bela was crowned in 1061, thanks in great part to the aid of the Polish troops.

SIECIECH (fl. late XI century). *Wojewoda* (governor, palatine), supposedly the "power behind the throne" during the reign of Władysław Herman. He was exiled sometime after 1097 by Władysław's sons Zbigniew and Bolesław Krzywousty ("the Wrymouthed").

SKAŁKA. In literal translation: Little Cliff, or Little Rock. A hill on the Wisła (Vistula) River not far from Wawel. Supposedly the site of a pagan temple, which was replaced by the Romanesque church of St. Michael the Archangel (hence references to the Bishop in Wyspiański's plays as an Archangel). Site of St. Stanisław's murder at the hands of Bolesław the Bold in 1079. Because of this, it became traditional for Polish kings to make an expiatory pilgrimage from Wawel to Skałka on the day before their coronation. Today, a Baroque church administered by the Pauline order stands on this spot; the grounds also contain the sacred pool with the statue of the bishop (referenced in the plays). Sculptures of the eagles who watched over the dismembered corpse of the bishop stand at all four corners of the pool. The crypts of St. Michael's contain the tombs of many distinguished artists and men of letters, including Wyspiański.

SKOTNICKI monument. Sculpted around 1810 by Stefano Ricci (a student of Canova) in honour of Michał Bogoria Skotnicki (1775-1805), a painter. It can be found in the Skotnicki chapel.

SOŁTYK monument. Designed in 1789 by the architect Domenico Merlini, and sculpted by Chrystian Piotr Aigner in honour of Bishop Kajetan Sołtyk (1715-1788), bishop of Kraków imprisoned by the Russians for his political activities. Portions of the monument depict his arrest and banishment.

ST. STANISŁAW (ze Szczepanów, or Szczepanowski, c. 1030—1079). Bishop of Kraków, martyr. His execution, at the orders of Bolesław Śmiały, who suspected him of treason (on behalf of the Czechs) led to the exile of the king and his replacement on the throne by his brother, Władysław Herman. Canonised by the Church in 1253, his feast day is April 11 (the traditional date of his death), although he is venerated with great pomp in Kraków on May 8 of each year, during which a procession with his relics travels from Wawel Cathedral to the church on Skałka where he was martyred.

ŚWIETLEC. A pagan god, referenced by Wyspiański as a sun-god, perhaps deriving the name from the substantive *światło* (light). Unmentioned by Brückner.

WAWEL. Complex of Royal and Ecclesiastical headquarters in Kraków. The castle on Wawel was the seat of the Kings of Poland from the late X century (Bolesław Chrobry) until the capital was transferred to Warsaw in the early XVII century by Zygmunt III Waza. The Cathedral of St. Wacław (Václav) and Stanisław (commonly known as Wawel Cathedral) remained the coronation church of Polish kings, and its crypts contain the tombs and cenotaphs of many rulers of Poland. The Polish national bards Adam Mickiewicz and Juliusz Słowacki are also buried in the crypts of the cathedral. Traces of human occupation of the hill have been dated to 50,000 BC. Many legends, such as that of the Wawel Dragon and Wanda, are associated with Wawel.

WELES. Although Wyspiański seems to identify Weles with the moon, Brückner suggests that he may have been a god of the Eastern Slavs associated with shepherding.

WISŁA (Vistula). The main river of Poland. Arising in the mountains of southern Poland, it winds over 1,000 kilometres through the country, including the cities of Kraków and Warsaw, before emptying into the Bay of Gdańsk.

WŁADYSŁAW JAGIEŁŁO (1377—1434). Grand Prince of Lithuania, whose marriage to Jadwiga of Anjou refocussed Polish politics from the Habsburg west toward the Balto-Slavic east. His tomb, which features an effigy of the king sculpted during his lifetime, is the work of an anonymous Italian sculptor. Art historians propose that the artist had been a student of Donatello.

WŁODZISŁAW (Władysław Herman, c. 1043—1102). Designated as the "King's Brother" in the plays, he ascended the throne when his older brother, Bolesław Śmiały, was exiled to Hungary in 1079 after the murder of St. Stanisław, Bishop of Kraków. Some historians accept the conspiratorial rumour that his accession to the throne was the result of the nobles' scheming against Bolesław. The *wojewoda* Sieciech is said to have been the power behind his throne. Shortly before his death he divided the Kingdom among his sons. A Romanesque cathedral was raised at Wawel during his reign, portions of which can be traced in the cathedral yet today.

ZYGMUNT. The most famous of all Polish bells. Cast in 1520 by bell-founder Jan Beham, it weighs some eleven tonnes, with a circumference of 8 metres and a diameter of 2.6. It is rung each Easter, as well as during other exceptional events of special significance to the nation.

ŻYWIA. The beautiful, yet fearful goddess seems to be Wyspiański's creation. Although she is mentioned by Jan Długosz in his catalogue of pagan deities, anthropologists and students of religion such as Brückner and Łowmiański do not find independent testimony to such a god having existed in the Slavic pantheon. The name is most likely derived from the words *życie* ("life") and *żywić* ("to nourish").

BIBLIOGRAPHY

Primary Sources

WYSPIAŃSKI, Stanisław. *Dzieła zebrane,* ed. Leon Płoszewski, et al. Kraków: Wydawnictwo Literackie, 1962-1982. Vol. 6: *Bolesław Śmiały, Legenda II, Skałka.*
— Vol. 7: *Akropolis, Achilleis.*
— Vol. 14: *Pisma prozą, juvenilia.*

Secondary Sources

ADAMCZEWSKI, Jan. *Kraków od A do Z.* Kraków: Krajowa agencja wydawnicza, 1986.

BRÜCKNER, Aleksander. *Mitologia słowiańska i polska.* Warszawa: Państwowe Wydawnictwo Naukowe, 1985.

BRZOZOWSKI, Stanisław. *Eseje i studia o literaturze.* Wrocław: Ossolineum, 1990.

ESTREICHER, Karol. *Kraków: przewodnik dla zwiedzających miasto i jego okolice.* Kraków: Towarzystwo Miłośników Historii i Zabytków Krakowa, 1938.

ŁOWMIAŃSKI, Henryk. *Religia Słowian i jej upadek.* Warszawa: PWN, 1986.

MIŁOSZ, Czesław. Miłosz. *Zaczynając od moich ulic.* Kraków: Znak, 2006.

OKOŃSKA, Alicja. *Stanisław Wyspiański.* Warszawa: Wiedza Powszechna, 1971.

PŁOSZEWSKI, Leon. *Wyspiański w oczach współczesnych.* Kraków: Wydawnictwo Literackie, 1971.

RÓŻEK, Michał. *Krakowska katedra na Wawelu.* Kraków: Wydawnictwo św. Stanisława, 1989.

SANDAUER, Artur. *Pisma zebrane.* Warszawa: Czytelnik, 1985. Vol. 1: *Studia o literaturze współczesnej.*

SINKO, Tadeusz. *Antyk Wyspiańskiego.* Warszawa: Instytut Wydawniczy Biblioteka Polska, 1922.

ABOUT THE AUTHOR

Stanisław Wyspiański (1869—1907). Poet, dramatist, theatrical director, painter, architectural restorer, furniture designer. In short, a Renaissance man of the early XX century. Wyspiański is of prime importance to the history of Polish art, as he is to the history of Polish literature. He is the central figure of Modernist painting in Poland. and the driving force behind the Młoda Polska (Young Poland) period in letters. A student of Jan Matejko, he was a professor at the Academy of Fine Arts in his home city of Kraków. During a period of study in Paris, he came to know, and be influenced by, Gaugin. His artworks are characterised by their decorative qualities and bright colours. He was especially fond of pastels. Many of his works may be seen in Kraków today. Of special importance are his stained glass windows in the Franciscan church. His designs for stained glass windows at Wawel Cathedral, including depictions of St. Stanisław, remained unrealised until the XXI century (when they were incorporated into the Wyspiański Pavilion on Grodzka St.) He is the author of nearly twenty verse dramas, chief among which is *Wesele* (The Wedding Feast, 1901), a poetic allegory concerning his contemporary Poland and the inability of his countrymen to act, in a concerted fashion, to win their independence from the partitioning empires of Austria, Russia and Prussia. His collected writings fill fourteen volumes. They include, besides his dramatic works, lyrical and narrative poetry, a strongly-interpreted translation of Corneille's *Le Cid*, the first great production of Adam Mickiewicz's *Dziady* (Forefathers' Eve), and a critical consideration of Shakespeare's *Hamlet* from the perspective of its stage realisation in modern Poland.

ABOUT THE TRANSLATOR

Charles S. Kraszewski (b. 1962) is a poet and translator, writing in both English and Polish. He is the author of three volumes of original verse; his translation of the entirety of Adam Mickiewicz's *Forefathers' Eve* was published by Glagoslav in 2016. He is a member of the Union of Polish Writers Abroad (London) and of the Association of Polish Writers (Kraków).

ILLUSTRATIONS

Stanisław Wyspiański, *Pastel Self-Portrait* (1903) Courtesy of the National Museum, Kraków.

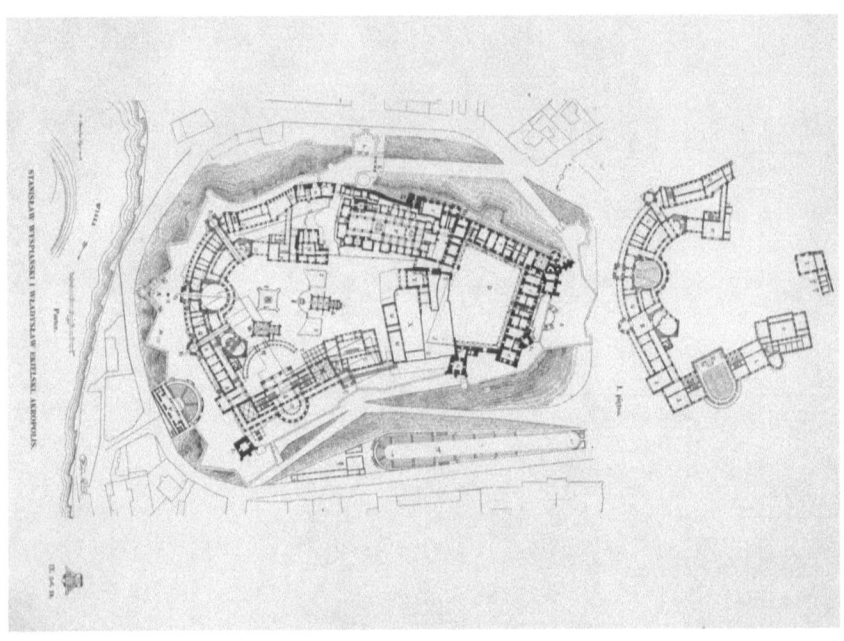

Stanisław Wyspiański and Władysław Ekielski, *Plan for the Renovation of Wawel Hill*. From *Akropolis: pomysł zabudowania Wawelu. Obmyślili Stanisław Wyspiański i Władysław Ekielski w latach 1904-1907* (Acropolis: An Idea for the Renovation of Wawel as Conceived by Stanisław Wyspiański and Władysław Ekielski between 1904-1907. Kraków: Jagiellonian University, 1908). Courtesy of the National Museum, Kraków.

Plaster model of the Wyspiański/Ekielski plan. Unrealised constructions, such as the Dome above the Senate (rear), the wooden Castle of the Bolesławs (left), and the hippodrome-like stadium along the lower right, are clearly seen. Courtesy of the National Museum, Kraków.

Architectural drawing by Stanisław Wyspiański to accompany the renovation plan. Dated 1904, it shows a portion of the "Cathedral Square" featuring the Bishop's Palace and Cathedral Canons' lodgings. From *Akropolis: pomysł zabudowania Wawelu. Obmyślili Stanisław Wyspiański i Władysław Ekielski w latach 1904-1907* (Acropolis: An Idea for the Renovation of Wawel as Conceived by Stanisław Wyspiański and Władysław Ekielski between 1904-1907. Kraków: Jagiellonian University, 1908). Courtesy of the National Museum, Kraków.

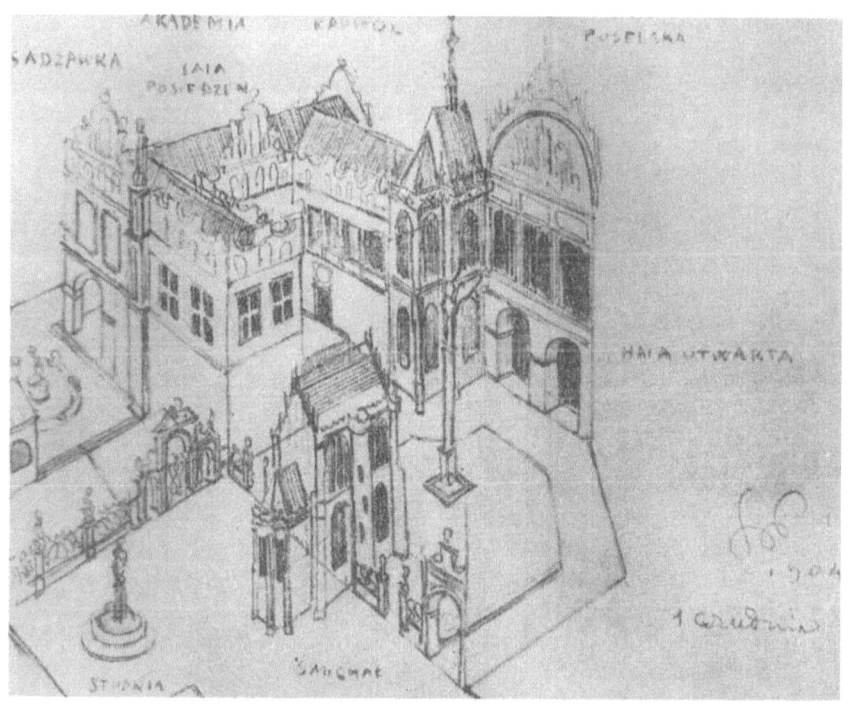

Architectural drawing by Stanisław Wyspiański to accompany the renovation plan. Dated 1904, it shows a portion of the "House of Representatives Square" featuring the Academy of Sciences building. From *Akropolis: pomysł zabudowania Wawelu. Obmyślili Stanisław Wyspiański i Władysław Ekielski w latach 1904-1907* (Acropolis: An Idea for the Renovation of Wawel as Conceived by Stanisław Wyspiański and Władysław Ekielski between 1904-1907. Kraków: Jagiellonian University, 1908). Courtesy of the National Museum, Kraków.

Architectural drawing by Stanisław Wyspiański to accompany the renovation plan, showing a portion of the planned Academy of Sciences. The note reads "Side podium; Stained glass window beneath the coffered vault." Courtesy of the National Museum, Kraków.

Cartoon by Stanisław Wyspiański for a stained glass window representing St. Stanisław (1900). The spectre-like head of the martyr emerges from a stylised torso similar to the silver panels of his reliquary tomb. Originally intended for Wawel Cathedral, the stained glass window remained unrealised until the XXI century. It can be seen today in the Pawilon Wyspiański 2000 on ul. Grodzka, near the Plac Wszystkich Świętych in Kraków. It is accompanied by two other stained glass windows based on the artist's cartoons, depicting King Kazimierz the Great and magnate Henry the Pious. Courtesy of the National Museum, Kraków.

Unfinished cartoon by Stanisław Wyspiański for a stained glass window representing Wanda (c.1900). Also intended for Wawel Cathedral, the dramatic cartoon in blue and green pastel presents Wanda in flowing lines that emphasise her connection to the River Wisła (Vistula). Courtesy of the National Museum, Kraków.

Stanisław Wyspiański, *Pastel Sketch of the Actress Władysława Ordon-Sosnowska in the Role of Krasawica* (1903). Courtesy of the National Museum, Kraków.

Stanisław Wyspiański, cover of *Skałka*, printed by the Jagiellonian University in 1907. Courtesy of the National Museum, Kraków.

Forefathers' Eve
by Adam Mickiewicz

Forefathers' Eve [*Dziady*] is a four-part dramatic work begun circa 1820 and completed in 1832 – with Part I published only after the poet's death, in 1860. The drama's title refers to *Dziady*, an ancient Slavic and Lithuanian feast commemorating the dead. This is the grand work of Polish literature, and it is one that elevates Mickiewicz to a position among the "great Europeans" such as Dante and Goethe.

With its Christian background of the Communion of the Saints, revenant spirits, and the interpenetration of the worlds of time and eternity, *Forefathers' Eve* speaks to men and women of all times and places. While it is a truly Polish work – Polish actors covet the role of Gustaw/Konrad in the same way that Anglophone actors covet that of Hamlet – it is one of the most universal works of literature written during the nineteenth century. It has been compared to Goethe's Faust – and rightfully so...

Buy it > www.glagoslav.com

www.ingramcontent.com/pod-product-compliance
Lightning Source LLC
Chambersburg PA
CBHW031052080526
44587CB00011B/661